WAR AND SOCIETY

VOLUME 2

WAR AND SOCIETY

A Yearbook of Military History

VOLUME 2

Edited by

BRIAN BOND and IAN ROY

HM HOLMES & MEIER PUBLISHERS NEW YORK

First published in the United States of America 1977 by
Holmes & Meier Publishers, Inc.
101 Fifth Avenue
New York, New York 10003

©1977 Brian Bond and Ian Roy

ISBN 0-8419-0293-3   LC 75-23095

Printed in Great Britain
79-6209

CONTENTS

Foreword

FOREWORD

This publication aims to provide a forum for the scholarly interest in war and its repercussions which has increased and broadened in recent years. Although, as some of the articles published in this issue indicate, we do not intend to exclude what might be termed the professional aspects of military history — such as tactical developments or staff training — the main emphasis will be placed on the inter-relationship of armed services, war and society. The articles in this volume by Professor V.G. Kiernan and Dr. N. Wynn, for example, represent a sophisticated approach to military studies which the editors would like to encourage, particularly among younger scholars just embarking upon research in this field.

Although the time-span covered by this volume is comparatively short, the editors would like to emphasize that in principle they are anxious to publish the best articles submitted irrespective of period or geographical area. Furthermore, although the *Yearbook* is published in English the editors would welcome contributions from outside the Anglo-Saxon world. It will be observed that, as in Volume 1, the articles in this issue are not related to a specific theme, but this possibility is being considered for the future. The main development since the publication of Volume 1 is the inclusion of review articles and reviews, and it is intended to expand this section of the *Yearbook* in future numbers.

Our readers will appreciate that this is an inauspicious time from the publishing viewpoint to embark on a new venture such as this, and as we go to press the future of the *Yearbook* appears somewhat uncertain. However, the Editors and Advisory Board are convinced that there is sufficiently wide interest and potential readership to justify the venture. We would appeal to all readers who have found our first two volumes interesting and academically valuable to ensure that the *Yearbook* is ordered by their College and University libraries.

B.J.B.

I.R.

THE AMERICAN NAVY IN THE WORLD OF FRANKLIN AND JEFFERSON, 1775-1826*

John B. Hattendorf

Ninety years ago, Alfred Thayer Mahan began his investigations into the elements of naval power. He took as his ground for study European history between the years 1660 and 1815, years which also saw the birth of the American Navy. By following a thread of history which was entwined on the interaction between maritime strength and the international relations among the great powers, Mahan attempted to deduce the essential elements by which navies were linked to the rise and fall of great nations. In summarising the ultimate failure of Napoleonic France to dominate Europe, he dramatically concluded, 'those far distant, storm-beaten ships, upon which the Grand Army never looked, stood between it and the dominion of the world'. This kind of thinking had a great impact on the developing navies in the late nineteenth century, particularly in the United States, Germany, Japan and Britain. Mahan's thoughts still reverberate today in the naval competition we see around us. But this is all the business of great powers.

In the first half century of independence, there was no realistic thought given in America to the possibility that the fledgling country would be an actor in the affairs of Europe or a power in the world at large. There was certainly no thought given to an American 'dominion of the world'. After all, it was to a large degree over a question of such power that the Revolution occurred. The American Revolution was not a contest between two rival nations, but in the colonists' eyes, an ideological struggle against what Americans perceived to be an encroachment of British rule on their liberties. Americans firmly believed in the wisdom of the English constitution and the traditional right and liberties which it preserved, yet they were anxious about the preservation of those liberties in the future. As Benjamin Franklin wrote to a friend.

I pray God long to preserve to Great Britain the English laws,

---

*This article is based on the text of the author's lecture at the British Museum in connection with the exhibition 'The World of Franklin and Jefferson', part of the observance of the American Bicentennial in Britain.

manners, liberties and religion, notwithstanding the complaints so frequent in your public papers of the prevailing corruption and degeneracy of your people. . .I hope the constitution is not so near a dissolution as some seem to apprehend.

In the eyes of many influential men in America, the growth of the power of the Crown in colonial matters, the substantial attempt to rationalise colonial government and the assertion of supremacy over colonial assemblies were serious threats to American liberty. The increase of British troops in the colonies and the use of the navy to enforce new regulations were seen as signs of the systematic corruption of Parliament and the destruction of a balanced constitution. As one colonial lamented in 1774: 'Alas, Power encroaches daily upon liberty, with a success too evident, and the balance between them is almost lost.' This antithesis between liberty and armed force was sustained in colonial thought by the experience of seventeenth-century England. With Englishmen, Americans centred their objections on a standing army, but also saw in their distant position the role of naval force in sustaining this 'exorbitant power'. One commentator of the day went on to describe military men as individuals who, although really the servants of the people, came to think of themselves as the King's men and quickly grew to become 'the means, in the hands of a wicked and oppressive sovereign, of overturning the constitution of a country and establishing the most intolerable despotism'. Such, they believed, had been the course of history in Rome, France, Spain, Germany, Poland, Sweden, Denmark, Russia, India, Egypt and Turkey. Now the last vestige of European liberty, the English constitution, seemed to be falling under the same shadow. This was the threat to America, that purer, freer England, 'sought and settled as an asylum for liberty, civil and religious'.

Given the experience of the American colonists in the context of their particular ideological views one must wonder why there ever was an American navy. Indeed, if the most prominent naval theorist would later link naval force almost exclusively to great power politics, it is a wonder that a small nation with no imperial ambition would seriously consider naval operations. In the fifty-year period between the outbreak of the American War and the death of Jefferson, there was only one ten-year period, 1785-94, in which the young country conducted no naval business. It was the only time in American history in which she did not have a navy. Much has been written on American naval history in the period between 1775 and 1826; it falls generally into two classes. One deals with the truly heroic exploits of John Paul Jones, Thomas

Truxton, Edward Preble, Oliver Hazard Perry, Stephen Decateur and others. The other deals with the American political scene in the struggle over naval construction, design and appropriations. I would propose that there may profitably be a third way to look at American naval history in this period, and that is to view the actual use of the navy, both in peace and in war, in relation to the international situation and the young nation's foreign policy and national goals. It is this aspect that I will attempt to sketch against the background just discussed.

Shortly after the outbreak of war, the Admiralty computed that there were already 50 vessels manned by 7,460 men on the North American Station. Just under one third of the Royal Navy was on station there, a prodigious force for rebellious colonies who had little naval expertise of their own. 'We cannot', William Ellery of Rhode Island wrote, 'with all the naval force we collect be able to cope with the British Navy.' That was not to say, however, that Americans would not try or that they were not adept sailors. Rebel fleets sprang up in a variety of places. In June 1775, Jeremiah O'Brien and his five brothers led a band of townspeople in the capture of HMS *Margretta* in a sea battle off Machias, Maine. George Washington's army in Massachusetts sent out armed vessels in the autumn of 1775 to search for war supplies. Another small fleet was built up on Lake Champlain under Benedict Arnold. Several ships were maintained on the Mississippi, and Benjamin Franklin, in Paris, directed raids on the British coast. Eleven of the thirteen colonies obtained warships of varying sizes and abilities. The major force, however, was commissioned by Congress as the Continental Navy. A naval committee was created to direct this fleet, ships were built and bought, sailors enlisted, and officers commissioned. Esek Hopkins became Commander-in-Chief and Abraham Whipple, Commodore of the Rhode Island Navy brought his flagship *Katy* to join the new force. At its height in 1777, it had 34 ships and something less than 5,000 men. As a naval force its accomplishments were limited. It had been unable to protect American commerce, which by the winter of 1777-8 was virtually extinct. It was unable to hold the Delaware River and so the principal naval base and government centre at Philadelphia was lost. Despite its weakness some important positive accomplishments were made in conjunction with the activities of privateers — ships privately owned and maintained, but commissioned by Congress. Some of these ships were merchant ships that were primarily engaged in commerce and preyed on enemy shipping only as the chance occurred. Others were full scale warships such as *Belisarius* of 500 tons armed with twenty guns and manned by 200 men. One historian has reported that of the 800 odd vessels captured by

Americans during the War, only 198 were taken by the Continental Navy and more than 600 were taken by privateers. Twelve regular warships were captured by the Continental Navy, and sixteen ships of the Royal Navy were prizes to privateers. Together with the privateers, the Continental Navy was thus able to divert some valuable resources to American use and to support the war of attrition against Britain. While the rebelling colonists could hardly command the sea lanes, the fleet action near Valcour Island under Benedict Arnold on Lake Champlain did save Washington from being caught between two converging armies. Naval vessels carried diplomats such as Benjamin Franklin to France where valuable diplomatic ties could be secured. Raids were made around the coast of Britain that caused a great deal of popular concern, even if they did not disrupt British trade to any great extent. In 1778, the American victory at Saratoga and the entry of France into the war dramatically changed the strategic view. A war of defiance could be turned to one of decision. As George Washington wrote to Lafayette, 'No land force can act decisively unless it is accompanied by a maritime supremacy'.

The establishment of a French naval base at Newport, Rhode Island, was the first move by which a local superiority was achieved and British sea lines of communication temporarily broken. The isolation of Britain in European politics, the addition of Spain, and then Holland, to the active alliance against her, and the growing discontent at home with the conduct of the war, all combined to create a situation in which King George III was obliged to recognise American independence. Alfred Mahan was correct; the key to American independence had been found in Europe.

With the peace the new nation let her navy fall into decay. Finally, the last ship, *Alliance,* was sold in 1785. The United States was without a naval force of her own. Throughout these years a debate was publicly waged over the propriety of a naval force. It was an argument marked by strong party sentiments, sectional differences and ideological conflicts.

On the wider stage, however, there is no question that the United States was 'a weak republic in a hostile world'. The policy of the young nation to rely on the physical expanse of the North Atlantic for protection and to nurture its liberties behind a few coastal fortifications had very serious flaws. George Washington had set the tone for this policy in his own administration as President, and summarised his views in his Farewell Address. 'Our detached and distant situation', he said, 'invites and enables us to pursue a different course from that followed by European nations.' In saying this he appealed to that popular image of America as a self-sufficient nation, unassociated with the rest of the world. Warning his countrymen of the dangers to be found in 'entangling alliances' which would inevitably draw the republic into the continual strife of European quarrels, Washington told them, 'the great rule of conduct for us in regard to foreign nations is, in extending our commercial relations to have with them as little *political* connection as possible'. At first glance one might think that the first President advocated an impossibly idealistic view. A more careful look, however, would reveal that he fully recognised that American prosperity rested largely on her maritime commerce and that peaceful commerce was open to depredation.

The period is not far off when we may take such an attitude as will cause the neutrality we may at any time resolve upon to be scrupulously respected; when belligerent nations. . .will not lightly hazard the giving us provocation; when we may choose peace or war, as our interest, guided by justice shall counsel.

The launching of the frigate *United States* in May 1797, followed shortly by *Constitution* and *Constellation,* was the movement in fulfilment of that prophecy. The threat of war with Algiers which had sparked this construction was not a remote matter. Thomas Jefferson calculated that in the time of uninterrupted trade with the Barbary States, those North African countries took one sixth of America's export in wheat and one quarter of her exported dry fish.

Peaceful American commerce was growing rapidly in other directions as well. In 1784, the New York ship *Empress of China* sailed for Canton to inaugurate American trade in the Orient. By 1790, a number of firms were engaged in this growing business, and American furs were being shipped directly from the Pacific coast in a lucrative commercial enterprise. The French Revolution and the outbreak of another European war marked the beginning of a period of great profit for neutral shipping. An index of American commercial success may be found in a few statistics. In 1792 custom house receipts from foreign trade stood at \$52 million, by 1801 they had nearly quadrupled to \$205 million. During the brief Peace of Amiens they slid to \$110 million in 1803. But with the renewal of the war, they rose again to \$246 million in 1807. The growth of this commerce was an essential part of American national interest. 'Peace, commerce and honest friendship with all nations', Jefferson had proclaimed in his inaugural address. Yet he worried. 'This exuberant commerce', he wrote on another occasion, 'brings us into collision with the other powers in every sea, and will force us into every war with European powers.' He was not wrong; the first seventeen years of the new navy would see not only the Barbary States, but France and Britain at war with America.

From the very outset the American position was based on her firm belief in neutral trade rights. With Americans particularly in mind, the popular new world poet David Humphreys thundered, 'it is time the ocean should be made what heaven intended it, an open highway for all mankind'. The fact remained that others had interests of their own which competed with such American idealism. Some opposition was just old-fashioned piracy such as that found in the West Indies and the situation which drew Edward Preble in USS *Essex* to the East Indies in 1800. However, the great danger, as Jefferson noted, was that American commercial success intruded in European politics. One need only remember that Lord Howe's great victory on the 'Glorious First of June' 1794 was occasioned by the expected appearance of a fleet of 116 ships carrying American flour to blockaded France.

In 1795 the Jay Treaty negotiated with Britain restored American commercial access to the British West Indies and gave preference to American goods traded to Britain. While beneficial to the growth of American commerce and Anglo-American relations, it was obviously detrimental to France, not only in the loss of trade, but in profit to her enemy. As a result of this situation, the French Directory began to take various measures which would prevent American trade from benefiting Britain. America saw these punitive measures as reason for resistance. With only a tiny naval force and privateers, Congress authorised reprisals to be taken against French ships, although not under a declaration of war. Remembered today as the 'Quasi-War with France', it was a brief affair in 1798-9, centred in the West Indies, and marked in American memory by the victory of Thomas Truxton's *Constellation* over the French frigate *Insurgente*. France saw quickly that if this conflict was allowed to spread to greater proportions, it would drive America firmly into alliance with Britain, a course which would be even less useful to France and certainly endanger French colonies in America. It was far better to maintain American neutrality by assuaging her grievances. In American eyes, this brave resistance to France was seen as good reason for a swelling national pride and greater respect from other nations.

In spite of Jay's Treaty, relations with Britain were not as happy as might be. American merchantmen were continually halted by ships of the Royal Navy and seamen taken from them to be impressed for service under the British flag. This was not entirely unjustified, as even American warships were manned by crews of which a significant percentage were not even naturalised Americans. Despite that, impressment could be a cruel business, and the continuation of it caused a great popular clamour in America.

Despite this difficulty, American trade continued to grow with some 6,000 merchant ships engaged in foreign trade and another 3,000 in coastal trade. By 1807, the extent of the trade had grown to such proportions that it was strategically useful that one side in the European war interdict that profitable trade with the enemy. Several of King George's Orders in Council did just that, and for America, matched Napoleon's Berlin and Milan Decrees. Each side placed severe penalties on any vessels which traded with the enemy. American trade was trapped between two great powers, each determined to stamp out American trade with the other. Neutral trade was a certain victim in the European struggle. In this situation, President Jefferson believed that the only way by which American independence and neutrality could be maintained was to ban American trade by embargo and retreat behind a defensive navy of gunboats. Following an incident between USS *Chesapeake* and HMS *Leopard* a few miles off the Chesapeake Capes, Jefferson was able to encourage Congress to pass the Embargo Act halting all foreign trade. The Act lapsed at the end of Jefferson's term, but it had certainly helped to preserve American neutrality. On the other hand, it was disastrous for the American economy. With very limited resources, the United States could not develop an adequate military and naval force which could deal with the great powers directly. The only feasible course seemed to be for her to withhold her commerce and to hope that this would create enough pressure to persuade the great powers to stop hindering American trade. It was a negative measure and as such, it was not particularly effective, but the Non-Intercourse Act of 1809 and Macon's Bill of 1810 were both designed to deal with this problem through that policy. Under these circumstances, the navy was employed in local defence and in protecting the American trade which remained at sea. While these national policies were being employed, sentiment in Congress was growing for the alternative of an active war policy against Britain.

Under the Macon Act, the United States banned trade only with England, and thus played into Napoleon's hands. He had readily seen that war between England and the United States would benefit his cause; he did not have to wait long. British impressment of American seamen continued. After the exchange of gunfire between HMS *Little Belt* and USS *President* off the Virginia coast in 1811, war was seriously considered by Congress. But it was not until June 1812, that the United States finally resorted to war in order to win 'free trade and sailor's rights'.

Actually, the situation was less serious than it had been five years earlier. England really did not want the war and neither did the New England merchants. It was supported enthusiastically only by the fervid nationalism of the frontiersmen who saw the opportunity to gain Canadian territory and to stop the Indian difficulties in the West. The assassination of Prime Minister Spencer Perceval opened the way for revoking the Orders in Council within a week of the American declaration of war. Perceval had adamantly insisted that the Orders against neutral trade be enforced, but even though this issue was opened to negotiation at his death, neither side would compromise on the issue of impressment. The war continued.

Within six months, Congress passed legislation which marked the final rejection of the Jeffersonian gunboat navy. With only sixteen ships in the Navy, Congress authorised a large building programme which included four 74-gun ships of the line. Although none were completed before the end of the war, America now intended to have a fleet which could, at least, be classed with the larger powers.

The American strategic decision to use force against the overwhelming power of Britain must undoubtedly have rested on the same view which an influential Baltimore newspaper, *Niles Weekly Register,* presented of the European war. Its pages clearly depicted a situation in which Britain was about to be defeated by France. It was reported that less than half of the Royal Navy's 254 ships of the line were operational, and only 96 were at sea. The war with Napoleon would clearly consume her energy so that the efforts of the American Navy would, in fact, be allied with an adverse situation for Britain. Privateering attacks on the maritime supply lines for Wellington's army in the Peninsula, and an incursion into Canada by relatively weak forces would have a decisive effect far beyond that expected for such small forces. By this means, America could forcefully assert her independence, remove the threats to her, and demand respect for neutral trade. Such a plan, however, was not based on a firm understanding of the situation in Europe.

The War of 1812 can be divided into three distinct phases. During the first period, from the opening of the war until the spring of 1813, Americans had a great deal of freedom and success at sea. At first the Royal Navy could not spare ships from the European theatre. The British Army in Canada could not be reinforced while Wellington's army needed men. However, in the second year and second phase of the war, Britain could afford·to establish a strong blockade of the American coast, even if she could not reinforce her army. The third phase was parallelled by the abdication of Napoleon and the final convulsion of the First Empire. The British could now afford to send a considerable force to America. Washington was burned, Maine invaded. American commerce and naval operations at sea were brought to a halt. Invasion from Canada through New York was prevented only by Thomas MacDonough's victory on Lake Champlain.

During the war, there were some spectacular American victories: Oliver Hazard Perry on Lake Erie, the USS *Constitution* over the *Guerriere,* the Battle of New Orleans, and the exploits of *Essex, Wasp* and *Enterprise.* In spite of these actions – which showed that ship for ship the Americans were superior to the British – the United States could still not contend with the overwhelming force of the Royal Navy. For America, most of the lessons of the war were negative ones, but they carried with them the promise of an improved military and naval administration that could more adequately deal with wartime situations. In the end, America was not crushed or returned to British domination. However, Canada did not become part of the United States. Britain had nearly ruined American commerce by her blockade. The British failure to control the Great Lakes and Lake Champlain combined with a general apathy on both sides to persuade the peace negotiators to agree to the *status quo ante.* 'Free trade and sailor's rights', the slogan on which the war was fought, was not even mentioned in the treaty.

In the years which followed the war, the United States was determined to build a strong navy and to provide for its gradual increase. American commercial interests began to grow again after the war, and the navy would be designed to protect them.

A continuous presence of American warships was established in the Mediterranean in 1815, and a permanent naval base created at Port Mahon. Unlike Britain, who obtained that same port in 1708, America sought no base for placing pressure on Europe. She chose this fine harbour because of its strategic location in relation to her own trade to the Levant and the Barbary States. One example of her detachment from European affairs may be seen in the Greek War of Independence which broke out in 1821 against Turkey. The war stirred great interest in the United States; many saw parallels to America's fight for freedom as well as romantic memories from the classical past. Strong political pressure urged that the United States Navy intervene. Although warships were readily available in the Mediterranean, and there was deep sympathy for the cause, no direct interference was made. Within two years, President Monroe clearly stated the American position. She disdained interference in a colony's disputes with its mother country, but once free, the United States was willing to support that freedom, particularly that of the newly created republics in South America.

When asked to comment on the proposals which would later become known as the 'Monroe Doctrine', the aged Thomas Jefferson wrote to James Monroe:

> The Question presented. . .is the most momentous which has ever been offered to my contemplation since that of Independence. That made us a nation, this sets our compass and points the course which we are to steer through the ocean of time. . .

> Our first and fundamental maxim should be, never to entangle ourselves in the broils of Europe. Our second, never to suffer Europe to meddle with cis-Atlantic affairs.

Shortly after the 'Monroe Doctrine' had been announced, President Monroe submitted to Congress his plan for a 'naval peace establishment'. In it, he took great pains to explain why he fully supported a relatively strong navy for the United States. Such a force would be totally unnecessary, he said, if either universal peace could be established or if the rights of neutrals in wartime could be guaranteed. The study of history and the experience of the United States in his own lifetime had demonstrated that neither was practicably possible.

It would be some years before the United States Navy was actually deployed in support of the regional policy which Monroe had outlined. But in the meantime, American warships had moved into worldwide stations guarding American commerce. Squadrons were stationed in the Atlantic, the Mediterranean and the eastern Pacific, purely for the protection of trade. A squadron, especially designed for shallow waters, was maintained in the West Indies expressly for the suppression of piracy. Occasional detachments were made from it to West Africa to help curtail the slave trade. The deployment of the United States Navy abroad was closely tied to diplomacy. It was a diplomacy which the first American diplomatic historian would describe in 1826 as 'altogether of a commercial character'.

By way of summary one might categorise the uses of the American Navy in the first years of its existence:

1. The new nation's independence was forcefully asserted in wartime by naval attack.
2. In peacetime, the presence of naval force abroad was used in an attempt to enhance American prestige.
3. The defence of the geographic boundaries of the nation was asserted

by coastal force and fleet action.

4. Diplomats were carried to their appropriate posts.
5. Commerce raiding by naval vessels and privateers was utilised in order to obtain necessary supplies from the enemy, as well as to disrupt the enemy's own source of supply.
6. World-wide naval presence was established for the protection of American trade at sea. Convoy protection was regularly used.
7. Overseas bases were acquired to support the protection of maritime trade.
8. Naval force was used to prevent European nations from interfering in American interests and in matters of American sovereignty.
9. Naval force was used to retaliate against the discriminatory policies of other nations.
10. Decisive political results from naval actions against a great power during wartime were limited to those situations where another great power was allied to the United States or when circumstances prevented a powerful nation from bringing its full military and naval resources against the United States.

All of these uses of naval power were consistent with the basic American outlook and were directly related in every case to foreign policy considerations. Of course, foreign policy may not be the sole reason for which a navy exists. Certainly in the present case, the existence of a viable national defence was crucial to the very unity of the federal republic. But even with such an additional factor, the uses of the American Navy in this period were significantly different from those which Mahan outlined for great powers, even though the basic naval elements involved were very similar. There was proper geographic position, overseas bases, maritime commerce, deployed squadrons, but the 'distant, storm-beaten ships' of the American Navy sought neither commercial nor political dominion. There was no thought given to command of the sea.

No body of naval theory has been written which will help us to understand fully why a small nation might wish to build a navy. In the American case, however, it seems apparent that the navy was used to secure a national identity amongst other nations as well as to assert, protect and defend those particular elements which were necessary to maintain that identity.

One may take as the refrain to the history of the American Navy in the years of its birth, the words of advice which Benjamin Stoddart gave to Congress in 1798:

The wisest, cheapest, and most reasonable means for obtaining the end we aim at, will be prompt and vigorous measures for the creation of a navy sufficient for defence, but not for conquest.

Bibliography

This essay is based on the following sources:

R.G. Albion, *Sea Lanes in Wartime* (1968).

G. Allen, *Naval History of the American Revolution* (1913).

American State Papers: Naval Affairs, Foreign Affairs (1832).

B. Bailyn, *The Ideological Origins of the American Revolution* (1967).

S.F. Bemis, *The Diplomacy of the American Revolution* (1935).

E.B. Billingsley, *In Defense of Neutral Rights* (1967).

A. De Conde, *The Quasi-War* (1966).

J.A. Field, *America and the Mediterranean World, 1776-1882* (1969).

J.C. Fitzpatrick (ed.), *Writings of George Washington* (1931-44).

R. Glover, 'The French Fleet 1807-14: Britain's Problem and Mr Madison's Opportunity', *Journal of Modern History,* 39 (1967), 233-52.

G.S. Graham, *The Empire of the North Atlantic* (1958).

F.H. Hayes, 'John Adams and American Sea Power', *American Neptune,* 25 (1965), 35-45.

D.W. Knox, *History of the United States Navy* (1936).

——, *The Naval Genius of George Washington* (1932).

C.L. Lewis, *Admiral Grasse and American Independence* (1945).

Liscomb, Bergh and Ford (eds.), *Writings of Thomas Jefferson.*

J.H. Macleod, 'Jefferson and the Navy: a Defense', *Huntington Library Quarterly,* 8 (1945), 153-84.

E.S. Maclay, *History of American Privateers* (1899).

G.J. Marcus, *The Age of Nelson* (1971).

A.T. Mahan, *The Influence of Sea Power upon History, 1660-1783* (1890).

——, *The Influence of Sea Power upon the French Revolution and Empire, 1793-1812* (1893).

W.J. Morgan, *Captains to the Northward* (1959).

—— (ed.), *Naval Documents of the American Revolution* (1964-).

C.O. Paullin, *Paullin's History of Naval Administration* (1968).

M. Smelser, *Congress Founds a Navy* (1959).

H. and M. Sprout, *The Rise of American Naval Power* (1939).

C.L. Symonds, 'Navalists and Anti-Navalists', unpublished PhD thesis, University of Florida, 1976.

U.S. Office of Naval Records and Library, *Naval Documents relating*

to the *Quasi-War between the United States and France* (1935-38).
——, *Naval Documents relating to the War with the Barbary Powers* (1939-44).
R.F. Weigley, *The American Way of War* (1973).

COLONIAL AFRICA AND ITS ARMIES

V. G. Kiernan

One of the prizes of empire has always been a supply of colonial soldiery, for use on the spot or elsewhere. It is likely to be cheap, and its employment draws off warlike elements that might make trouble. All the old empires raised troops from subjugated provinces; some, like the Assyrian and the Roman, came to rely far more on colonial levies than on their own manpower. Tribesmen from Numidia or Mauritania were among Rome's innumerable recruits, and involvement in the wars of other countries has been through the ages one feature of a vast African diaspora. In Muslim India, whose rulers could seldom rely on their own subjects, African as well as many other foreign swordsmen were familiar figures: they were known as 'Habshis' — blacks, or Abyssinians. An English traveller in the seventeenth century came on them in Ceylon, at the capital of the king of Kandy. 'He hath also a Guard of Cofferies or Negro's, in whom he imposeth more confidence, than in his own People.'[1] As late as the end of the nineteenth century the Nizams of Hyderabad kept a disorderly rabble known as the 'African Bodyguard'.[2]

In Europe a Negro battalion took part in the French siege of Gaeta in 1806, and for a bonus of fifty centimes the men were encouraged to run and pick up enemy shells and try to remove the fuses before they could explode.[3] Before the twentieth century Africans were frequently made use of in the Americas, though there were obvious risks in arming members of the slave race. Individual masters would hesitate, as French planters did,[4] but governments at a pinch were bolder. Brazilian Negroes fought well against Dutch and French invaders in the seventeenth century. In Jamaica in 1728, when the authorities could not depend on their poor whites, mostly Irish, in case of Spanish attack, they formed a corps of Negroes who were to be posted behind them and ordered to shoot any who turned tail.[5] To Tom Cringle, watching a militia parade in Kingston, the blacks looked a good deal more martial than either the white men or the mulattos.[6] Argentina during its struggle for independence made use of free Negroes and Mulattos, and then filled the gaps with slaves.[7] Later on the dictator Manuel Rosas, aided by his amiable daughter Manuelita, won the impulsive loyalty of the blacks, who furnished him with spies inside every family, and with retainers not to be bribed by any rival.[8] North Americans too drew on

Negroes in the course of their War of Independence, which was to bring so little freedom to the black man; and when Melville served in the navy he found a slave among his messmates.[9] Long after emancipation, black men in the American army represented a sort of 'colonial' soldiery.

Thus, long before the 'scramble for Africa', the fighting qualities of some of its people had been known abroad, while its discords made it easy for outsiders to secure a following. Warfare in many forms was endemic, from tribal skirmishes to quite large-scale encounters. An eighteenth-century Portuguese explorer was impressed by the power of one Kazembe or ruler in the Congo whose troops were 'remarkably well disciplined, and very orderly in their behaviour'.[10] Although the continent had lagged far behind in weaponry it showed a precocious quickness to learn. West Africa's long history of organised warfare was enlivened from the Middle Ages onward by the advent of horse and gun, and states and dynasties rose and fell on the tides of conquest. An early Dutch agent there warned his employers of African skill in the use of 'muskets and carabines', and deplored the facility with which these weapons could be obtained.[11]

Portugal, the pioneer, was always short of manpower, and defended its scattered strongholds in Africa as in Asia chiefly with local levies or mercenaries. A victory over the Congolese was won in 1665 by an army of '3,000 African bowmen, 200 European troops, 150 settlers, and 100 African riflemen'.[12] Defoe's Captain Singleton, crossing the continent, could only trust his captured porters with bows and lances, and wanted them to think the white men's firearms supernatural;[13] but the Portuguese leaders had no fear of putting them into the hands of black recruits, too divided among themselves to think of combining against their masters.

By the nineteenth century Angola had a second-line force known as the *guerre preta* or black army, 'raised on a vassal basis by chiefs of the coastal belt whom the Portuguese had terrified, corrupted, or otherwise persuaded into co-operation'.[14] For any expedition against a tribe of the interior it proved easy to obtain soldiers from another tribe hostile to it. There were normally more black troops than white,[15] despite Angola's growing number of white settlers, while a visitor to Guinea in 1936 paid tribute to Portugal's success in running it with 264 African volunteers under six white officers and eleven NCOs.[16] For some years after rebellion broke out in Angola in 1960 there was hesitation about relying on black troops, but by 1968 they were back in the line. According to an official statement in that year a quarter of them were still volunteers, but opponents asserted that the proportion was really far smaller.[17]

As a rule, in colonial Africa, only limited forces were required for policing heterogeneous populations with little or no national character. Resort to formal conscription was exceptional; indirect modes of compulsion were commoner. In either case there were affinities with slavery, and these revealed themselves from time to time, not only in the Portuguese empire where enslavement of black man by white lingered longest. Cut off in Egypt with a dwindling army — a premonition as it were of France's later dwindling manpower — Bonaparte ordered all Mamelukes from eight to fourteen years of age to be drafted and trained for service.[18] For more immediate purposes he was asking the sultan of Darfur in the Sudan to send shiploads of black slaves down the Nile,[19] to be turned into defenders of liberty, equality and fraternity. There was always likely to be a sub-Saharan ingredient in armed forces in northern Africa. When Mehemet Ali of Egypt was building a European-style army he invaded the Sudan partly in search of supplies of slaves to swell its ranks;[20] unluckily for him, all but 3,000 of the 20,000 brought to Assouan by 1824 cheated him by dying. Dinka tribesmen continued to be inducted as slaves into Sudanese units of the Egyptian army.[21] Servitude in indigenous forms went on. In the Great War a Sierra Leone chief thought himself entitled to impound the bounties due to seven of his 'domestics' who joined or were pushed into the army, had any of them survived; and most of the carriers raised both there and in French West Africa were bondsmen.[22]

From the commencement of the long-drawn-out French conquest of Algeria, a generation later, native levies were being enlisted. Some Turkish *spahis (sipahi, sepoy)* marooned there joined, and *chasseurs spahis* began to be set on foot from material partly French, partly local. By 1914 there were seven regiments, and the corps lasted until Algeria regained independence. A Kabyle tribe, the Zwawa, which had been in the habit of supplying mercenaries to the Turks, in 1830 offered them to the French; though a few years later they deserted to the enemy under the influence of religious fanaticism, and from 1841 the 'Zouave' corps was exclusively French.[23] Other local recruits became the *tirailleurs algériens.* A British officer observing the operations against the Kabyles in the late 1850s noticed how easy it was to enroll defeated tribesmen as irregulars eager to join their conquerors in plundering other villages with which they were feuding.[24] He noticed also that while the French stimulated zeal by allowing a few natives to win commissions, they took care — unlike the British in India before the Mutiny — not to trust their native soldiers with artillery.[25] After all of northwest Africa came under French rule, opinion held Moroccan recruits to be 'by far the best', with Algerians second, and Tunisians last.[26]

Senegal was occupied by the French in the time of the Second Empire, and in 1857 its first administrator, Faidherbe, set on foot the first battalion of *tirailleurs sénégalais*. From 1885 there was a regular mode of recruiting, through chiefs who 'often resorted to tyrannical methods to impress their young subjects into French service'[27] – methods destined in the long run to undermine their own ascendancy. It was with the troops thus acquired that the rest of French West Africa was subdued. Reliance on local fighting men obliged the French to fall in with local custom. Hope of plunder was the volunteer's chief inducement, 'and the regular distribution of captives was the most efficient way to secure his continued loyalty. That female prisoners were euphemistically called *épouses libres* did not make them any less a form of payment.'[28] In 1890 *tirailleurs soudanais* were added, in 1891 Hausas. In 1900 all black African units were incorporated in the army under the generic title of *tirailleurs sénégalais,* though the Senegalese were now only the biggest single contingent.[29]

Britain depended both at home and in India on voluntary enlistment, and it was natural for the same practice to be followed in Africa. In West Africa the military mind was never entirely satisfied with the material to hand. Burton referred disparagingly to a Gold Coast Corps disbanded after mutinying in 1862.[30] 'The West African people', according to two very recent writers, 'may be broadly divided into Negro, or debased races, and the finer types'; though they add that both species shared, when in uniform, 'the useful attributes of cheerfulness and loyalty'.[31] Experiments began early. During and after the Napoleonic wars Africans were enrolled in several units, most prominently in the West India Regiments which after 1840, with a Royal African Colonial Corps reconstituted as one of them, took over garrison duties in both West Africa and the Caribbean.[32] In 1963 some freed Hausa slaves were formed into 'Glover's Hausas', or the Lagos Constabulary, and in 1873 some of these served under Wolseley in the sixth Ashanti war. They were, it was said, so scared of guns that 'they would hang them up in trees and actually worship them', but a Scots officer succeeded in licking this unpromising material into shape.[33] In 1897 a group of units were amalgamated into the West African Frontier Force.

As British control spread over Nigeria the Muslim north offered a recruiting ground which must have reminded Britons of northwest India. In 1914 the Nigeria Regiment, as one constituent of the West African Frontier Force, was formed out of a miscellany of earlier formations, like the one put together by the Niger Company.[34] It had not been intended to serve outside its own region, and when in 1916 it was decided to raise a Nigerian Brigade for the campaign in German East Africa men from each company were invited to come forward. Many northerners did, 'but in the south matters were not nearly so good'. An NCO assured an officer that they would go wherever they were ordered, but they would not *volunteer* to go so far from home: 'a man was a fool to leave his wife and family, home and comfort, for war and discomfort'.[35] A more sensible attitude, or one further removed from the instincts of the true fighting breeds, could scarcely be imagined. There were still Europeans who deemed Nigerians and West Africans at large only fit for porter work.

Europe's standing armies were often built up in the sixteenth century round a nucleus of foreign mercenaries, and this pattern can be found repeating itself in Africa. A police force was set up in the German Cameroons in 1891 which included Hausas and Dahomans, to whom were added men from Togo and the Sudan. In 1895 a regular *Schutztruppe* or 'protective force' was instituted.[36] It was kept up to the mark by flogging, but its function was to protect German interests, not the population, against which it was guilty of much high-handed conduct. 'Natives have an almost innate tendency to exploit their fellows', one scholar commented,[37] somewhat fatuously. Germans could virtuously point to their 'Protectorate Troops Law' of 1896, which restricted native levies to the scale needed for police duties, and eschewed any militarising policy like that of the French.[38]

In the Congo Free State the first non-white soldiers were collected from Zanzibar, Nigeria and elsewhere;[39] then men were drawn from certain provinces whose inhabitants the Belgians regarded as 'martial races'. Grogan, the Cape-to-Cairo traveller, accused them of tapping the wrong tribes, degraded and vice-sodden cannibals. 'Most natives can be touched in their pride or sense of the responsibility of a soldier's position', he wrote. 'But these brutes are mere brutes.'[40] It might be replied that they were wanted, in the bad early days of the Congo, for brutal business. Grogan alleged also that instead of being supplied with provisions they were too often left to supply themselves, by 'commandeering'.[41] Subsequently each province was called on for a quota, but down to 1914 some furnished more men than others, and even after that date more sergeants.[42]

In eastern Africa too European power found its first props in soldiers from outside. But many areas were well stocked with 'martial races' of their own. Livingstone's letters reflect a very marked dichotomy between two types of peoples, one remarkably pacific, the

24

other aggressive and predatory. This was a situation favourable to intruders, with the slave dealers from the coast, Arab or Portuguese, in the lead. They were attended by fighting men culled from 'such tribes as exhibited the qualities of ruthlessness and courage of a far higher order than that possessed by their victims'.[43] These 'more virile' natives were of Wakuma, Masai, Yao and Zulu stock. An unfriendly witness, a South African officer writing on 'The Natives and their Military Value', paid the Wakuma and Masai the compliment of crediting them with physiognomies 'much closer to those of Europeans' than most Africans could boast; and he pointed out that British, Belgian and German *askaris* – this Arab word became the standard term for soldier in the whole region – were drawn from the same districts, some far off in the Sudan.[44] That some peoples, or classes, are more 'martial' than others is a fact, but one due to social circumstances and conditioning, and liable to rapid change. Europeans were too apt to see it as an unchanging genetic fact, on a par with their own inborn superiority.

Askaris of the true breed 'simply loved being soldiers'.[45] Army life was the one least out of harmony, in this new age, with their old habits: they took no interest in the schools and clerkships that European rule brought, and that other African communities eagerly clutched at. There were marked differences of temperament among the martial races themselves, with a dividing line between those amenable to strict army training and those impatient of it. Organised drill and discipline have been the hallmark of modern European warfare, and were giving Europe the mastery of the world. Willingness to submit to them is a social phenomenon of complex origins, but must be connected with habituation to authoritarian rule. Zululand was developing both a despotic monarchy and a code of military obedience not equalled perhaps anywhere in old Asia. Masai, semi-nomadic pastoralists, shone as irregulars, or as scouts or guides. By contrast, some of the men who put on uniform took so readily to the parade ground that they could be seen going on with their exercises in their free time. 'For drilling and parade', a British observer concluded, 'the native mind shows great keenness and aptitude. . .Smart and well-disciplined they are most punctilious in all military services.'[46]

It was out of this stuff that the King's African Rifles (KAR) were embodied in 1902: by 1914 they mustered 21 companies, veterans of a long series of minor compaigns.[47] This regiment was a fusion of three that had come into being in Britain's East African territories. These too started with a nucleus of outsiders. The Central Africa Regiment, in Nyasaland, began with Indian soldiers, mostly Sikhs; the Uganda Rifles with a very mixed bag of Sudanese, among them Egyptians and

25

tribesmen; the first East Africa Rifles were another hotchpotch, taken over from the private army of the Imperial British East Africa Company.[48] It was the same story with the Northern Rhodesia Regiment; it consisted at the outset, in 1894, of 200 Sikhs, volunteers from the Indian army, 40 Zanzibaris, 40 Arabs, 69 Makua recruited with Portuguese permission in Mozambique, along with 'negro irregulars' from a medley of local tribes.[49] There would be obvious difficulties in the way of turning such a scratch lot into an effective force, but at least its motley ingredients would never combine either with one another or with the surrounding population against their paymasters.

In German East Africa, where the last revolt was not quelled until 1907, the first members of the *Schutztruppe* set up in 1891 were likewise strangers, most of them Zulus, Somalis, Sudanese, Swahilis or coast 'Arabs'.[50] As German power pushed inland it drew on tribes like the Wasakuma and Angoni. 'Particularly fruitful was the area around Tabora, in the centre of the territory, the land of the Wanyamwezi, which produced a large proportion of the German force.'[51] Others came from British territory, among them men previously in battalions of the King's African Rifles disbanded in 1911 as superfluous;[52] an illustration of the artificiality of colonial frontiers in Africa. Enlistment was for five years, and could be renewed; native NCOs were usually long-term men. The German authorities, it was credibly enough reported, 'assiduously encouraged their Askaris. . .to consider themselves in every way superior to the mass of non-military natives and as a class apart from their fellows'. They proved very 'receptive of the military cult', behaved like men of a higher caste, and looked altogether different from the rest, 'in whose demeanour the sense of inferiority and the timidity engendered by years of oppression was very noticeable'.[53] This was not much unlike the relative status of army and civilians in Hohenzollern Germany. Every two askaris shared a 'boy' or batman. They were 'very vain and proud', their commander from 1914, von Lettow-Vorbeck, found, and there was no getting rid of such customs.[54] Like all the other forces, they had besides an indispensable train of carriers, 'ruga-ruga', who might be given some military lessons. When the censorious Grogan reached a post in Tanganyika he was for once delighted with what he found. 'The German black troops keep splendid order, and the station has the most flourishing air. I am a great believer in the Germans' African methods.'[55]

After their initial duty of helping to 'pacify' their own region, colonial levies might be utilised further afield. Angolan troops were used in the 1880s against rebels in Mozambique.[56] When the Italians attacked Ethiopia a large part of the army defeated at Adowa in 1896

26

was composed of men from their African possessions.[57] Ethiopia itself had been expanding of late by methods akin to those of the European empires, absorbing into its army warriors from areas over-run by the dominant Amharas. In the British case it was the strain of the Boer War a year or two later, with white men alone in action, that led to East African detachments being employed far away from their homes. In 1899 some men of the Central Africa Regiment were sent to Mauritius; they were allowed to take one wife each, but fell foul of the Creole inhabitants. Next year others from the same corps found themselves in the Gold Coast, and in Somaliland fighting the 'Mad Mullah'.[58] Somalis of northern Kenya made useful soldiers and policemen, though they tried to insist on being accorded a better status than ordinary Africans;[59] and it was lamented that some of 'the riff-raff to be found about the bazaars of sea-port towns' had been allowed to get into the army and infect the solid, reliable 'up-country' Somalis.[60] The French had started earlier, using Algerians in their Crimean and Italian wars, and at the end of 1913, of 76,000 men engaged in the occupation of Morocco, 12,000 were Senegalese.[61] Here was the same process that India had gone through, a kind of snowballing through which a small investment of European manpower could yield large returns.

The Great War embroiled Africa as well as Europe, and, unlike the Boer War, it ranged European and African together on both sides — a disagreeable surprise to 'those who said that hostilities would be confined to Europe, and that war between two white races in a black man's country was unthinkable'.[62] Nigerian and Gold Coast units helped to round up the Germans in the Cameroons before joining in the vastly more arduous campaign in East Africa. They were wanted there because of heavy mortality from sickness among the white troops. Nigeria's first contingent, in 1916, was made up of 2,402 African soldiers with 125 British officers and 70 British NCOs; their own mortality was to be heavy enough.[63] Indians taking part, including Baluchis, Kashmiris, Panjabis, Pathans, were joined by Portuguese and Belgians with their African auxiliaries. Besides all these there were South Africans, who gave deep offence to the Nigerians by addressing them as 'boys', as they were accustomed to do with all black men at home;[64] and for part of the time the commander-in-chief was Smuts. Altogether, if Leipzig was a Battle of the Nations, this was a war of the races.

As in the Boer War, a huge sledgehammer was being brought to bear on a very small band of opponents, but now most of these were black men. While the Indian corps was getting ready its commander, Brigadier-General A.E. Aitken, stated tersely: 'The Indian Army will make short work of a lot of niggers.'[65] Lettow-Vorbeck's memoirs describe the capture of four Indian companies and their British officers, and 'the warlike pride with which our Askari regarded the enemy; I never thought our black fellows could look so distinguished'.[66] It was thanks in great measure to the quality of these men that his tiny army 'engaged, from first to last, the attention of 372,850 British, and surrendered twelve days *after* the Armistice'.[67] He began the contest with 2,540 askaris, and enrolled 11,000 more in the course of it; he could scrape together about 3,000 Germans.[68] There were times when the 'splendid bearing' of the Africans breathed fresh confidence into despondent Europeans,[69] and in the remnant which finally laid down its arms, reduced to 1,323 men, askaris outnumbered Germans by nearly eight to one. An English settler who served against them testified that 'as a rule the German, black or white, fought us clean and fair'.[70]

Immense devastation fell on some areas, thousands of villagers were carried off by the rival forces as porters. Kenya alone paid for the war with an estimated 46,000 African lives.[71] Meanwhile the KAR expanded to a strength of nearly 32,000, including some captured German askaris,[72] and at the end of the war their victory parade at Nairobi was a stirring occasion.[73] Glory had been dearly bought, but there was at least the novel sensation of a spectacle in which ordinary Africans could take pride.

In the Great War, writes Lord Wavell, 'For the first time in history coloured troops were used in warfare on the continent of Europe'.[74] They came mostly from India or Africa. Their coming was not unforeseen. Britain's regular army was small, and France, in the best position to tap the African supply, was heavily outnumbered by Germany. Use of colonial troops to make good the deficiency had found its loudest advocate in Colonel Mangin, most of whose career before 1914 was spent in the colonies. In 1910 he wrote a book, *La Force noire,* which made a strong impression on many other army men and politicians. In the same year he headed a mission charged to explore the potential of West African manpower as the raw material of war, and the Assembly approved a plan to raise 20,000 more *tirailleurs* within the next four years.[75] From 1912 any shortage was made up by compulsion: district headmen had to supply quotas of *appelés,* for four years with the colours. The burden was depicted as a light one, only one man per thousand it was said officially. Similar measures were introduced in Madagascar and Indochina. It was becoming a cliché to refer complacently to Africa as 'un immense réservoir d'hommes, prêts à défendre la patrie'. When the expected war came it brought 1,918,000 men from the colonies to France, 680,000 of them combatants, and for Frenchmen the reality of their empire became for the first time thrillingly alive.[76] There had always been critics who urged the folly of sending the country's soldiers away to remote corners of the globe; now empire was proving itself an asset, instead of a liability, to national defence.

In French black Africa about 215,000 soldiers were mobilised during the Great War, of whom 157,000 were sent abroad and about 30,000, a very high ratio, killed.[77] To bring in recruits considerable pressure was exerted, both in this and in the Second World War, through chiefs or headmen, who were government catspaws, and through Muslim religious leaders who, having a status of their own, could drive bargains with the French in return for inducing their disciples to take service instead of helping them, as they often did at first, to dodge it.[78] In 1915 some of these soldiers were at Gallipoli, and the Muslims among them, as among the Indian units, were pitted against their Turkish co-religionists. Sir Ian Hamilton, the Allied commander, was not much pleased to see them. 'These niggy-wigs were as awkward as golly-wogs in the boats', he confided to his diary after watching practice landings,[79] and he was soon disgruntled because 'the proportion of white men in the French Division is low; there are too many Senegalese'.[80] He objected again when the French withdrew some of their own troops, and noted that 'the Turks dropped manifestoes from aeroplanes along the lines of the Senegalese calling upon these troops to make terms and come over now that their white comrades had left them to have their throats cut'.[81] Turkish propaganda filtering through the Sahara combined with discontent at home against the French demands for more men to cause a serious revolt in 1916.[82]

But it was on the western front that most of the French African troops were deployed. During the retreat from Mons Haig observed that a neighbouring French corps included Moroccans, 'chilled and depressed' in their light tropical wear.[83] A vanguard of Senegalese reached the trenches of Artois that same autumn, and 'literally died of cold';[84] their superiors had not troubled to think about climate or clothing. Winter camps were then formed for them on the Riviera, and they did much good service; their habit of massacring prisoners struck alarm into the enemy.[85] It was in 1917, after the costly failure of many offensives, that the highest hopes were pinned on them, as men who could be counted on to break through any line, to display something like the *furia francese* of former days, or the whirlwind of a Highland charge. They were known as 'Mangin's blacks'; he was now at the head of the sixth Army, cast for a prominent role in the great new attack mounted by Nivelle, and was impatient to make good his doctrine of

Africa as the sword arm of France. 'Mangin was a killer, and he looked the part',[86] but most of his victims were to be his own men. 'In the spring', wrote Brigadier-General Spears, who was with a British corps on the flank, 'long trains hauled their cargoes of black chattering happy sub-humans to the area where presently the heaviest fighting would take place'[87] – language graphically expressive of the white man's feelings about his black cannon fodder.

But instead of a 'wild savage onrush', when their day of glory arrived on 16 April, 1917, they were so numb with icy rains that they could scarcely crawl forward. 'They got quite a long way before the German machine-gunners mowed them down.' In the confusion, French as well as German guns were firing on them. Of 10,000 engaged, 6,300 were casualties, the rest broke into panic flight. It was a 'heart-breaking spectacle', says Spears, but he adds consolingly: 'As they ambled back they soon recovered their composure. Fear had probably never penetrated their thick skulls.'[88] On the murderous battles of July and August the following year Ludendorff was to comment: 'The French had sent into action a remarkably large number of Senegalese and Moroccans and had endeavoured to spare their own people.'[89] As Spears remarked, the French turn of mind was 'unsentimental'; and their own men had sometimes mutinied. We are told that they have 'gratefully remembered' Senegal and its sacrifices;[90] but gratitude seems to have confined itself after 1918 to monuments in Dakar in honour of the 'morts pour la patrie'.[91]

When Smuts was laying down the command in East Africa he paid tribute to 'the native troops, who make splendid infantry. . .they have done magnificent work'.[92] At the end of the war he sounded a warning against allowing the Germans back into Africa, where they might raise formidable armies and use them to conquer other territories and build an economic and military power which 'might yet become an important milestone on the road to world Empire.'[93] At the peace conference when the mandate system was being devised, governments administering backward populations, especially in central Africa, were forbidden to militarise them. This was meant to protect whites at least as much as blacks, but the French strongly objected to any such restraints.[94] Fears continued to haunt the South African mind of 'hordes of native soldiers', trained by white rulers, who might be 'a grave menace to European civilisation on the continent'; the Italian conquest of Ethiopia would make possible 'the rapid preparation of a native army formidable in numbers and military spirit'.[95] Norman Angell believed that this had indeed been Mussolini's prime motive: 'we shall find Italy with a million black conscripts, not to fight in Africa but in Europe.'[96]

France's occupying forces in the Rhineland after 1918 included some blacks, partly it must be supposed as a means of rubbing their defeat into the Germans. Others were being employed in 'pacifying' Syria and Morocco. Recruiting diminished after 1920, and in the inter-war years averaged only about 10,000 annually — one sixth of what the army had pressed for — of whom two men in three were conscripts. Economically and socially 'the results of conscription were generally condemned as disastrous';[97] they were vividly depicted by the anthropologist Gorer.[98] It was General Franco who brought African soldiers to fight again in Europe, this time in a civil war. His Moors appear to have been supplied by their feudal chiefs, at so much a head. According to a pro-Franco Spanish writer about 80,000 were raised; he adds that 'The "Moorish" soldier was generally excellent, showing blind obedience towards his Spanish officers'.[99] George Padmore warned the left in Europe to be on its guard against similar use of African soldiery elsewhere, and pointed out that 'one-third of the French standing army garrisoned in France is composed of colonial professional troops'.[100]

In the Second World War black Africa supplied the French with 160,000 men. In Nigeria 121,652 men were raised. Chiefs and notables were expected to persuade young men to come forward, and 'possibly "moral pressure" was sometimes used'[101] — which may possibly be an understatement. Both Nigerians and KAR took part in 1940 in the liberation of Ethiopia, where prisoners included 11,732 Africans along with 10,350 Italians.[102] Later they served in Burma; and they demonstrated what had often been questioned, that complicated modern equipment was not beyond their ability to master.[103] During 1945-54, 56,000 black troops were sent to fight for France in Indochina, and then 30,000 in Algeria. Portugal went on with the same tactics until 1974; in 1976 Rhodesia is trying uneasily, under the spur of necessity, to raise more black mercenaries.

Egypt, never formally annexed, had to be allowed officers of its own. A training school for officers in the Sudan was set up in 1905.[104] But this was exceptional. The KAR came out of the Great War under the leadership of 1,423 British officers assisted by 2,046 British NCOs.[105] That only white men could be qualified to command was a general axiom of colonial armies; not mainly because of educational or technical requirements, which India for example could easily meet, but because white status had to be kept up and large-scale mutiny made improbable. This was still more essential in Africa because of the absence of large numbers of European troops to provide a counterweight. Since native troops had no leaders of their own it was

31

easy to maintain that without white officers they would always be helpless. This was only a logical extension of a conviction that European peasants or workmen could only make good soldiers when led by men of the higher classes. Any broad gulf whether of class or of race is likely to foster a mystique of 'leadership'.

Both Senegalese and north Africans could stand heavy shellfire, Spears considered, but when their officers were knocked out 'they were apt to become a general nuisance if not a danger'.[106] 'No single factor is of greater importance with colonial troops than the choice of suitable European leadership', writes the historian of the KAR, and he finds one reason for the Italian collapse in Africa in 1940 in 'the poor quality of many of the officers and NCOs serving with the native regiments'.[107] He describes the inexperienced British askaris of that time as shaky at first. 'Africans tend to be better in attack than in defence', and to be 'credulous' and 'quickly affected by rumour', easily unnerved by tactical retreats.[108] Clearly this is likely to be the case with any soldiers who have no leaders of their own kind. In East Africa, as in most areas, chiefs seldom joined the army, preferring to ingratiate themselves with authority by getting others to join instead. Bechuana and Basuto soldiers in the Second World War had an advantage here: some of their chiefs were with them, with the rank of RSM, and could 'lead and advise, exhort, bring news, explain difficulties' — and being largely Christians they had native pastors with them as well.[109]

Between white officer and black private, one stumbling block was language. In the British case, ability to communicate with the men was less readily acquired in Africa, where most officers were regulars who came out from their own regiments for a short term only, than in India. East Africa's *lingua franca*, 'kitchen Swahili', was very simple, a member of the KAR in its later days remarked, but some officers and NCOs never learned it; this he thought 'totally unforgivable', the more so as many askaris had to learn it as a new language, besides a modicum of English.[110] To one Englishman washed into the KAR by the Second World War, relations between the regular officers, despite their very poor linguistic attainments, and their men seemed reasonably good: those between British regular NCOs and Africans much less so, because they were apt to be puffed up by their novel importance.[111]

How army service affected Africans and Africa is a question too little explored. Colonial forces were small at most times, and recruiting grounds as a rule restricted; they were likely to be — as in the Panjab, or for that matter in the British Isles — the poorest, most backward areas, outside the mainstream of African life. This was so in French West Africa; in Nigeria 'the best recruiting areas were those furthest from the regional capitals, in economically depressed parts',[112] chiefly in the north and the 'middle belt'. In Uganda they lay in the north, 'among ethnic groups possessing a reputation for martial skills and few other economic opportunities'.[113] On the other hand, this very backwardness could mean that army life had all the more effect in shaking up the individual or group, and through them the archaic societies they belonged to. It could be, as for Amerindians and other pre-industrial peoples, an introduction, for want of a better, to a modern world of gadgetry, of time regulated by clocks and watches; it was a bridge between past and present. In British eastern and central Africa 'it is difficult to over-estimate the significance of the European military machine' in mixing together members of different communities, scattering people far and wide in the same way as work in the mines did.[114]

Soldiering and mine working had much in common, in the recruit's removal from his home, isolation, subjection to discipline; of the two, the army may be thought, in peacetime at least, the more humane employer. In western Africa it did something to undermine indigenous slavery, by offering one of the new occupations that bondsmen could run away to.[115] To men from very poor districts a very modest allowance of food and clothing was luxury. A force like the KAR provided an elementary education, as well as medical care, and some training in hygiene and domestic science for soldiers' wives; all this could give the recruit a better opinion of himself, along with an improved physique.[116] In its later days it had a training school where men leaving the ranks could turn themselves into craftsmen or welfare officers.[117] There was always a trickle of men ending their service after a shorter or longer term, carrying their new acquirements with them; it was noticeable in the Congo that they were often so completely detached from their old moorings that they preferred to settle in the towns instead of going back home.[118] After both World Wars the trickle became a flood. In the Second World War especially, with its far more complex requirements, recruits had to be sought from wider sections of society, as well as in greater numbers; from south as well as north, in Nigeria as in India. Men who went abroad often came home with altered ideas about themselves and their world. After 1945 an observer wrote of Africans, whose horizons till lately had been bounded by their villages, returning from battlefields in Europe or Burma with new vistas before them, and a thirst for education, the 'white man's juju', as the bringer of 'wealth, power, and success', the three things needed for happiness in life.[119]

Politically the consequences of the colonial army system may have been on the whole less good, but they were very mixed. Sometimes service might intensify old tribal loyalties and rivalries. These could hamper smooth running, as an officer noted,[120] but they had their uses too. It was for a long time the practice of the KAR to have half of a company made up of Yao, half of hereditary foes of theirs like the Angoni, although by 1926 it could be said that 'all the Nyasaland troops have proved themselves so reliable that such a precaution is not really necessary'.[121] Mutinies between 1895 and 1900 made the Belgians decide that the Congo army must be 'ethnically integrated down to the squad level'; when another outbreak in 1944 disclosed that there had been carelessness about this, 'it was reiterated that at least four ethnic groups had to be represented in each platoon'.[122] It must have been largely due to such measures that mutinies were on the whole uncommon, by comparison with India up to 1857.

Conversely, army service, with this shuffling up of elements, might have a detribalising influence, and make for a new, wider union. In East Africa it was sometimes found that men serving British and Germans did not hesitate 'to fight against their blood brothers'.[123] Or members of diverse tribes might come together in a common loyalty, cemented by a regiment's traditions, ceremonies and songs.[124] In an epoch when old social ties were loosening, and many individuals were cast adrift, this might supply a new brotherhood or 'family'. And in some degree such coming together might contribute to the moulding of Africa's new nations. In the Belgian Congo the 'Force publique', with its wide catchment from all the provinces, could be deemed 'the most truly national Congolese institution'.[125] Nevertheless, it broke up the moment independence came, partly for want of an officer cadre of its own. During the World Wars, especially the Second, colonial governments in need of recruits had to make some appeal, as in India, to 'national' feeling, and when Nigerian troops were fighting far away from home it was easier to think, or talk, of 'Nigeria' as an entity. Yet on the whole few Nigerians came to think of the army as 'theirs', as a part of a nation.[126]

Dividing and ruling might be practised between army and people, as well as between soldier and soldier. Sometimes its results came about without intention, as at Freetown at the end of the nineteenth century when there was rioting between the West African Regiment and the populace.[127] Soldiers culled from backward areas 'were quite ready to suppress rebellions against colonial rule that might arise elsewhere'.[128] In Morocco the French could be accused of utilising Berbers from the hills against Arabs of the towns.[129] In Mozambique towards the end the Portuguese were playing on tribal enmities, hiring Makua against

Makonde;[130] the worst atrocities of the repression may have been caused by these tactics. In Guinea, Fula tribesmen were set against the rebels, and attempts were made to set Cape Verdeans against mainlanders.[131]

Colonial forces did contribute to emergent nationalism, indirectly or directly. Their achievements in foreign wars could stimulate African self-respect; in the early 1920s West African spokesmen were declaring that if black men had been good enough to take part in the Great War they were good enough to take part in running their own governments.[132] In Senegal 'blacks who had been feted by whites in France for their victories over another white race, began to doubt the "innate" superiority of the whites'.[133] France, like Portugal, went on with the game too long, and again ignored religious feeling. There was resentment at the use of black troops in Algeria: a serious matter for a government 'well aware that the Algerian and Moroccan troops which were used in Indochina' were now 'the hard core of the rebel army in North Africa'.[134] In British Africa, where this goad was lacking, things went differently. As in India, the 'martial races' played little part in freedom struggles. Kikuyu were not taken into the KAR, John Gunther found, because like Bengalis they were reckoned 'too intellectualized and unreliable'.[135] Only six years later another visitor to Kenya was writing: 'The Kikuyu, so long contemptuously dismissed as a rabble of cowardly "Kukes", have gone through fire' — one tenth of their whole community, he thought, had been killed or arrested.[136]

A decree of 1889 authorised Senegalese to be commissioned,[137] but few were in fact commissioned until after 1949, when officer training was embarked on as part of a programme of black army expansion.[138] When the French left Africa they planned to retain military control. The British might have been expected towards the end to see their interest in training plenty of African officers, to leave behind as pillars of British influence and stability. Whether from lack of political foresight, or from army prejudice, they trained very few. Absence nearly everywhere at independence of a competent and socially influential officer class — such as emerged in India during the Second World War — was by no means an unqualified misfortune. But in sum the armed forces bequeathed to the new Africa by the colonial régimes were small, badly equipped and poorly led. So far they have been, as those of Latin America have always been, more of a nuisance than an asset.

Notes

This essay grew out of a paper written for a seminar at the Institute of Commonwealth Studies in December 1975, presided over by Professor G.N. Sanderson. I learned much from the discussion which followed. My other chief indebtedness is to Mr C. Fyfe, of the Centre of African Studies at Edinburgh University, who has been unsparing of advice, criticism and information.

1. Robert Knox, *An Historical Relation of Ceylon* (1681; new ed., Dehiwala, Ceylon, 1966), p.65. I owe this reference to Dr T. Barron.
2. J.E. Harris, *The African Presence in Asia* (Evanston, 1971), pp.102-5. Lord Macarthey found at Macao in 1794 an unimpressive company of Negro or mulatto infantry; see *An Embassy to China,* ed. J.L. Cranmer-Byng (london, 1962), p.219.
3. P. de Ségur, *Un Aide-de-camp de Napoléon* (1873; Nelson ed., Paris, nd), p.303.
4. E. Fieffé, *Histoire des troupes étrangères au service de la France* (Paris, 1854), vol.1, pp.278-81.
5. H.O. Patterson, 'Outside History: Jamaica Today', in *New Left Review,* no.31 (1965), p.39.
6. M. Scott, *Tom Cringle's Log* (1836), Chap.xi.
7. T.H. Donghi, 'Revolutionary Militarization in Buenos Aires 1806-1815', in *Past and Present,* no.40 (1968), pp.87, 97.
8. See D.F. Sarmiento, *Facundo* (1845), and A.W. Bunkley, *The Life of Sarmiento* (Princeton, 1952), pp.84-5.
9. Herman Melville, *White Jacket* (1850), Chap.xc.
10. B. Davidson, *In the Eye of the Storm. Angola's People* (London, 1972), p.77.
11. B. Davidson, *Africa in History* (London, 1968), p.194.
12. D.M. Abshire and M.A. Samuels (eds.), *Portuguese Africa. A Handbook* (London, 1969), p.43.
13. Daniel Defoe, *The Life Adventures and Piracies of the Famous Captain Singleton* (1720; Everyman ed., 1922), pp.62, 65.
14. Davidson, *In the Eye of the Storm,* p.111.
15. Abshire and Samuels, op.cit., pp.209-10; cf. p.407.
16. Ibid, p.103.
17. Davidson, *In the Eye of the Storm,* p.112.
18. J.C. Herold, *Bonaparte in Egypt* (London, 1962), pp.211-2. A 'Mameluke corps' of Copts and others, who accompanied the French when they went home, was later formed (pp.241, 391).
19. Ibid, p.316.
20. H. Dodwell, *The Founder of Modern Egypt. A Study of Muhammad 'Ali* (Cambridge, 1931), pp.63-5.
21. R. Davies, *The Camel's Back. Service in the Rural Sudan* (London, 1957), pp.129-30.
22. J. Grace, *Domestic Slavery in West Africa. . .1896-1927* (London, 1975), pp.166, 221.
23. W.H. Chaloner and W.O. Henderson (eds.), *Engels as Military Critic* (Manchester, 1959), pp.81-2.
24. H.M. Walmesley, *Sketches of Algeria during the Kabyle War* (London, 1858), pp.344 ff.
25. Ibid., pp.29 ff., 51.
26. C.G. Haines (ed.), *Africa Today* (Baltimore, 1955), p.57.
27. S.P. Davis, *Reservoirs of Men: a History of the Black Troops of French Africa* (Chambéry, 1934), p.64.
28. A.S. Kanya-Forstner, *The Conquest of the Western Sudan. A Study in French Military Imperialism* (Cambridge, 1969), p.272.

29. See War Office *Handbook of the French Army*, 1914 ed., pp.71-3; *Larousse* encyclopaedia, 'Sénégal'.
30. Sir R. Burton, *A Mission to Gelele, King of Dahome,* ed. C.W. Newbury (London, 1966), p.187n.
31. Col. A. Haywood and Brig. F.A.S. Clarke, *The History of the Royal West African Frontier Force* (Aldershot, 1964), p.11.
32. C. Fyfe, *A History of Sierra Leone* (OUP, 1962), p.215. Numerous references to military history will be found in the index, under 'Army'.
33. W. Baird, *General Wauchope* (Edinburgh, 1901), p.41.
34. N.J. Miners, *The Nigerian Army 1956-1966* (London, 1971), pp.12, 26.
35. Capt. W.D. Downes, *With the Nigerians in German East Africa* (London, 1919), p.44.
36. H.R. Rudin, *Germans in the Cameroons 1884-1914* (London, 1938), pp.193-4.
37. Ibid., p.197.
38. Dr H. Schnee (an ex-Governor of German East Africa), *German Colonisation Past and Future* (London, 1926), p.79.
39. V.A. Olorunsala (ed.), *The Politics of Cultural Sub-nationalism in Africa* (New York, 1972), p.206.
40. E.S. Grogan and A.H. Sharp, *From the Cape to Cairo* (1900; Nelson ed., nd), p.294.
41. Ibid., p.295.
42. Olorunsala, op.cit., pp.201, 281.
43. Brig.-Gen. J.J. Collyer, *The South Africans with General Smuts in German East Africa 1916* Pretoria, 1939), p.18.
44. Ibid., pp.16-17.
45. I. Grahame, *Jumbo Effendi. Seven Years with the King's African Rifles* (London, 1966), p.56.
46. Capt. R.V. Dolbey, *Sketches of the East Africa Campaign* (London, 1918), p.23. Cf. W. Lloyd-Jones, *KAR Being an unofficial account of the origin and activities of the King's African Rifles* (London, 1926), p.106: 'The African askari loves drill. . .he is a real joy to a good "drill".' Haywood and Clarke, op.cit., p.323, tell of West Africans giving themselves extra drill.
47. Lt.-Col. H. Moyse-Bartlett, *The King's African Rifles. A Study in the Military History of East and Central Africa, 1890-1945* (Aldershot, 1956), p.259.
48. Ibid., pp.3, 11, 51.
49. W.V. Brelsford, *The Story of the Northern Rhodesia Regiment* (Lusaka, 1954), p.4.
50. Brig.-Gen. J.H.V. Crowe, *General Smuts' Campaign in East Africa* (London, 1918), p.27; Maj. J.R. Sibley, *Tanganyikan Guerrilla: East African Campaign 1914-18* (London, 1973), pp.17-18.
51. Sibley, op.cit., p.18.
52. Crowe, op.cit., p.29.
53. Collyer, op.cit., pp.18-20.
54. Gen. von Lettow-Vorbeck, *My Reminiscences of East Africa* (London, nd), p.24.
55. Grogan and Sharp, op.cit., p.121.
56. R.J. Hammond, *Portugal in Africa 1815-1910* (Stanford, 1966), p.183.
57. See A.H. Atteridge, *Famous Modern Battles* (London, nd), Chap.x, 'Adowa'. Other accounts differ as to the ratio of African troops in Baratieri's army.
58. Moyse-Bartlett, op.cit., pp.29-30, 33.
59. I owe this to a seminar paper by Miss Mahassin El-Safi on Somalis in Kenya, at Edinburgh University, in Feb.1971.
60. Lloyd-Jones, op.cit., pp.216-7.
61. *Handbook of the French Army,* pp.114-5.

62. C.J. Wilson, *The Story of the East African Mounted Rifles* (Nairobi, ?1938), p.9.
63. Downes, op.cit., p.46.
64. Ibid., pp.54-5.
65. B. Gardner, *German East. The Story of the First World War in East Africa* (London, 1963), p.17.
66. Lettow-Vorbeck, op.cit., p.61.
67. J. Terraine, *Douglas Haig. The Educated Soldier* (London, 1963), p.136.
68. Lettow-Vorbeck, op.cit., p.19.
69. Ibid., p.142.
70. Wilson, op.cit., p.28.
71. Sir C. Lucas (ed.), *The Empire at War,* vol.IV, *Africa* (OUP, 1925), pp.236-7, 272-3; Davidson, *Africa in History,* p.255.
72. Sibley, op.cit., p.116.
73. Moyse-Bartlett, op.cit., p.415.
74. *New Cambridge Modern History,* vol.XII (1960), p.263.
75. S.P. Davis, op.cit., pp.109-10; S.H. Roberts, *History of French Colonial Policy (1870-1925)* (London, 1929), p.332.
76. Roberts, op.cit., p.605.
77. Exact figures are not known, and estimates vary somewhat; this is by S.P. Davis, op.cit., p.156.
78. C. Cruise O'Brien, 'Chefs, Saints et Bureaucrates. La politique coloniale au Sénégal', in Anouar Abdel-Malek (ed.), *Sociologie de l'impérialisme* (Paris, 1971), pp.212-4.
79. General Sir Ian Hamilton, *Gallipoli Diary* (London, 1920), vol.1, p.104.
80. Ibid., vol.1, p.192; cf. p.195.
81. Ibid., vol.II, pp.226, 236-7.
82. V. Thompson and R. Adloff, *French West Africa* London, 1958), p.120.
83. Terraine, op.cit., pp.96-7.
84. Brig.-Gen. E.L. Spears, *Prelude to Victory* (London, 1939), p.203.
85. A. Horne, *The Price of Glory. Verdun 1916* (new ed., Harmondsworth, 1964), p.308.
86. Ibid., p.228.
87. Spears, op.cit., pp.264-5.
88. Ibid., pp.490, 504-6.
89. *My War Memories, 1914-1918* (English ed., London, 1920), p.676.
90. M. Crowder, *Senegal. A Study of French Assimilation Policy* (revised ed., London, 1967), p.95.
91. There were long delays after the Second World War before any compensation was awarded to black veterans: Thompson and Adloff, op.cit., pp.228-9.
92. Downes, op.cit., p.267.
93. Introduction to Crowe, op.cit., p.xvi. Cf. a long memorandum by Curzon, in December 1917, on the perils of a German militarisation of Africa: W.R. Louis, *Great Britain and Germany's Lost Colonies 1914-1919* (Oxford, 1967), pp.94-5.
94. League Covenant, Art.XXIII, Clause 5; H.W.V. Temperley (ed.), *A History of the Peace Conference of Paris,* vol.II (London, 1920), pp.239-40.
95. Collyer, op.cit., pp.16-17, 19.
96. Quoted in G. Padmore, *Africa and World Peace* (London, 1937), p.236.
97. Thompson and Adloff, op.cit., pp.227, 232; cf. Roberts, op.cit., p.332.
98. G. Gorer, *Africa Dances. A book about West African Negroes* (London, 1935).
99. R. de la Cierva y de Hoces, 'The Nationalist Army in the Spanish Civil War', in R. Carr (ed.), *The Republic and the Civil War in Spain* (London, 1971), p.199.
100. Padmore, op.cit., p.235.

101. Miners, op.cit., p.14.
102. Brelsford, op.cit., p.83.
103. Moyse-Bartlett, op.cit., p.573.
104. Sir H. Macmichael, *The Anglo-Egyptian Sudan* (London, 1934), p.147.
105. Moyse-Bartlett, op.cit., p.413.
106. Spears, op.cit., p.265.
107. Moyse-Bartlett, op.cit., pp.573, 685.
108. Ibid., p.572.
109. See D.H. Barber, *Africans in Khaki* (London, 1948), pp.86-7; B. Gray, *Basuto Soldiers in Hitler's War* Naseru, 1953; also published in Basuto), pp.52-3. Mr C. Himsworth kindly lent me a copy of this work.
110. Grahame, op.cit., p.35.
111. Information from Prof. G.A. Shepperson, 3 December 1975.
112. Miners, op.cit., p.27.
113. Olorunsala, op.cit., p.80.
114. G.A. Shepperson, 'Military History of British Central Africa' (a review of Moyse-Bartlett, op.cit.), in *Rhodes-Livingstone Journal,* vol.26 (1959), pp.24, 26.
115. Grace, op.cit., p.168.
116. I am indebted for this to an article, kindly shown me in advance of publication by the author, Dr A. Clayton, of the Royal Military Academy, Sandhurst: 'Communication for New Loyalties. African Soldiers' Songs'.
117. N. Farson, *Last Chance in Africa* (new ed., London, 1953), p.177.
118. Olorunsala, op.cit., pp.200-1.
119. D.M. McFarlan, *Celabar. The Church of Scotland Mission 1846-1946* Edinburgh, 1946), pp.165-6.
120. Grahame, op.cit., pp.56-7.
121. Lloyd-Jones, op.cit., p.47.
122. Olorunsala, op.cit., p.201.
123. Dolbey, op.cit., p.23.
124. This is the main theme of the article referred to in note 116 above.
125. Olorunsala, op.cit., p.241.
126. Miners, op.cit., p.32; cf. p.30, on complaints of disorderly behaviour by some recruits, especially during the Second World War.
127. Fyfe, op.cit., p.596.
128. Miners, op.cit., p.2.
129. S. Smith, *U.S. Neocolonialism in Africa* (Moscow, 1974), pp.153-4.
130. Abshire and Samuels, op.cit., p.423.
131. B. Davidson, *The Liberation of Guiné* (Harmondsworth, 1969), p.62.
132. Davidson, *Africa in History,* p.277.
133. S.P. Davis, op.cit., pp.166-7.
134. Thompson and Adloff, op.cit., p.231.
135. J. Gunther, *Inside Africa* (London, 1955), p.364.
136. E.S. Munger, letter from Nairobi, Mar.14, 1955, in E.S. Munger (ed.), *African Field Reports 1952-1961* (Cape Town, 1961), p.247.
137. S.P. Davis, op.cit., p.66.
138. Thompson and Adloff, op.cit., pp.231-2.

WAR AND SOCIAL CHANGE:
THE BLACK AMERICAN IN TWO WORLD WARS

Neil A. Wynn

I

A number of writers in recent years have recognised the significance of the Second World War as a 'progressive force' for change in the lives of black Americans: most have followed Richard Dalfiume in seeing 'The "Forgotten" Years of the Negro Revolt' in terms of rising black militance; others, like myself, have argued that the war brought equally important changes in all aspects of Afro-American life.[1] While such writings, whatever their different emphases, have drawn attention to a long-neglected period of American and Afro-American history, they have also removed something of the sense of historical continuity. Moreover, several questions about the nature of war and the factors which can effect social change have been left unanswered. In both respects a comparison between the two World Wars and their different impacts on the situation of black Americans can provide the answers.[2]

By the end of the nineteenth century, blacks in the South (over 90 per cent of the black population) were subject to physical discrimination, disenfranchisement and economic deprivation. After the 1870s both the American government and the people had lost interest in the Afro-Americans' plight and were concerned more with industrial growth, westward expansion and imperialism. Racial prejudice was encouraged by imperialism, with its justification of the white man's burden, and by the pseudo-scientific writings of the period, which confirmed the racial superiority of the Aryan race. Progressivism, when it came, did little for the blacks, and under Woodrow Wilson's 'New Freedom' blacks actually suffered setbacks. The traditional patronage which had provided a few federal and diplomatic appointments for blacks was ignored and from 1913 onwards, segregation was introduced to government departments in the nation's capital. Dependent on southern support in Congress in order to pass his reform measures, Wilson was not likely to argue the case for civil rights legislation. Besides, he was himself a southerner who believed in the separation of the races and as President of Princeton had barred blacks from attending the university. At meetings with his Cabinet the President delighted in telling the members, five out of ten of whom were also from the South, 'darky stories'. Even if he had been concerned with the situation of black Americans, with the outbreak of war in Europe Wilson's attention was increasingly diverted from domestic matters. As Kelly Miller, the Dean of Howard University, later observed, Wilson reversed the old motto: for him 'charity began abroad rather than at home'.[3]

Blacks themselves were in no position to demand change in the years before the war. With a predominantly rural and ill-educated black population there was not the base on which to build a strong, viable racial organisation. At the same time, the pre-eminence of Booker T. Washington, with his public emphasis on racial separation, vocational training and evolutionary change, encouraged acceptance of the existing patterns among both blacks and whites. Although his views were being increasingly challenged by men like the Boston journalist, William Monroe Trotter, and W.E.B. DuBois, they still held sway after his death in 1915. New organisations like the NAACP (organised in 1909) and the National Urban League (1911) were still trying to formulate policies and establish themselves when America entered the First World War.

The preconditions for change were not promising and given the weakness of the black population and the prevailing attitudes of most whites, it is not surprising that Afro-Americans met with strong opposition to their demands for equal treatment even after America's entry into the war in April 1917. Black volunteers for armed service were accepted only as long as there remained places in the four black Army regiments established under the Army Reorganization Act of 1866: once those places were filled, the Afro-Americans were turned away.

Despite the long history of black participation in America's armed forces, many whites, including government and military officials, felt that blacks made poor soldiers, that equal service would degrade white troops, or that blacks might use their military training and weapons at home. This last point was expressed forcibly in the debates on the Selective Service Act of May 1917 which declared that all men between the ages of 21 and 30 should be liable to the draft. Senator Vardaman of Mississippi opposed universal conscription because 'millions of Negroes who will come under the measure will be armed, [and] I know of no greater menace to the South than this'.[4] However, the Act was passed and of the 2,290,525 blacks registered, some 370,000 were called into service. In fact, nearly 31 per cent of the registered blacks were drafted, compared with 26 per cent of the white registrants, because of discrimination by certain boards on the question of deferments.

Once accepted, the range of service open to blacks remained limited.

In the Navy black men could work only as mess men, cooks or heavers of coal; they were barred entirely from the Marine Corps, the Coastguard and from the Army Aviation Corps. Although in theory all branches of the Army were open to them, in practice some 380,000 of the 400,000 black soldiers were members of Services of Supply regiments acting as stevedores, drivers, engineers and the like. Only a small number actually saw combat duty, and then beside French troops who had experience of dealing with colonial forces of their own. Even in such limited roles, blacks were subjected to discrimination and insult. Many training camps were situated in the South where the soldiers had to accept local Jim Crow laws and suffer harrassment from neighbouring white civilian populations. Within the camps they were often maligned by their officers, many of whom were white southerners chosen because they 'would understand the Negro temperament'.[5] (Only after a struggle was a segregated black officer training camp established but there were still only 1,200 black officers at the end of the war.) In Houston, Texas, black soldiers finally responded to a series of racial insults and in November 1917 were involved in a race riot in which 17 whites died. Sixty-four black soldiers were accused of murder and after a one-day trial thirteen were sentenced to death and the rest to life imprisonment.

Even overseas, with all the hazards of the trenches, blacks found discrimination. While the French population was often prepared to treat the black soldier as a social equal, such attitudes were discouraged. In August 1918, in a secret memorandum, the French liaison officer at the American HQ warned his compatriots against dealing with blacks 'on the same plane as with the white American'. He also suggested that blacks should not be commended too highly in front of white Americans. There were reports that in Britain Americans reacted violently towards inter-racial couples.[6]

Despite the various barriers and obstacles in their way, black troops did serve with some valour and distinction. Three regiments of the black 93rd Infantry Division were awarded the Croix de Guerre, as were more than 100 individual black soldiers. However, such records tended to be forgotten in military circles. Instead the collapse and disintegration of a regiment of blacks from the 92nd Division in the face of the enemy was remembered and emphasised, even though an official investigation in 1919 blamed inexperience, poor leadership and lack of artillery rather than racial inferiority. Similarly, rumours of inefficiency, of numerous incidents of rape and disorder, persisted long after the war — again despite evidence to the contrary. While blacks were given few opportunities to demonstrate their equality, real or supposed cases of poor performance confirmed the prejudices of many whites.

If there was little change within the armed forces, there was much more on the domestic front — but as a consequence of spontaneous and unguided change rather than official action. The most important and dramatic was the 'Great Migration' of blacks from the South to the North which, as Allan Spear has pointed out, caused some historians to see World War I 'as the major turning point in the history of Negroes in the North'.[7] There had been a slow, but steady movement of blacks from the South to the North during the twenty years preceding World War I. However, with the outbreak of war the demand for labour to meet the immigration from Europe added a pull to the already existing push to poverty and discrimination in the South, turning the trickle of black migrants into a flood. Actual estimates of numbers vary from 150,000 to over 2,000,000, but a more likely figure lies somewhere between 400,000 and 600,000. Some of those who moved during the war returned home following the peace. Even so, the black population in the North rose from 1,036,000 in 1910 to 1,551,000 in 1920. Over 61,000 blacks entered Chicago alone and it was to the major cities that most of the migrants went.[8] While the migration did become one of the major social issues of the day, destroying the idea of race as a purely southern problem, some 77 per cent of the black population still lived in the South in 1940 and, as we shall see, a more diverse movement occurred during World War II.

Occurring 'without organisation or leadership' the migration during the First World War was encouraged by letters from earlier migrants, by appeals in the widely-circularised black paper, the *Chicago Defender,* and by labour agents from northern industries.[9] Many of the new arrivals in the North found that they had been misled by the labour agents or exaggerated advertisements, but by and large there was a considerable demand for workers and it was not too difficult to find employment during the war. Both the *Chicago Defender* and the National Urban League acted as clearing houses for job information and, with or without such guidance, 'some 255,000 blacks found new jobs in the wake of the war emergency'.[10] The conditions of employment were, as letters from migrants suggested, much better than those in the South. Blacks spoke of daily wages of from six to eight dollars a day, often equivalent to weekly wages in the South. In Chicago the average rate of pay was 50 cents an hour compared to 75 cents a day in the South: as the *Chicago Defender* commented, 'The opportunity we have longed for is here. . .The war has given us a place upon which to stand.'[11]

The opportunity existed not just to earn higher wages, but also to work in occupations previously restricted to whites. During the war black workers secured their first foothold in industry, semi-skilled and clerical jobs opened up, and there was some shift away from traditional types of employment. In Chicago in 1910, 51 per cent of black men worked in service industries as domestic servants, hotel and restaurant waiters or janitors; by 1920, the percentage had dropped to 28 per cent. Black women too, made some progress, replacing white women (who were themselves replacing white men) in textile, clothing, food and tobacco industries. Between 1910 and 1920, the number of black women in manufacturing and mechanised production rose from 67,937 to 104,983.[12]

However, the gains for both sexes were not without their limits. For men, the majority of jobs were in the unskilled sections of industry and were concentrated in a few fields such as iron and steel, meat packing, ship building and the automobile industry. In 1910 blacks constituted 6.4 per cent of the unskilled labourers in the steelworks, but by 1920 their percentage had increased to 17: a new stereotype of the black performing hot and heavy tasks had arisen. For black women, restrictions still applied and for those with high school or even college educations there was no real alternative to domestic services. Moreover, the gains made during the war proved to be tenuous and during the recession of 1919-20 there were massive lay-offs with the wholesale displacement of black workers.[13] Although some jobs were regained later in the twenties, the vulnerability of black workers persisted and was revealed again during the Depression. In a series of articles in the *Journal of Negro Education* in the summer of 1943 comparing the World War I employment situation with that of World War II, all writers agreed that little progress had been made in the earlier war. One of the contributors summed up by concluding that the 'Negro laborer had failed to become a part of the American war industrial scheme' because neither employer, fellow employee, nor government would act to enable full participation'.[14]

If the migrations did not lead to full economic opportunity, they did not necessarily result in better living conditions either. With a cutback or even cessation in housing development during the war years, many of the northern cities suffered shortages in accommodation. For blacks, the situation was compounded by the racial prejudice which confined them to already existing black areas. As Robert C. Weaver, a leading authority on black housing, later wrote, it was during the war years and after that 'the idea of Negro ghettos in northern cities became fixed'.[15] Conditions within the ghettos, because of overcrowding and the low economic status of the inhabitants, were deplorable. In Chicago 'the core of the black belt was a festering slum', while in Harlem the situation of the blacks was reflected in the figures which showed that between 1923 and 1927 the death rate was 42 per cent in excess of that of the rest of the city. Twice as many Harlem mothers died in childbirth as in other districts. Little wonder that blacks often found urban life 'debilitating'.[16]

II

The alteration in the population and employment patterns of blacks caused some reaction among their white countrymen. Writing about race relations during World War II, the Swedish sociologist Gunnar Myrdal, observed that the earlier conflict had 'stirred up people's minds and prepared them for change'.[17] In actual fact, however, there were many indications that the American people were prepared to resist change, particularly in racial affairs. The psychological impact of the war led to a heightened sense of national unity, but with an intensification of 'in-group' feelings reflected in hostility and intolerance towards foreigners or racially 'un-American' groups. The Ku Klux Klan, revived in 1915, grew in strength during the war and was only part of the widespread attack on minority ethnic and racial communities. Blacks specifically were the victims of increasing violence throughout the war years as whites fought to prevent changes in the *status quo.*

The migration of blacks from the South, at first welcomed as a possible cure for the racial problem, soon attracted mounting opposition from all parts of the country. In some areas of the South, whites, concerned about the loss of their labour supply, attempted to prevent blacks from leaving, outlawed the activities of labour agents, and tried to discourage the sale and distribution of the *Chicago Defender.* Lurid tales of conditions in the North were also intended to discourage would-be migrants. In the North, too, the arrival of large numbers of blacks was viewed with alarm. Some newspaper headlines spoke of 'half a million darkies' swarming to the North and suggested that they were 'incited by German spies', while members of labour organisations feared that blacks would be used as strikebreakers or that their employers were creating a surplus in manpower in order to undermine existing working conditions.[18] Competition in work was equalled by competition for housing and conflict over both led to the riot in East St Louis in 1917 in which at least forty blacks were killed. Other smaller clashes occurred in New York and Philadelphia, and in Chicago between 1917 and 1919 there were over 24 bombs thrown at homes occupied by blacks or the real estate agents who sold to blacks.

The continued friction between the races in Chicago exploded in 1919 with the riot in which 38 people lost their lives and over 500 were injured. Across the country, blacks were subjected to an increasing wave of violence as the number of lynchings rose from 38 in 1917 to 64 in 1918, and 83 in 1919, and during the Red Summer of 1919 there were more than 20 race riots.

Following the riot in East St Louis, the NAACP staged a silent protest march in New York city. Among the banners was one which asked 'Mr President, why not make America safe for Democracy?' The answer was a stony silence and despite repeated requests from blacks for some action on race relations, Wilson remained unresponsive, 'unwilling to make any formal statements that would seem to ally him with black leaders'.[19] Not until July 1918 did the President make any statement deploring mob violence – and then without mentioning the racial context.

The federal government was not completely unconcerned with the situation of the Afro-American. As Joel Spingarn, in his capacity as Army intelligence officer, pointed out,

> The co-operation of this large element of our population in all civilian and military activities is of vital importance; the alienation, or worse, of eleven million people would be a serious menace to the successful prosecution of the war.[20]

Such practical considerations were not ignored by one of the more liberal Cabinet members, the Secretary of War, Newton D. Baker. In October 1917, following the East St Louis riot, he appointed Emmett J. Scott, former secretary to Booker T. Washington, as Special Assistant to advise on racial matters. In May 1918 George E. Haynes, professor at Fisk University, was made Director of Negro Economics within the Department of Labor to assist with the mobilisation of manpower on the homefront. Both appointments were a considerable departure from the Wilson administration's previous lily-white policy, but they were also entirely war-oriented, primarily morale boosting exercises designed to increase contributions to the war effort rather than to bring long-term changes in race relations. Scott's chief function was to provide liaison between the government and black leaders, to tour training camps and to investigate complaints. He did initiate action against discriminatory draft boards in the South, but otherwise had little real effect as he 'became a faithful and often uncritical servant of the war effort'.[21] Haynes, too, concentrated on public relations, organising meetings and committees to discuss racial problems. In some cases such bodies helped to place black workers in employment and Haynes himself secured several black appointments within the Labor Department bureau. However, like Scott, he attempted little reform and even within federal offices discrimination and segregation continued.

Even sympathetic whites tended to speak of blacks in terms of the stereotyped 'uncle', 'Hottentot', 'pickaninny', as 'boys who do not grow up even under shell fire', and an Army Signal Corps film, *Training of Colored Troops,* presumably made for recruiting purposes, is full of such images.[22] The dramatised story of a black soldier from induction to training, it concentrates on the comic aspects, including shots of a watermelon eating competition and showing the black soldiers dancing to their band. The soldier concerned is, of course, joining the engineers. More encouraging were the attempts of some southerners to counteract racial tensions by forming inter-racial committees. During the violence of 1919 some of these committees came together under the Commission on Inter-racial Co-operation headed by a white southerner, Will Alexander. Although attacking only discrimination and not segregation, the Commission was, until World War II, the chief voice of southern moderation. Sadly, it was struggling against the tide in the 1920s and could only reach a small minority of people. For the majority of white Americans the fact of black participation in the war effort was either ignored or resented. Rather significantly the major study of the impact of the war on America, Frederic Paxson's three volume *American Democracy and the World War,* has the very barest mention of blacks, with no reference at all to their role in the armed forces or in industry, nor any comment on wartime racial violence.

Despite their treatment in society and in the armed services, the majority of black Americans were only too willing to support the war effort and to demonstrate their loyalty. While the *Chicago Defender* could demand 'let us, too, make America safe for democracy' it could also, the following week, say that the black man's duty was 'to keep a stiff upper lip and make the most out of the situation'.[23] Refusing to 'rock the boat', the *Defender* urged blacks to set aside grievances until the war was over for, 'If we again demonstrate our loyalty in the face of injustices. . .those injustices will disappear'.[24] This view was shared by W.E.B. DuBois, editor of the NAACP's magazine, *The Crisis.* Like the *Defender,* DuBois suggested that 'First Your Country, Then Your Rights', should be the black man's order of priorities because 'Out of this war will rise, too, an American Negro with the right to vote and the right to work and the right to live without insult.' It was this belief which led him to call 'Close Ranks' in July 1918 and to ask blacks to forget their grievances while the war was on: 'When men fight together and work together', he said, 'this foolishness of race prejudice disappears.[25]

Although criticised by some fellow blacks for the 'Close Ranks' editorial and his desire to continue as editor while holding a commission in the Army (an offer neither pursued by the Army nor taken up by DuBois), DuBois reflected the views of most civil rights leaders and of blacks generally — a fact demonstrated by their willingness to volunteer for armed service and the contribution of over $250,000 in war loans from blacks. Some black leaders were, indeed, even less critical than DuBois. Robert Russa Morton, Booker T. Washington's successor at Tuskegee, assured President Wilson in 1917, probably rightly, 'that you and the nation can count absolutely on the loyalty of the mass of Negroes'.[26] In 1918 the government sent Morton to France to investigate the conditions of black soldiers and he later reported that a policy of equal treatment and equal service had been 'adopted by the War Department and with very satisfactory results'. In an address to black soldiers he expressed the hope that 'no one will do anything in peace to spoil the magnificent record you have made in war' — a message taken by his audience to imply acceptance of the *status quo*.[27]

The views of men like Morton and Scott were often criticised after the war. In all fairness, however, the difference between the accommodationists' stance and that of the other black leaders was only one of slight degree. Basically both camps were saying support the war effort and you will be rewarded. Only a very few blacks rejected this philosophy during the war (although more did after it). Among them were A. Philip Randolph and Chandler Owen, the editors of the *Messenger,* a socialist journal. Randolph and Owen endorsed the position of the American Socialist Party and argued that the war was a direct result of capitalism from which only capitalists could benefit. The *Messenger* repeatedly pointed to the discrimination and segregation applied to blacks and rejected the idea that blacks would be rewarded for service in the war. 'Since when', they asked, 'has the subject race come out of a war with its rights and privileges accorded for such participation?'[28] Their writings and outspoken comments attracted the attention of the Justice Department and in 1918 both men were arrested. The judge who heard their case could not believe that the young men were other than the innocent dupes of white radicals and he dismissed the charges. In August Owen was drafted and sent to a camp in the South where he spent the remainder of the war and Randolph only avoided a similar fate because the war ended when his call up was due.

In a minority during the war, Randolph and Owen were more in line with the general black mood once the war had ended as other Afro-Americans saw that their hopes of recognition were not to be fulfilled. Rather than the subjects of white gratitude, blacks were instead among the victims of the post-war xenophobia and hysteria which swept the country. Among the 83 blacks lynched in 1919 were ten soldiers, some still in uniform. Well might a young black war veteran who had been chased by a mob during the riot in Chicago ask,

> Had the ten months I spent in France been all in vain? Were those white crosses over the dead bodies of those dark skinned boys lying in Flanders fields for naught? Was democracy merely a hollow sentiment? What had I done to deserve such treatment?[29]

In February 1919 the *Chicago Defender* found it hard to believe that men who had fought in Europe would 'tamely and meekly submit to a program of lynching, burning and social ostracism', and following the Chicago riot, in which 15 whites were among the 38 dead, the paper commented that blacks were 'no longer content to turn the left cheek when smitten upon the right'.[30] W.E.B. DuBois was equally disillusioned and bitter. Calling upon blacks to 'marshal every ounce of our brain and brawn', he coined the slogan 'We *return, we return from fighting,* we *return fighting'* and privately he remarked, 'I did not realize the full horror of war and its wide impotence as a method of social reform.' More optimistically he concluded that perhaps 'passive resistance by 12 million to war activity might have saved the world for black and white'.[31]

But the war had brought some change: the black man who had held his grievances in abeyance during the war was not prepared to do so when it was over. The 'New Negro' who said 'I ain't looking for trouble, but if it comes my way I ain't dodging' had arrived, and during the riots in Chicago, Washington DC and elsewhere there were many instances of blacks retaliating to white attacks.[32] The post-war mood was best captured by the ebullient and arrogant Marcus Garvey whose Universal Negro Improvement Association (UNIA), with its stress on black pride and the African culture, seized the imagination of many among the masses of ordinary blacks. But like the UNIA, the 'New Negro' was not in evidence for long and for most Afro-Americans 'normalcy' did mean a return to the pre-war situation. However, the experiences of the First World War were not forgotten and they were recalled in 1941 by men who vowed not to make the same mistakes again.

III

If the Second World War did have a greater impact on the Afro-American than the First, it was because the former was a more total war which had a greater effect on American society generally. Lasting twice as long, the Second World War cost 330 billion dollars compared to the 32 billion of World War I and involved over 14 million people in the armed forces as opposed to the earlier 5 million. The demands for manpower in defence industries resulted in the addition of more than 10 million people to the labour force, led three million women who would otherwise have stayed at home into the workforce, and encouraged the movement of more than five million people from one area to another in search of employment. The effects of these different developments can be measured in a variety of ways: in the higher wage levels, the growth in trade union membership, or the rise in marriage, divorce and birth rates, or the increase in juvenile delinquency. So great was the impact of the war that one recent writer has suggested that the six years of conflict brought more social change than did the six years of the New Deal.[33]

But if the difference in impact of the two World Wars was significant, so too was the difference in the situation of the black population. The urbanisation and migration of blacks, which continued in the interwar years, led to a greater sophistication and self-consciousness reflected in the literary movement of the Harlem Renaissance, the rising circulation of the black press and the increased strength of civil rights organisation. By 1940 the combined circulation of more than 150 black newspapers totalled 1,276,600, and the *Chicago Defender,* only established in 1905, had sales of over 82,000. Similarly, the NAACP had a membership approaching 90,000 and a budget of over 60,000 dollars.[34] During the 1930s the Association had fought and won several cases in the Supreme Court which were to help shape race relations for the next decade.

Blacks, too, were beginning to feel and to exercise their growing economic and political power in the years before the war. As well as the rise of black trade unionists, like A. Philip Randolph, the 'Jobs-for-Negroes' movement and the boycotts of stores were signs of a growing self-awareness and the ability to mobilise blacks at grass-roots level. More decisive though, was the swing of black voters away from the Republican party and into the New Deal coalition. Although Franklin Roosevelt's actual commitments to the blacks were slim, his general humanitarian and liberal outlook benefited Afro-Americans as part of the general population. His position on race relations was certainly more favourable than that of Woodrow Wilson, and his wife Eleanor was able to speak and act for blacks and to provide moral leadership in the country. Men like Harold Ickes, Will Alexander and Harry Hopkins, sympathetic to blacks, could lay special emphasis on their needs within their particular agencies. The participation in government of a number of black advisers, including Robert C. Weaver, Mary McCleod Bethune and others, did ensure that blacks received some consideration in policy-making. Despite all this, however, there was still discrimination in New Deal agencies and blacks did suffer disproportionately during the Depression. When the mobilisation for war began in 1940, it seemed again that blacks were to be excluded from both the military and industrial sectors and remain the last hired and first fired.

In January 1940 there were still seven million whites and one million blacks unemployed and the large pool of white labour meant that blacks could be, and were, ignored in the early industrial mobilisation. While the rate of unemployment amongst whites dropped from 17.7 per cent to 13 per cent between April and October 1940, for blacks it remained static at 22 per cent. Indicative of the extent of discrimination was the fact that only 240 blacks were employed in the entire aircraft industry in 1940 and as late as January 1942, 51 per cent of several hundred of the largest war contractors refused to employ blacks.[35] The situation was not so different in the armed forces. The four black regular army regiments had been run down in strength until by 1939 there were only 3,640 black soldiers with only five black officers, three of whom were chaplains. In the Navy, even the number of black mess men had been reduced, and there was still no change in the policy of exclusion from the Air Corps, Marine Corps and Coastguard.

The black response to this situation was an immediate demand for equal participation. As early as 1939 the traditional civil rights bodies were joined by first the Committee for the Participation of Negroes in National Defense, and later by the National Negro Defense Program and other bodies, to press for an end to discrimination. Their vocal protests, coming in a presidential election year and seized upon by the Republicans, had some effects. In October 1940, following meetings with black representatives, the White House issued a statement on military policy which declared that blacks would be used in 'each major branch of the service' and in proportion to their numbers in the population. Segregation, however, was to be maintained as it had 'proved satisfactory over a long period of years' and changes 'would produce situations destructive to morale and detrimental to the preparation for national defense'.[36] This statement was met with anger from blacks not prepared to accept segregation and in an attempt to repair the damage, the government made further concessions. Colonel

Benjamin O. Davis was appointed the first black general and plans for the formation of an aviation training school were announced. Following the precedents of the First World War, William H. Hastie, Dean of Howard University Law School, was appointed civilian aide to the Secretary of War. Unlike his earlier predecessor, however, Hastie remained an outspoken critic of military racial policies. In 1943 he resigned, amid much publicity, because he felt he was being continually ignored within the War Department.

Despite Hastie's feelings to the contrary, there was some change in military practices. An Army Air Corps school for blacks was established at Tuskegee in 1941 and the first black air squadron flew in combat in 1943; black officers were trained with whites in integrated camps because of the difficulties involved in providing separate facilities; and in line with the 1940 policy statement, the Marine Corps and Navy accepted blacks for general service from 1942. Further protests and outbreaks of racial violence led to the desegregation of some Army recreational facilities and bus services and the implementation of an educational programme of 'morale building information on the stake and role of the Negro in the war'.[37] But despite these changes, and high-level discussions on the best use of black troops, there was no change in the overall policy of segregation until challenged by the demands of the war.

In December 1944, during the Battle of the Bulge, the need for fresh replacements for front line troops led to the integration of 37 volunteer black platoons with larger white units. This experiment lasted until the war in Europe ended and proved very successful. Surveys revealed that rather than increasing racial prejudice, integration served to reduce it.[38] Although the integrated groups were disbanded once the war was over, the experience was not forgotten and the old arguments in favour of segregation were considerably weakened. In the Navy too, the need to utilise all available manpower led to experimentation. In an effort to use black sailors fully, but still preserve segregation, two ships were manned with all-black crews. The impracticability of this solution led to the integration of a number of vessels in 1944 and then the entire auxiliary fleet. Again the way for greater integration had been prepared.[39]

By the end of the war, more than one million blacks had served in different branches of the armed forces. While discrimination and prejudice had persisted, it had not been as powerful a force as in the earlier war. For many blacks, the forces had provided an education in technical programmes and, for some, a basic course in reading and writing. Many thousands served overseas where they often were treated as equals for the first time in their lives. One certain reward for armed service was the GI Bill of Rights with its provision for loans to support education, or home purchase, or to buy farms and businesses. Although there is no record of the number of blacks who used the Bill (but considerable evidence of discrimination in its application), a significant number were among the several million veterans to have made use of the Bill's provisions by the 1950s. For some black veterans the best avenue of opportunity remained the armed services and in 1946 blacks accounted for some 25 per cent of all re-enlistments.[40]

In industry, the pattern of progress was like that in the forces: concessions in the period prior to American entry into the conflict as a result of black protest, followed by change which occurred spontaneously in response to the necessities of war. In 1940, the question of discrimination in defence industries had not been dealt with and despite constant pressure from blacks, Roosevelt refused to take any action. At the beginning of 1941, A. Philip Randolph suggested that 10,000 blacks should march on Washington to demand the right to work in war industries. By May 1941, Randolph had been joined by despairing leaders of the NAACP, Urban League and other organisations and the date of the march was set for 1 July 1941. Failing to persuade the blacks to back down, Roosevelt gave way and on 27 June 1941, he issued Executive Order 8802 stating that there should be no discrimination in defence industries and establishing a Fair Employment Practices Committee to see that the policy was carried out. Although the first executive action of its kind since Reconstruction, in actual practice the Committee had little real power and could only rely on the publicity created by its public hearings. It did, however, hear thousands of cases and the example it set was copied by a number of local and state governments.

Employment opportunities for blacks did increase during the war, but as one writer pointed out, they did so as a result of 'the general appearances of stringencies in the supply of labor' rather than government efforts. Most gains were made after 1942 and in areas of acute labour shortage.[41] Whatever the cause, the number of blacks in work rose from 4.4 million to 5.3 million during the war and by 1944 the number unemployed was only 151,000. The numbers employed as skilled craftsmen, foremen and semi-skilled operatives doubled. Black women also found new opportunities, and some additional 600,000 entered the labour force.[42] One crucial area of progress for both sexes was in employment in government service and by 1944 19.2 per cent of all persons in federal departments were black. A great many of these were working in the traditional janitorial and custodial positions, but the proportion was much less than it had been. In one of the best departments, the Office of Price Administration, more than 70 per cent of the 1,250 black workers held clerical or administrative posts.[43] With blacks in almost every government agency and with advisers in Selective Service, the Office of War Information, the Office of the Secretary of War, the Department of Labor, Office of Education and the Housing Agency, Afro-Americans were in a position to assert their claims in the post-war period.

With full employment, many black homes had more than one wage earner and as wage levels were rising anyway, there was a considerable jump in family incomes. The average earnings of the black urban worker rose during the war from about 400 dollars a year to over 1,000 dollars; in Atlanta, one survey revealed that average black family incomes had increased by over 65 per cent.[44] Typical of the changes taking place was the case of the black woman whose income rose from 312 dollars to 2,477 dollars after she gave up domestic service to become a drill operator. Although by 1945 the average money income of all black families was only half that of whites, this was the highest it had ever been, and was the highest it was to reach for some time. However, there were not the lay-offs in 1945-6 that had occurred following World War I. The increase in the number of blacks in trade unions by 700,000 to 1,250,000 afforded some protection; employers too, were now more prepared to use black workers and one survey showed that of 300 war industries, 253 intended to continue to employ blacks.[45] The generally high levels of employment in the post-war years made it possible for blacks to maintain the gains they had made and it was not until the recessions of the early 1950s that there was any real slipping back.

IV

Once again, the increased employment opportunities in areas outside of the South led to a rise in the migration of blacks. However, the movement which occurred during the 1940s was neither just a repetition nor a continuation of the earlier migration. It was, in the first instance, part of a general shift in population and came only after whites had flocked to the cities. There was little need this time for encouragement from friends or the press, nor was there any call for labour agents, although a few were reported in the South.[46] The movement of the forties was not simply from the South to established ghettos in the North either: among the new destinations were smaller cities such as Rochester, Buffalo, Denver, Milwaukee and Pontiac where the black populations increased by 100 per cent or more. The area which attracted most migrants was the West coast, the site of much of the aircraft and ship-building industry. Between 1940 and 1944 more than 500,000 people moved to the San Francisco Bay area alone – 45,000 of them were black. In the country as a whole, 14 per cent or 1.8 million blacks had moved out of state between 1940 and 1947 and by 1950, 62 per cent of the black population were urban dwellers and only 68 per cent remained in the South.[47] Now race relations *had* become a national concern.

As in the earlier war, the migrations had disruptive consequences. Housing was once more in short supply and competition between the races created friction. In Buffalo, New York, Catholic priests encouraged their white congregations to oppose black housing projects; in Chicago, between 1944 and 1946 there were 46 cases of arson bombings of black homes; in Detroit black families moved into houses in the Sojourner Truth project only under the protection of National Guardsmen.[48] Despite the provision of homes for black defence workers by the Federal Public Housing Authority, the problems of black housing intensified. In Chicago, Detroit, Cleveland, Buffalo, St Louis and other cities, conditions 'changed on the whole from bad to worse', and one study showed that in general residential segregation increased between 1940 and 1950.[49]

As well as the problems in housing, there were the strains of the war itself; adjustments to new occupations and environments, long working hours, the irritations of rationing and shortages, and worries about friends and relatives in the forces. On top of this, blacks had to suffer the additional burdens of discrimination. In 1943 these pressures exploded in 242 race riots in over 47 cities. The worst of these occurred during June in Detroit where the problems of housing and employment were exacerbated by the influx of whites from the South and by the racist leadership of a number of 'religious political demagogues' including Father Charles Coughlin and the Reverend J. Frank Norris.[50]

The Detroit riot, like many riots, began with one small incident which was then coloured and added to by rumours among both races. In the three days of violence which followed, blacks looted and destroyed white-owned stores, while whites attacked blacks caught outside of the ghetto. The riot only ended after federal troops had entered the city, by which time 25 blacks and nine whites were dead. Just over a month later, in August, another riot broke out in Harlem, but unlike the Detroit affair violence was confined purely within the ghetto and involved few whites: it was an expression of the black anger and bitterness built up over a number of years and increased under the pressures of war. Five people, all black, died, 500 were injured, and 500 were arrested; an estimated five million dollars worth of damage was committed in the attacks on white property.[51]

The *Pittsburgh Courier* referred to the Harlem riot as 'an orgy of vandalism without reason, without excuse and without defense'.[52] However, given the background of conditions in Harlem and the constant reports of discrimination in all sectors of the war effort, the riot was not so difficult to explain. Moreover, there was during the war an increase in black militancy, actually encouraged to some extent by the black press, which, when faced with constant frustration, was almost certain to lead to such outbursts. Indeed, the *Pittsburgh Courier* was at the forefront of this militant mood with its extremely popular slogan of a 'Double V' for victory at home as well as abroad, while the *Chicago Defender* urged 'Remember Pearl Harbor and Sikeston, too' in a reference to the lynching of a young black in Sikeston, Missouri. The *Crisis* emphasised 'that now is the time *not* to be silent about the breaches of democracy here in our own land'.[53] Very different from the views expressed in the earlier World War, a variety of surveys revealed that the majority of blacks supported this position. Over 88 per cent of those polled by the *Courier* agreed that the black man should 'not soft pedal his demands' during the war; a government survey of black opinion in New York found that 42 per cent of those questioned felt it *more* important to achieve democracy in America than to defeat Germany and Japan, and while groups which refused to serve in the 'whiteman's war' (such as the Black Muslims) were dismissed as 'Foolish Fanatics', men like Winfred Lynn, Ernest Calloway and Lewis Jones, who refused to serve in segregated forces, received widespread sympathy.[54]

The white response to these black demands was in some ways similar to that of World War I. After the pre-war concessions of 1940 and 1941, Roosevelt was concerned primarily with the war and unwilling to take any further action which might jeopardise support for his policies in Congress. In 1942 he refused to meet black leaders to discuss the status of Afro-Americans in the war and in reply to a request for a commission to examine race in the world struggle he outlined his priorities thus: 'I think we must start winning the war with all the brains, wisdom and experience we've got before we do much general or specific planning for the future.'[55] Even after the riots of 1943 Roosevelt dropped plans for a government investigation and committee on race relations in favour of the appointment of a white aide, Jonathan Daniels, to correlate information on racial affairs. Yet the question of black morale was a serious one and in a message to the National Urban League's annual conference in 1943, the President pointed out that the 'integrity of our Nation and our war aims is at stake in our attitude towards minority groups at home'. Racial strife, he said, 'destroys national unity at home and renders us suspect abroad'.[56] In order to boost black morale and counter enemy propaganda, the government embarked on a programme to ease race relations. Early in the war the Office of War Information produced a 70-page illustrated record of black life, *Negroes and the War,* which stressed the progress made by blacks and contrasted the ideologies of the United States with those of Nazi Germany. The commentary was written by Chandler Owen who, like Randolph, was now working to ensure that blacks *did* participate in the war.[57]

After the riots of 1943 the government produced a series of films, *The Negro Soldier, Negro Colleges in Wartime, Henry Brown, Teamwork* and the *Negro Sailor.* Like *Negroes and the War,* these films emphasised the part blacks had played in past wars, and were playing in present wars. Although they overlooked many of the contradictions in the American creed, never mentioning segregation for instance, the films lacked the patronising air of earlier efforts and did reveal something of the extent of black involvement in the war effort and could only help to further racial harmony. In fact, several of the films were popular with audiences: the *Negro Soldier* was shown in more than 300 theatres in New York alone.[58] Joe Louis, the black heavyweight boxer, also played his part in bolstering the morale of black troops by touring army camps in America and abroad and talking to the black soldiers. By the end of the war he was a sergeant and had been awarded the Legion of Honour.

The war forced others, as well as those in government, to recognise the importance of race relations in American life. Several popular magazines, notably *Fortune, New Republic* and *Survey Graphic,* devoted entire issues to blacks and the prominence they had achieved during the war. Many books were written on the same subject by both blacks and whites: Gunnar Myrdal's *An American Dilemma* (1944), Lillian Smith's novel *Strange Fruit* (1944), Carey McWilliams' *Brothers Under the Skin* (1943), and a collection of essays edited by Rayford Logan called *What the Negro Wants* (1944) were just a few. Also significant were the white leaders who spoke on the black man's behalf. Wendell Willkie, the Republican presidential candidate in 1940, urged Americans to fight for democracy at home as well as abroad in his speeches and in his best-selling book *One World* (1943); the novelist Pearl S. Buck attacked American hypocrisy in a widely publicised letter to the *New York Times* as early as November 1941; and in April 1942 the *Times* took up the same issue in an editorial headed 'A Minority of Our Own'. Like others, the editor urged that the racial problem had to be solved if America was to avoid 'the sinister hypocrisy of fighting

57

abroad for what it is not willing to accept at home'.[59] Some attempts to remedy the situation were made by the more than 200 race relations committees and organisations established throughout the country following the riots in 1943. While such bodies did little to remove the root causes of racial violence they did help to bring a greater awareness and degree of understanding through the dissemination of educational materials and through meetings.

In the South, too, liberal editors such as Hodding Carter, Thomas Sancton and Virginius Dabney, spoke out in favour of change, even urging the repeal of segregation laws in some instances because they did not work under the stress of war conditions. In 1944, following a number of conferences, several black and white leaders in the South joined together in the Southern Regional Council to work for better racial understanding, and other inter-racial committees were formed throughout the South. Still, there were many instances of prejudice and discrimination and old prejudices died hard. A bus sign in Charleston went so far as to suggest that observance of Jim Crow laws would help to ensure victory by reducing friction between Americans; in 1944 the South Carolina House of Representatives issued a declaration which reaffirmed their belief in white supremacy, and in the immediate aftermath of the war it appeared that the Red Summer of 1919 was to be repeated as some whites used violence to enforce such beliefs.[60]

The violence which broke out with the end of the war was not on the scale of that of 1919 but was horrific nonetheless. During 1946 there were small-scale riots and racial disturbances in Columbia, Tennessee, Athens, Alabama, Philadelphia and Chicago. In July 1946, two black men, one of them a veteran, and their wives, were brutally murdered in Georgia; shortly afterwards another black veteran was shot to death for voting in local elections in the same state. In South Carolina, Isaac Woodard, a black soldier who had served for three years, was blinded by a white policeman. However, these incidents caused a widespread revulsion and in August 1946 a National Emergency Committee Against Mob Violence was formed by blacks and whites from various civil rights and other bodies. Led by the executive secretary of the NAACP, Walter White, members of the Committee met with the new President, Harry S. Truman. Shocked by what he heard at the meeting, Truman promised action and on 5 December 1946, he set up a Committee on Civil Rights to study, report and recommend means of guaranteeing civil liberties. This was a major departure in federal policy and was a far different response from that of Woodrow Wilson over 25 years earlier.

V

Truman's actions on civil rights went far beyond those of any other president in the twentieth century. In speeches to Congress in 1947 he called for civil rights legislation and for a permanent Fair Employment Practices Commission. Later that year, at a rally in front of the Lincoln Memorial, he became the first President to address the NAACP in person. In his message, which was broadcast on national radio networks and shown in cinema news programmes, he demanded that the federal government should show the way in the field of civil rights. In October the Committee on Civil Rights published its report, *To Secure These Rights,* which condemned segregation and discrimination in every walk of life. The President incorporated many of the recommendations made in a Civil Rights Message to Congress in February 1948, when he emphasised that 'the world position of the United States in the world today makes it especially important that we adopt these measures. . .'[61] International attention had been drawn to the state of American race relations by *An Appeal to the World,* a petition presented to the United Nation's Commission on Human Rights by the NAACP. Although not acted upon because of American opposition, the petition caused considerable embarrassment.

But as well as the pressure of external factors, Truman was also confronted by blacks at home who had emerged from the war with greater organisation and unity and a determination to maintain and advance gains made during the emergency. During the debates on the reintroduction of Selective Service in 1947, A. Philip Randolph threatened to lead a campaign of massive civil disobedience unless segregation in the forces was ended. Although other black leaders were reluctant to back Randolph, an NAACP poll found that 71 per cent of black students were prepared to support him and several blacks, including Lester B. Granger of the Urban League, warned that they would no longer work with the Defense Department unless there was a change of policy.[62] After meetings with black leaders, on 26 July 1948 Truman issued an executive order that declared that there should be 'equality of treatment and opportunity for all persons in the armed services' and a committee was established to see this policy implemented. Truman made it clear publicly and in his instructions to the Committee that he intended that segregation be ended. On the same day he established a Fair Employment Board within the Civil Service.[63] The President also encouraged his Attorney General, Tom Clark, to prepare *amicus curiae* briefs against restrictive housing covenants and in 1948 the Supreme Court ruled that such covenants were unconstitutional.

The legal battle against segregation in education received additional impetus during this period too. The war had focused 'the attention of the nation on the educational deficiencies of the Negro' and in 1948 the President's Commission on Higher Education found that segregation usually led to discrimination and inequality and suggested that the time had come to make public education at all levels equally accessible.[64] Just as blacks had to wait until 1954 for the Supreme Court to confirm these findings, so too most of the recommendations made by Truman and the Civil Rights Committee were delayed until the 1950s by the conservative coalition in Congress. However, these various developments, and the continuation of the economic progress made during the war, were sufficient to maintain black expectations. This was the crucial period of progress before reaction which culminated in the 'Negro Revolt' of the 1960s.

It was surely no coincidence that the first president since Lincoln to take a stand openly sympathetic to Afro-Americans, and at the risk of dividing his party, should do so in the immediate aftermath of the Second World War. Clearly, the impact of the two World Wars was very different. World War I was not sufficient a test of American institutions and patterns of behaviour, nor was black participation sufficient, to sweep away long-ingrained stereotypes and prejudices. It brought little real change in the status of blacks other than some distribution in their population. World War II was more total, 'a wholly engrossing commitment'[65] in which the participation of blacks, both as soldiers and industrial workers, was a much greater necessity. The war effort required that blacks be recognised as an integral part of the nation subject to the same duties — and therefore the same rights — as other citizens. But it is still unlikely that blacks would have gained as much if the preconditions had not changed. The urbanisation of the 1914-20 period and after, provided a stronger base for political and economic organisation. Bodies such as the NAACP, Urban League and black trade unions were stronger and more experienced while black newspapers had greater circulations and reached a better educated and more sophisticated audience. As a result, blacks were a much more conscious, homogenous group capable of mobilising support for a March on Washington or a campaign to end segregation in the forces. They also had more electoral power and during the 1930s they had become an important constituency of the Democratic Party. Blacks too, had learned from the lessons of the First World War and were much more outspoken in their demands for equal participation. As a consequence of this political strength and militance, and because of the ideological nature of the war, many whites were more aware of the black plight.

The aftermath of the war was also important for the black American. Whereas the First World War had been followed by a return to isolation, the Second determined finally that America was to be fully involved in world affairs and as Malcolm X suggested, Stalin maintained the pressure for change that Hitler had exerted.[66] Conspicuous as the leaders of democracy, outside pressures encouraged Americans to continue the progress in civil rights. At the same time, economic commitments to the rest of the world enabled the continuation of the wartime American industrial boom and so made it possible for blacks to hold on to their economic gains. It was only in the late 1950s that black hopes for further change were finally exploded. Just as the impact of the Second World War on black Americans cannot be fully understood without some appreciation of the 1930s and late 1940s, neither can sense be made of the 'revolt' of the 1960s unless seen from the perspective of wartime changes.[67]

Notes

1. Dalfiume, 'The "Forgotten Years" of the Negro Revolution', *Journal of American History*, LV, 1, June 1968, pp.90-106; Harvard Sitkoff, 'Racial Militancy and Interracial Violence in the Second World War', *Journal of American History*, LVIII, 3, December 1971, pp.661-81; Neil A. Wynn 'The Impact of the Second World War on the American Negro', *Journal of Contemporary History*, VI, 2, 1971, pp.42-52; Richard S. Kirkendall, *The United States, 1919-1945* (New York, 1974), pp.219-32; Richard Polenberg, *War and Society. The United States, 1941-45* (New York, 1972), pp.99-130.
2. For suggestions on approaches to the study of war and social change see K.L. Nelson, *The Impact of War on American Life* (New York, 1971), pp.1-7, and Arthur Marwick, *War and Social Change in the Twentieth Century* (London, 1974), pp.6-14.
3. Kelly Miller, *The Everlasting Stain* (Washington DC, 1924), p.10; Nancy J. Weiss, 'The Negro and the New Freedom: Fighting Wilsonian Segregation', *Political Science Quarterly*, LXXXIV, 1, March 1969, pp.61-79.
4. Vardaman quoted in J.L. Scheiber and H.N. Scheiber, 'The Wilson Administration and the Wartime Mobilization of Black Americans, 1917-18', *Labor History*, X, 3, 1969, p.441.
5. Chester D. Heywood, *Negro Combat Troops in the World War: The Story of the 371st Infantry* (1928, New York, 1969 ed.), p.46; W.E.B. DuBois, 'An Essay Toward a History of the Black Man in the Great War', *The Crisis*, June 1919, pp.69-72.
6. French liaison officer quoted in Edward M. Coffman, *The War To End All Wars: The American Military Experience in World War I* (New York, 1968), pp.231-2; for race riots in Britain see *Chicago Defender*, 21 June 1919.
7. Spear, *Black Chicago; The Making of a Negro Ghetto, 1890-1920* (Chicago, 1967), pp.ix, 129.
8. Spear, *Black Chicago*, pp.138-41; Emmett J. Scott, *Negro Migration During the War* (New York, 1920), p.3; Mary Ellison *The Black Experience: American Blacks Since 1865* (London, 1974), pp.81-92.
9. U.S. Dept. of Labor, Division of Negro Economics, *Negro Migrations in*

1916-17 (Washington DC, 1919), pp.95, 22-30.

10. Nancy J. Weiss, *The National Urban League, 1910-1940* (New York, 1974), p.178.

11. *Chicago Defender,* 29 December 1917; Spear, *Black Chicago,* p.157.

12. E. Franklin Frazier, *The Negro in the United States* (New York, 1969 ed.), p.598, St Clair Drake and Horace R. Clayton, *Black Metropolis: A Study of Negro Life in a Northern City* (New York, 1970 ed.), pp.232-35; Chicago Commission on Race Relations, *The Negro in Chicago: A Study of Race Relations and a Race Riot* (Chicago, 1923), pp.87-104.

13. Spear, *Black Chicago,* pp.151-5.

14. Leo A. Ransom, 'Combatting Discrimination in the Employment of Negroes in War Industries and Government Agencies', *Journal of Negro Education,* XII, 3, Summer 1943, p.407.

15. Weaver, *The Negro Ghetto* (New York, 1948), p.4.

16. David Trask (ed.), *World War I At Home: Readings on American Life, 1914-1920* (New York, 1970), p.10; Spear, *Black Chicago,* p.24; Gilbert Osofsky, *Harlem, The Making of a Ghetto: Negro New York, 1890-1930* (New York, 1968), p.141.

17. Myrdal, *An American Dilemma* (New York, 1944), p.193.

18. 'Report to the Illinois State Council of Defense on the Race Riots at East St Louis by the Committee on Labor', *American Federationist,* XXIV, 1917, pp.622-5; Drake and Cayton, *Black Metropolis,* pp.59-61.

19. Scheiber and Scheiber, 'The Wilson Administration and the Wartime Mobilization of Black Americans', p.447.

20. Spingarn quoted in Scheiber and Scheiber, p.440.

21. Scheiber and Scheiber, p.446.

22. *Training of Colored Troops,* Signal Corps Films, in National Archives Film Library, (NA 111H-1211-PPSA-1); see also articles by Kingsley Moses and John Richards in Trask (ed.), *World War I at Home,* pp.131, 140-42.

23. *Chicago Defender,* 17, 24 November 1917.

24. *Chicago Defender,* 6 April 1917, 4 May 1918.

25. *The Crisis,* May, June, July 1918.

26. *New York Age,* 22 March 1917.

27. Morton, *Finding a Way Out: An Autobiography* (Garden City, 1921), pp.245, 263; also see John Hope Franklin, *From Slavery to Freedom: A History of Negro Americans* (New York, 1969), p.469.

28. Quoted in Jervis Anderson, *A. Philip Randolph: A Biographical Portrait* (New York, 1973), p.112.

29. Chicago Commission on Race Relations, *The Negro in Chicago,* p.483.

30. *Chicago Defender,* 22 February, 2 August 1919.

31. *The Crisis,* May 1919, and DuBois quoted in Roi Ottley, *New World A'Coming* (New York, 1943), p.318.

32. Chicago Commission, *The Negro in Chicago,* p.481; Miller *The Everlasting Stain,* p.31.

33. Geoffrey Perrett, *Days of Sadness, Years of Triumph: The American People, 1939-1945* (New York, 1973), pp.11-12; Polenberg, *War and Social Change,* p.4.

34. Florence Murray (ed.), *The Negro Handbook, 1942* (New York, 1942), p.201; Langston Hughes, *Fight for Freedom: The Story of the NAACP* (New York, 1962), pp.197-8.

35. Frazier, *The Negro in the United States,* p.606; Fair Employment Practices Committee Hearings, Los Angeles, 20-21 October 1941, in FEPC file National Archives Record Group 228.

36. Press Release, 9 October 1940, in Franklin D. Roosevelt Library, Hyde Park, File 93, Box 4.

37. Military Policy Implications of Report by Research Branch, Special Services Division, on 'Attitudes of the Negro Soldier', 31 July 1943, in Office of Assistant Secretary of War, (OASW 230), in National Archives Record Group 107.

38. War Dept., Troop Information and Education Division, Report b-157, 3 July 1945, 'Opinions About Negro Infantry Platoons in White Companies of 7 Divisions', in War Department file 47, National Archives Record Group 330.

39. For a fuller treatment of desegregation of the forces, see R. Dalfiume, *Desegregation of the U.S. Armed Forces: Fighting on Two Fronts, 1939-1953* (Columbia, Missouri, 1969). For film of the naval experiment see my Open University television programme, 'The Afro-American and World War II', A301, programme 15.

40. Charles G. Bolté, 'He Fought For Freedom', *Survey Graphic,* XXXVI, 1, January 1947, p.117.

41. William J. Schuck in Chapter IX, 'Eliminating Employer Discriminatory Hiring Practices', of unpublished and incomplete *History of the Mobilization of Labor for War Production,* in War Manpower Commission records, National Archives Record Group 211, p.60; see also Louis Ruchames, *Race, Jobs, and Politics: The Story of FEPC* (New York, 1953).

42. President's Committee on Fair Employment Practices, *First Report* (Washington DC, 1945), p.92; Department of Labor, *Negroes in the United States: Their Employment and Economic Status,* Bulletin 1119 (Washington DC, 1952), pp.43-5.

43. 'The Employment of Negroes in Federal Government', Report, March 1944, in FEPC 408, National Archives Record Group 228.

44. Dept. of Labor, *Negroes in the United States,* p.25; Dept. of Labor, 'Annual Family and Occupational Earnings of Residents of Two Negro Housing Projects at Atlanta, 1937-44', *Monthly Labor Review,* vol.61, 6, December 1945, p.1070.

45. National Urban League, 'A Summary Report of the Industrial Relations Laboratory: Performance of Negro Workers in 300 War Plants', New York 1944, in Moorland-Spingarn Collection, Howard University.

46. Memo. Robert C. Weaver to Robert Taylor, consultant, Defense Housing Co-ordinator, 6 June 1941, reporting agents in Chatanooga and Nashville, in Housing and Home Finance Agency, Box 23, National Archives Record Group 207.

47. Dept. of Labor, *Negroes in the United States,* pp.3-5; Weaver, *The Negro Ghetto,* p.83.

48. William L. Evans, *Race Fear and Housing in a Typical American Community,* National Urban League (New York, 1946), Weaver, *The Negro Ghetto,* pp.92-5.

49. 'A Crucial Problem in Race Relations – Housing: Negro Housing Conditions in Five Cities of the North, 1940-45', *Race Relations: A Monthly Summary of Events, and Trends,* IV, 4, November 1946, p.117; Donald O. Cowgill, 'Trends in Residential Segregation of Non-Whites in American Cities, 1940-1950', *American Sociological Review,* XXXI, 1, February 1956, p.46.

50. Earl Louis Brown, *Why Race Riots? Lessons From Detroit,* Public Affairs Pamphlet 87 (New York, 1944), pp.6-8.

51. For the Detroit riot, see Harvard Sitkoff, 'The Detroit Race Riot of 1943', *Michigan History,* LIII, 3, 1969, pp.183-206; Alfred M. Lee and Norman Humphrey, *Race Riot* (New York, 1943). For Harlem see Walter White, *A Man Called White* (New York, 1948), pp.224-39; *New York Times,* 3, 8 August 1943.

52. *Pittsburgh Courier,* 14 August 1943.

53. *Pittsburgh Courier,* 7 February 1942; *Chicago Defender,* 28 February 1942;

The Crisis, January 1942; Lee Finkle in 'The Conservative Aims of Militant Rhetoric: Black Protest during World War II', *Journal of American History,* LX, 3, December 1973, pp.692-713, has argued that the militant expressions of the black press masked a basic conservatism of aims and that the black people were often more militant than their leadership.

54. See Wynn, 'Black Attitudes Towards Participation in the American War Effort, 1941-45', *Afro-American Studies,* III, 1, June 1972, pp.13-21.

55. Roosevelt to Edwin R. Embree, 16 March 1942, in reply to letter of 3 February, in Franklin D. Roosevelt Library, File 93, Box 5.

56. Letter of address, 7 September 1943, in NUL 'Victory Through Unity: Annual Conference', 28 September - 3 October 1943, in Schomburg Collection, New York Public Library.

57. Office of War Information, *Negroes and the War,* Washington DC, nd.

58. Florence Murray, *The Negro Handbook, 1946-47* (New York, 1947), p.265; also see Open University programme 'The Afro-American and World War II' for film clips.

59. *New York Times,* 3 April 1942, Pearl S. Buck's letter on 15 November 1941.

60. *Public Papers of the Presidents: Harry S. Truman 1948,* pp.125-26; William C. Berman, *The Politics of Civil Rights in the Truman Administration* (Columbus Ohio, 1970), Donald R. McCoy and Richard T. Ruetten, *Quest and Response; Minority Rights and the Truman Administration* (Kansas, 1973).

61. Sterling A. Brown, 'Count us in', in Logan (ed.), *What the Negro Counts* (Chapel Hill, 1944), pp.318-22.

62. Murray, *The Negro Handbook 1946-47,* p.206; *New York Times,* 23 March 1948.

63. *New York Times,* 27 May, 27 July 1948.

64. Frazier, *The Negro in the United States,* p.446; President's Commission on Higher Education, *Higher Education for American Democracy* (New York, 1948), pp.34-8.

65. Thomas C. Cochran, *Social Change in Industrial Society: Twentieth-Century America* (London, 1972), p.148.

66. Malcolm X, *Autobiography* (Harmondsworth, Middlesex, 1968), p.344.

67. A version of this article, entitled 'War and the Black American', was given as a paper at an Open University History Seminar at the Institute of Historical Research in February 1975.

THE FAILURE TO RESOLVE THE PROBLEM OF VENEREAL DISEASE AMONG THE TROOPS IN BRITAIN DURING WORLD WAR I

Suzann Buckley

In Britain in the mid-nineteenth century the experiences of the Crimean War (1854-1856) stimulated concern with reforming various aspects of the Army. One part of this interest was the medical conditions of the military. In conjunction with this topic the heretofore virtually ignored problem of venereal disease among the troops attracted attention. By 1860 some medical and military authorities, the *Times and Lancet,* were stressing that the high incidence of venereal disease among the troops was detrimental to the national defence. Their arguments were adopted by members of Parliament whose pressure brought about the passage, between 1864 and 1869, of a series of Contagious Diseases Acts.[1]

The CD Acts, as they were commonly known, were supervised by the Admiralty and the War Office and were implemented by a special body of plain-clothed policemen. The Acts required prostitutes who resided in or near designated towns to undergo medical examination and, if necessary, to remain in hospital for a maximum of three months. Although this arrangement apparently reduced the incidence of venereal disease among the military in the prescribed towns, the drawbacks soon became obvious. Any substantial reduction of the disease among the troops would require the costly extension of the CD system to all towns in Britain. Also, the Acts engendered bitter protest. Opponents condemned them for violating the divinely ordained order by which venereal disease punished illicit intercourse, for demoralising the state by having it recognise vice, and for discriminating against women. This opposition and the Government's disinclination to assume greater financial obligations led to repeal of the Acts in 1886.[2]

After the repeal of the CD Acts the military authorities handled the venereal disease problem by exhorting the forces to shun promiscuity and by providing more attractive living conditions for the troops. The civil authorities were thus left to deal with prostitutes. But although the Criminal Law Amendment Act of 1885 enabled the police to take measures against brothels, there was no legislation recognising transmission of venereal disease and prostitution as crimes. Suspected prostitutes could be arrested only if they indulged in indecent behaviour or created a public nuisance by either soliciting or loitering. The testimonies of the arresting officer and the woman were thus the chief criteria for determining guilt or innocence.[3]

In 1887 this dependence upon the veracity of the parties caused a problem for the Home Office when Miss Cass, a twenty-one year-old dressmaker, was arrested for soliciting. At her trial she denied the charge and produced commendations of her upstanding moral character. Consequently, the magistrate did not fine her the customary 40 shillings. However, he did not exonerate her. Expressing belief in the policeman's testimony, he dismissed her with a warning. This action was seized upon by some Liberal members of Parliament. Evidently hoping to embarrass the Conservative Government by raising the issue of police policy towards prostitutes, they demanded that the Home Secretary, Henry Matthews, institute an enquiry into the Cass case. Matthews refused, but the House of Commons forced the Government to hold an investigation. As a result, the policeman was tried for perjury. He was acquitted, but subsequently the police were reluctant to take action against prostitutes.[4]

In the ensuing decades, although prostitutes were left almost unchecked, the rate of venereal disease among the Army and Navy in Britain declined. Those concerned about venereal disease ceased to regard it as chiefly a phenomenon among the military and began to consider it in connection with civilians. In 1913 the Royal Commission on Venereal Diseases was appointed to investigate means for diminishing the 10 per cent venereal disease rate among civilians. Although it was chiefly interested in this element, the Commission did mention the military. The decline of venereal disease among the forces, the Commission concluded, demonstrated that there was no need to revive the CD Acts.[5]

As a result of the Commission's conclusion doubtless the linking of medically examined prostitutes with the reduction of venereal disease among the military would have remained a dead issue. However, the substantial rise in the number of cases of venereal disease among the troops during World War I revived the question. The British Government attempted to deal with the problem among the British and imperial forces in France by allowing men access to the state-controlled brothels staffed by medically inspected prostitutes.[6] In Britain this approach could not be taken. Brothels were illegal and the medical examination of prostitutes had been ruled out by Prime Minister Asquith's desire to avoid further confrontations with some of the suffragettes. In October 1914 he assured one of the suffragette groups, the Women's Freedom League, that his government would not re-enact the CD Acts and that none of the Defence of the Realm Regulations conferred any powers 'which would have the effect of reviving the CD Acts in letter or spirit'.[7]

Other possible means of dealing with venereal disease among the troops in Britain included official issuance of prophylactics, and punitive action against men and women who spread the disease. The British and some imperial military leaders were reluctant to sanction the former approach officially lest the public view such action as encouraging promiscuity.[8] The latter course did not appeal to the Home Office or to the War Office. The Home Office did not wish to propose legislative action against civilians,[9] and the War Office steadfastly maintained that soldiers and sailors suffered sufficiently by the loss of pay occasioned during hospitalisation for treatment.[10] With respect to women, both departments were convinced that public opinion would not tolerate action against women who were 'outwardly respectable [and] only occasionally immoral'.[11] This conclusion left prostitutes as possible targets, but neither department wanted to do much about this element.

In November 1914 Sir Thomas Barlow, the President of the Royal College of Physicians, suggested to the Home Office that legislation should be enacted empowering the police to remove or to exclude prostitutes from military areas.[12] The Home Office merely referred the matter to the War Office who replied: 'the question. . .is one in which the Department is not primarily concerned or at present desirous of intervening'.[13] The reluctance of the departments to sponsor this type of measure stemmed from the unanimous desire of the members to avoid stirring up either 'a crop of Cass cases'[14] or 'the old controversy over the CD Acts'.[15] Also, some felt that it would be harmful to the preservation of the moral and physical well-being of the troops. As Sir Ernley Blackwell, an assistant under-secretary in the Home Office, pointed out: 'if prostitution in a reasonable manner is rendered impossible we are likely to see an increase in [such] worse forms of vice [as a] number of young officers [committing acts of] indecency with young males'.[16] Besides this factor, the removal of prostitutes, Blackwell feared, would increase the spread of venereal disease. There would be greater contact with girls who were much more liable to contract and spread venereal disease 'than an experienced prostitute who knows her business'.[17] General B. Wyndham Childs, who became the director of Army personnel services in 1917, concurred in this assessment. The Criminal Law Amendment Act of 1885 and the repeal of the CD Acts had, in his view, already done enough harm by depriving men of getting 'value for money [from women who] were more or less clean'.[18] Additional repressive measures against prostitutes would exacerbate the situation by swelling the ranks of the unclean 'enthusiastic amateurs'.[19]

Rather than suppress prostitutes the Home Office and the War Office preferred to check the spread of venereal disease among the troops by other means. The Home Office encouraged the female patrols, which had been formed by a number of suffragettes, to continue dissuading women from promiscuous behaviour with soldiers and sailors.[20] For their part, the War Office expanded the peacetime programme of recreational facilities and lectures on the moral and physical dangers of promiscuity.[21]

These approaches to the problem would have remained the *modus operandi* had not the representatives of the Dominions demanded greater efforts to keep diseased women from spreading venereal disease among the troops. From mid-1915 to 1918 the British were thus placed in an awkward position. The military necessity of preserving harmonious relations with the Dominions and of keeping the British and imperial forces fit for battle required action. Any measures, however, might incite opposition, particularly from the Women's Freedom League. A detailed examination of the efforts to resolve this dilemma can provide the means for assessing the behaviour of the War Office with respect to protecting the health of military manpower. The assessment, in turn, can add another dimension to accounts of British military ineptness in prosecuting the war.

I

By mid-1915 the Canadian military was agitating very strongly for the British to take action. Their arguments ranged from moral duty to military efficiency. On the moral level, some Canadian commanders argued:

> . . .these young men come over here as officers or soldiers, many of them fresh from the fields and farms, thinking only of a soldier's life and of the defence of the Empire, they know nothing of the temptations and dangers they are to be subjected to, and fall an easy prey; therefore they ought to be protected.[22]

In a more cogent contention, other Canadian officers denounced the financial and military waste involved when thousands of Canadian soldiers contracted venereal disease in Britain.[23]

One suggestion offered by the Canadians was for the British to use the Defence of the Realm Act (DORA) as authorisation to take up transient women in the Kent area and to retain them for treatment if they were found to have venereal disease. In July this recommendation was endorsed by the Chief Constable of Kent who asked the Home Office and the War Office to sanction it. Both refused on the grounds that it would be a re-enactment of the CD Acts.[24]

Despite their rejection of the Canadian plan, the Home Office realised that something must be done. Consequently, Blackwell put aside his adverse views about driving away prostitutes in order to recommend that the Home Office should ask the Army Council to sponsor a new regulation of DORA. This would permit the military to remove from certain areas all women who had been convicted of offences related to prostitution.[25] Agreeing to action along these lines, on 11 September 1915 the Army Council drafted a regulation empowering the military authorities to prohibit certain types of women from entering or residing in any specified area. The categories of women comprised those who had been convicted of managing or assisting in the management of a brothel and those known prostitutes who had been convicted of any offence.[26] On 22 September, however, General Sir H.C. Sclater, the Adjutant-General, decided to delay proceeding with this proposal until the Secretary for War, General Kitchener, had been consulted.[27]

While the War Office were hesitating over action, Blackwell met with Harold Tennant, the War Office parliamentary under-secretary, to discuss modification of the draft regulation. But this was barely touched upon because Tennant quickly indicated his disapproval of a new measure. The existing provisions of DORA were, he argued, sufficient to deal with the problem. Aware of the limited use made of DORA by the military because the present regulations did not give them legal powers against prostitutes, Blackwell maintained that it was 'better to proceed openly. . .against well defined classes. . .'.[28]

No decision was taken at this meeting, but in October the Home Office sent a circumspect revision of the draft regulation to the Army Council. Lest the Women's Freedom League be antagonised, the Home Office proposal referred to 'persons' rather than to 'women', thereby making it 'appear [that the regulation was not] aimed at women only'.[29] More important, the Home Office would not approve the broad authority to prohibit entrance or residence 'in any area' unless the Army Council were satisfied that they could 'control the use of power so as to prevent any indiscreet action on the part of the local military authorities'.[30] In effect, the Home Office intended that the regulation should be applied only to 'undesirable'[31] women who had appeared in Folkestone and in the adjoining neighbourhood since the outbreak of the war.[32]

By this time, however, opposition to the measure had been

marshalled by those within the War Office who, because of their fears of public criticism, resented the burden for action against prostitutes being placed upon the military. The Army Council therefore rejected the proposal on the grounds that 'any possible benefits which might result from the proposed action are more than counterbalanced by the very grave objections which have always been apparent'.[33]

Refusing to let the issue be dropped, the Canadians obtained a good deal of support from various British sources. The English Home Commanders backed the idea. The measure would, after all, protect their men as well as the Canadians.[34] The Archbishop of Canterbury, apparently having accepted the Canadian rhetoric of 'innocents abroad', threatened to bring the matter before Parliament 'if something were not done'.[35] These pressures could hardly be ignored. The Home Office strongly urged the Army Council to reconsider their decision.[36] In January 1916 the Army Council acquiesced. However, the War Office emphasised that 13A of DORA would be 'merely auxiliary'[37] to existing measures for preventing the spread of venereal disease among the troops. Obviously, the War Office did not intend to employ the regulation extensively. As far as they were concerned, the onus for action against women lay with the Home Office.

As part of the attempt to place the burden on the Home Office, in August 1916 Lord Derby, the new Secretary for War, wrote to Herbert Samuel, the Home Secretary. Specifically, Derby wanted Samuel to encourage the police to exercise their powers 'more drastically'[38] and to increase the number of female patrols so that they might assist the police in apprehending suspected prostitutes. Sir Edward Troup, the Home Office permanent under-secretary, advised Samuel to respond negatively. Little further action could be taken by the police, he argued, without 'running the grave risk of false arrests'.[39] Furthermore, the greater use of female patrols was questionable. Women could call upon a constable to make an arrest, and the public 'might be less disturbed in the event of a mistake being made if the person who originated the mistake were another woman'.[40] Nonetheless, even under these circumstances, the Home Office might find themselves embroiled in another Cass case controversy.[41] What was needed, Troup suggested, was legislative power to assist the police in keeping women from spreading disease among the troops. Consequently, he and the rest of the Home Office began to draft a bill to deal with the situation.[42]

On 15 February 1917 the Criminal Law Amendment Bill, which had been written chiefly under Samuel's supervision, was introduced into the House of Commons by Sir George Cave, the new Home Secretary. According to some of its many provisions, convicted brothel keepers were to receive heavier fines and possibly jail sentences; prostitutes, on a second conviction for soliciting or loitering, could be jailed for a month instead of being fined. In addition to greater punishment of these elements, the Bill stipulated that any person who was suffering from venereal disease in a communicable form should not have sexual intercourse with any other person or solicit or invite any person to have sexual intercourse. No one was to be convicted if proof could be brought forward to show reasonable grounds for believing that one was free from the disease when the offence was committed. However, any person whom a doctor had certified as diseased within the past three months would be considered still infected. If a person were convicted, the court could order a medical examination in order to ascertain if the person was suffering from the disease. Conviction carried a sentence of a prison term of six months to two years.[43]

The whole bill provoked much discussion, and the provision pertaining to venereal disease was denounced by all. Those who wanted a return to the CD Acts ridiculed the clause as 'a pill to cure an earthquake'.[44] It was a 'half-hearted'[45] measure which they correctly perceived would be virtually unenforceable. They did little to block opposition to it. As a result the clause was rendered even more meaningless by opponents to it. These successfully demanded the insertion of corroboration of evidence against the accused and the elimination of certification as evidence of infection.[46]

At about the time when Cave was floundering with the Home Office proposal, the Army Council reluctantly yielded to the demands of the officers in the home command for a new provision for DORA.[47] Among other things, 35C empowered the military to exclude persons from camp areas if their presence was 'likely to prejudice the training, discipline, administration, or efficiency'[48] of the forces. By not requiring conviction of offences related to prostitution before exclusion, the English commanders intended that this regulation would give them broader powers than 13A.

While the War Office was deciding whether 35C could be used against prostitutes, the representatives of the Dominions at the meetings of the Imperial War Conference of 1917 in April were discussing the problem of diseased women 'swarming'[49] around the troops. By now the Australian and New Zealand forces, who had arrived in 1916, were also suffering to a great extent from venereal disease. Aware that the incidence of venereal disease among some of the imperial troops was as high as 287 per 1,000 per annum,[50] the representatives were outraged that no adequate steps had been taken by the British. The Canadian Prime Minister, Sir Robert Borden, abandoned his generally dispassionate manner to threaten that if effective steps were not taken soon, he would speak about it publicly 'in a way that [would] not be forgotten'.[51] Warning that failure to protect the troops had sufficiently antagonised Canadian public opinion so as to hinder recruitment and to jeopardise assistance to Britain in future wars, Borden emphatically stated: 'if [he] should be Prime Minister of Canada on the outbreak of another War [he] would not send one man overseas if the conditions were such as have prevailed here during the progress of this War'.[52] It was, after all, difficult to believe that nothing could be done: 'we are in the midst of a War which may shatter this whole Empire, and surely a measure [to curb diseased women] would not be too drastic whatever consequences it might produce'.[53] This choice, he argued, was better than letting the 'disease be carried to every Dominion of the Empire, and the future of our race damaged beyond any comprehension or conception'.[54]

Borden's opinion, which was shared by spokesmen for the other Dominions, greatly perturbed the British. Already beset by difficulties with conscription, low morale among the military, and unsuccessful campaigns, they did not wish to compound these problems by incurring the disfavour of the representatives of the Dominions. By describing the controversies over the Cass case and the CD Acts, the British therefore tried to convince Borden and his imperial colleagues that they were powerless to take action. Sir Edward Henry, the Head of the Metropolitan Police, pleaded that the existing laws were 'wholly unsatisfactory'.[55] Of 20,000 women charged with offences related to prostitution since August 1914, in four fifths of the cases the magistrate had only been able to impose a fine. To recoup this financial loss, the women left court 'to ply their trade harder than before'.[56] The police, General Childs contended, were not alone in this predicament because the Army Council were also 'perfectly impotent to deal with the conditions of affairs under the laws of this country'.[57] Although given to speculating that 'if the country were under military government, the question would be settled in a week',[58] Childs would not advocate any action by the military. He would only concede: 'if legislation is adopted. . .the military will see that it is carried out as far as the Army is concerned'.[59] Annoyed by the negative attitude of the British, the Conference pressed for action by endorsing the following veiled censure:

That the attention of the authorities concerned be called to the temptations to which our soldiers on leave are subjected, and that such authorities be empowered by legislation or otherwise (1) to protect our men by having the streets in the neighborhood of camps, and other places of public resort, kept clear so far as practicable of women of the prostitute class, and (2) to take any other steps that may be necessary to remedy the serious problem that exists.[60]

In the hope that this resolution would assist passage of the Criminal Law Amendment Bill. Walter Long, the Colonial Secretary, sent a copy of it to the Lord Advocate.[61] But nothing could save that Bill. The whole matter had been handled badly. In December 1916 dissatisfaction with Asquith's conduct of the war had contributed to the downfall of his government. The new government of Prime Minister Lloyd George was pledged to more vigorous prosecution of the war. The Home Office and the War Office, working together, should therefore have taken advantage of the advent of the new government in order to obtain strong measures for dealing with diseased women. Supported by the War Office, the Home Office could have pushed for Henry's proposal to empower magistrates to order the medical examination of women who were convicted of offences related to prostitution and to send them to institutions for treatment.[62] The Home Office realised that 'the parliamentary difficulties in obtaining [such] legislation were not so great. . .'.[63] Equally important, the new government was not bound by Asquith's assurances to the Women's Freedom League.

Samuel had not consulted with Derby about the type of legislation to sponsor. He was aware of the reluctance of the War Office to have anything to do with legislation approximating the CD Acts, and he probably doubted that Derby would render assistance. The War Office continually issued public statements that the military rate of venereal disease of 48.3 per 1,000 per annum was slightly lower than before the war.[64] Without the admission by the War Office that this figure, based on rate rather than on actual cases, was mere claptrap in view of the great expansion of the forces since 1914, the Home Office would not have been able to justify the need for a straightforward piece of legislation.

Denied the argument vital to justification of greater powers for magistrates, the Home Office had presented comprehensive legislation which seemed to bear no relation to a wartime emergency. To many, in fact, the venereal disease clause had appeared to be an unnecessary addition to two measures taken by the Local Government Board to implement the recommendations of the Royal Commission on Venereal Diseases.[65] These were the Venereal Disease Act (1917), which prohibited the advertisement of quack remedies, and the system instituted in 1916 by which the Government underwrote most of the costs for local authorities to establish clinics to provide free diagnosis, treatment and distribution of medicines.[66]

The Home Office realised the unlikelihood of securing parliamentary approval of the Criminal Law Amendment Bill during the present session. They therefore returned to their previous policy of looking to the military to take action. In response to the request of the Chief Constable of Grantham for police power 'to interfere at once where we have no doubt that one of these women is suffering from an infectious disease',[67] Cave asked Derby to summon a conference between officials of the Home Office, War Office and Colonial Office in order to discuss whether 35C 'could be made useful in dealing with prostitutes without exciting a hostile public sentiment'.[68] But Derby was 'hesitant when faced with a dilemma and his amicability rendered him liable to the influence of whoever counselled him last. . . .'.[69] In this instance he was advised by Childs. He pointed out that summoning a conference would have undesirable implications. It would suggest that the censure of the Imperial War Conference was directed at the War Office and that the military alone were the immoral part of the community.[70]

In August 1917 the Home Office deferred to Derby's refusal to hold the conference and they sponsored the meeting between Troup, Blackwell, Henry, Childs and Edward Harding, a Colonial Office clerk. Childs argued that the use of 35C was 'quite impracticable'[71] because the main difficulty was in protecting men on leave in London. Henry and the Home Office representatives once again explained that the police had little power to deal with prostitutes in London. Unable to get around this stalemate, the representatives agreed that the only means of alleviating the problem of venereal disease among the troops lay in developing existing agencies for educating the civilian and military population to the dangers of the disease, in treating infected persons before they could communicate the disease, and in providing the military with prophylactics.[72]

Soon after the conference had come to these limited conclusions, the Home Office and the War Office began to battle with the Colonial Office. Anxious to 'get something out of the Departments to show the Dominions that the resolution [had not been] overlooked',[73] the Colonial Office asked the Home Office and the War Office for suitable statements which could be forwarded to the Dominions. The Home Office suggested that the conclusions of the August conference should be sent,[74] but Childs urged the War Office to delay their reply until they knew what Cave intended 'to do to later the conditions which exist in this country among the civil population'.[75] In September the Home Office informed the War Office that they were looking into measures.[76] Having made his point that the disease was not solely a military phenomenon, Childs agreed that the report of the August Conference should be sent. However, 'because the suggestion of prophylatic measures if it ever sees the light of day would raise the Devil in the House of Commons',[77] he stipulated that under no circumstances should the Dominions be told that this represented the opinion of the Army Council.[78]

The forwarding of the report to the Dominions in October did not close the issue. In November the Foreign Office asked the Home Office what to tell the American military authorities who were 'anxious to obtain the assistance of municipal and other authorities in London and other large towns relative to the control of prostitution'.[79] The Home Office advised the Foreign Office to send a report of the August conference, and Cave requested Long to call a conference between Henry and officials of the War Office, Home Office and Colonial Office in order to discuss the feasibility of adding a new regulation to DORA.[80] In December at this meeting, Blackwell pointed out that Cave envisaged a regulation similar to the revised venereal disease clause of the Criminal Law Amendment Bill. In this case, however, the regulation would not apply to the whole populace. It would only affect soldiers, sailors and women:

No soldier or sailor who is suffering from venereal disease in a communicable form should have sexual intercourse with any woman or invite or solicit any woman to have sexual intercourse with him; no woman who is suffering from venereal disease in a communicable form shall have sexual intercourse with any soldier or sailor or invite or solicit any soldier or sailor to have sexual intercourse with her.[81]

In defending the proposal, Blackwell contended that although the venereal disease clause of the Criminal Law Amendment Bill had been approved by a Grand Committee of the House of Commons, nothing could be done until action had been taken on the whole Bill. In contrast, the proposed addition to DORA 'could be made at once on the ground of promoting military efficiency'.[82] In addition to this advantage, the provision, Blackwell argued, would resolve the problem of diseased women. Although 'it was necessary for political reasons to create similar offences for women and men, in fact, the proposed Regulation would be actually operative only to deal with cases of women'.[83] Furthermore, in practice 'the Magistrates would give the women charged the alternative of (a) remand for medical examination or (b) conviction, and that thus, in effect, the result would be what was desired'.[84] No decision was taken at this meeting, but the proposal was referred to the

War Office.

Childs did not show the proposal to the other members of the War Office.[85] He claimed that soldiers and sailors would object strongly to a regulation which punished them while leaving civilians 'free to contaminate any woman. . .'.[86] His major objection to the regulation, however, was that it would 'throw upon the War Office and the Admiralty the responsibility which obviously rests with the Home Office'.[87]

Fearful that the representatives of the Dominions would be furious if nothing were done, Long tried to break the *impasse*. He threatened Derby that he would bring the matter before the War Cabinet if the War Office did not consider the Home Office proposal. To appease Long, Derby sent Childs to talk with him and with Cave. A compromise was reached. On 7 February 1918 officials of the War Office, Home Office, Admiralty and Colonial met to approve the following suggestion of the Home Office: a provision should be added to DORA making it a summary offence to solicit, invite or perform sexual intercourse with any member of His Majesty's Armed Forces. A woman charged would, if she agreed, be remanded for medical examination.[88]

On 21 February, W. Hayes Fisher, the President of the Local Government Board, warned Long that the one-sidedness of the measure would provoke opposition. Long agreed, but he would waste no time trying to resolve the problem. As he explained to the War Cabinet, who had been asked to sanction the regulation because of its controversial nature, immediate action was necessary in order to appease the Dominions.[89] Long did, however, mention to the War Cabinet that considerable sentiment outside the Army endorsed applying the regulation to soldiers and sailors as well as to women. The War Cabinet therefore approved the provision, known as 40D, with the stipulation that Derby should be prepared to explain to Parliament why it did not include the military.[90]

The War Cabinet's approval of 40D triggered a new battle between the departments: who was to be responsible for it? Because it involved women, Long felt it was a matter for the civil authorities. Cave protested that 40D could be defended only as a military measure. Consequently, 'if the military authorities do not approve or desire the Regulation. . .it should be abandoned'.[91] Not surprisingly, Derby disagreed.[92] Cave then suggested that the War Cabinet should resolve the issue.[93] Sir Maurice Hankey, the secretary to the War Cabinet, urged Cave, Derby and Long to settle the matter among themselves. His plea that he was 'continually being told by the War Cabinet that [he brought] questions onto the Agenda that never ought to reach them'[94] fell on deaf ears. Aware that it would be extremely difficult to reach agreement, Long demanded that the War Cabinet should handle the dispute.[95] On 13 March the War Cabinet reaffirmed approval of 40D and decided upon a compromise: the representatives of the War Office, supported by those of the Home Office and the Colonial Office should defend the regulation in Parliament; and the initial action in a prosecution should lie with the military, but the prosecution itself should be conducted by the police.[96]

Displeased with receiving the main responsibility for 40D, the War Office retaliated by ignoring it. This perturbed the Colonial Office who were 'getting into frightful hot water with the Dominions over the delay'.[97] On 22 March the War Office eventually yielded to strong pressure from the Colonial Office and announced that 40D was in effect.[98] After years of squabbling, it appeared that the military and civil authorities were going to take concerted action to stop the spread of venereal disease among the troops.

Within a few months it was evident that appearances belied reality. In June, when Long asked the War Office, the Admiralty and the Home Office to submit reports on the enforcement of 40D, he encountered a classic manifestation of 'the "circumlocution office" game'.[99] The Home Office argued that the War Office and the Admiralty should supply the material because these authorities were responsible for the initiation of all proceedings of 40D.[100] The Admiralty claimed that the Home Office should provide the information, and the War Office maintained that 'it would hardly be in order for the Army Council to circularise the chief constable seeking information of this description from the civil authorities'.[101]

Fearful that 'something sensational'[102] would happen if the departments did not stop evading the issue, the Colonial Office pressed them for information. But no statistics were available on 19 July when the matter was discussed at the Imperial War Conference of 1918. Cave merely informed the representatives of the Dominions that there had been 'a great number of prosecutions. . .and a good many convictions'.[103] He also hinted that further action might be possible if the Criminal Law Amendment Bill, which had been reintroduced in February 1918, were passed. Thus the fact that less than 100 convictions had been obtained[104] and that little action had been taken to push the Criminal Law Amendment Bill[105] was not disclosed. Accepting Cave's assurances that something was being done and that further action might be possible, the imperial representatives were willing to disperse without passing another censure resolution.[106] However, they still made it plain that they wanted greater efforts to stop diseased women from 'lying in wait for clean young men who come to give their lives for their country'.[107]

By the time of the discussion at the Imperial War Conference, much of the anger of the imperial authorities had, in fact, been vented in talks with the War Office. On 10 May and 18 July some of the High Commissioners of the Dominions and members of the Australian, Canadian and New Zealand medical corps had met with representatives from the War Office, the Admiralty, and the American Army. The War Office had intended to consider what steps might be taken with respect to men who had venereal disease at the time of demobilisation, but the representatives of the Dominions had turned the meetings into forums for criticising the War Office. The two major grievances involved the failures to curb diseased women and to follow the example of the Dominions in setting up clinics in Britain where the military could go for medical treatment within a few hours after exposure to venereal disease. The Australians had been especially annoyed that the lack of early treatment centres for venereal disease continually prevented 2,000 or 3,000 men from being 'ready and fit for the first line'.[108] Emotions had run so high that General Sir Neville Howse, the senior Australian medical officer had hinted that the British were remiss because their troops did not run the same risk with regard to infection as the Australians who had 'more virility' [109]

The War Office had ignored the question of early treatment depots, but they had promised to urge the Home Office to use 40D in order to obtain more convictions of women. Some British, however, were becoming disturbed by the regulation. On 1 August 1918 George Barnes, Labour's representative on the War Cabinet and spokesman for the Women's Freedom League, denounced 40D before the Committee on Home Affairs. This Committee was chaired by Cave and included the President of the Board of Trade, the President of the Local Government Board, the Minister of Reconstruction, the President of the Board of Education, the Minister of Labour, the Secretary for Scotland and a representative of the Treasury. It had been appointed on 10 July 1918 to handle matters which were of such importance that they would otherwise have been considered by the War Cabinet.[110] Claiming that 40D was discriminatory against women, an encouragement to promiscuity, and ineffective, Barnes urged the Committee to recommend suspension of the regulation until Parliament had decided upon the Criminal Law Amendment Bill. In contrast to Barnes, Ian Macpherson, the War Office parliamentary under-secretary, recommended that 40D be retained. It was, he contended, 'a regrettable necessity'[111] which was vital to appease the Dominions and the

Americans. W.A.S. Hewins, the Colonial Office parliamentary under-secretary, reiterated the need for preserving good relations with the Dominions by keeping 40D. Accepting the arguments of Macpherson and Hewins, the Committee decided that 40D should be retained.[112]

Dissatisfied with the outcome, on 7 August Barnes called the attention of the War Cabinet to public opposition to 40D.[113] After some effort to postpone consideration of the matter, on 20 August the War Cabinet decided upon a course of action: Cave should circulate a memorandum on possible improvements in the administration of 40D; Macpherson should prepare a statement 'for propaganda purposes'[114] showing that the military did not go unpunished if they contracted venereal disease; and the legal counsellors should be asked to advise the Government on the question of extending 40D to civilians.[115] But on 28 August the War Cabinet paid little attention to the opinion of Sir Gordon Hewart, the Solicitor-General, that there should be no serious difficulty in applying 40D to civilians. Instead attention focused on the point made by Lord Robert Cecil, the Foreign Office under-secretary: 'Agitation in the country was very strong and in the event of a general election considerable pressure would be put on candidates'.[116] This implication that 40D would cause the Government to lose the support of the recently enfranchised six million women convinced the War Cabinet that the issue had to be regarded as 'one of political expediency'.[117] They therefore accepted Cecil's recommendation that, subject to the approval of Prime Minister Lloyd George, the King should be asked to appoint a royal commission to decide what amendments of 40D were desirable and whether it should apply to civilians.

Neither Cave nor Derby were disturbed by this decision, but Long was greatly distressed by the *de facto* abrogation of 40D. Although expediency had been his chief motive in pushing for the measure, he did not feel that it should be eliminated for this reason. In order to absolve the Colonial Office of responsibility for this action, he sent the War Office a memorandum which argued that the decision was likely to create 'great and legitimate disappointment and dissatisfaction in the Dominions'.[118]

The Government, perhaps because the representatives of the Dominions had not passed a censure resolution at the Imperial War Conference, refused to be intimidated by Long's protest. Lloyd George agreed to the idea of a royal commission, but apparently pressure from Barnes, Cave and Cecil for a report as soon as possible resulted in the establishment of a committee rather than a commission.[119] Also the question of extending 40D to civilians was eliminated from the Committee's terms of reference.[120]

On 3 October the Committee was appointed. It was chaired by Lord Moulton, a Lord of Appeal, and it included Mrs H.B. Irving and Mrs Found, who had been active in social work, Dr Flora Murray, Sir Malcolm Morris, the vice-president of the National Council for Combating Venereal Disease, Sir Francis Lloyd, the commander of the First Guards Brigade in London, and the Bishop of Southwark. From 10 October to 14 November the Committee held five meetings. Before much evidence had been taken from religious, lay, medical, military and civil authorities, proceedings were abruptly suspended. The Committee decided to adjourn when they were informed by Lord Moulton that taking further evidence might be a waste of time because of the likelihood that 40D would be abrogated as a result of the Armistice. Furthermore, they decided to cease their investigations and to recommend that 'in view of the advent of peace the regulation should be dropped'.[121]

This abandonment of the sensitive question of 40D presumably should have restored harmony between the departments. But, in a fitting epilogue, they engaged in one last skirmish. Shortly after the Armistice, a committee composed of Barnes, Cave, Lord Milner (the new Secretary for War), the Secretary for Scotland, and the Secretary for Ireland, was appointed to consider which regulations of DORA should be abrogated. Learning that the Committee wanted the War Office to agree to the dissolution of Lord Moulton's Committee and to the repeal of 40D, Macpherson demanded that the Colonial Office must also approve these recommendations. This was necessary, he contended, in order that the War Office would not be 'saddled with full responsibility for the regulation'.[122] Long believed that the Dominions would be annoyed at having no provision to protect the troops during demobilisation, but he perceived the futility of further protest.[123] There was no major outcry from the Dominions, and on 26 November 1918 it was announced that 40D had been taken off the books.

II

The failure to cope with the problem of venereal disease among the troops in Britain can be attributed in varying degrees to the Home Office and to the War Office. Faced with the alternatives of 'damned if you do, damned if you don't', they opted for the latter course. When this situation became untenable, the War Office made matters worse. By virtually refusing to deal with the problem, the War Office forced the Home Office to try to resolve what was essentially a military concern. The War Office then hampered the efforts of the Home Office by refusing to admit that an emergency existed.

In 1917 had the War Office presented honest figures and worked with the Home Office emergency legislation to keep women from spreading the disease might have been approved. Even had this failed, some improvement in the situation could have been effected if the War Office had agreed to apply DORA to soldiers and sailors as well as to women. Had the War Office made clear that they were willing to share with the Home Office responsibility for the regulation, the costly delay in implementing the measure would have been avoided. More importantly, it is quite possible that opposition to this procedure might have been less severe than that levelled at 40D.[124] With co-operation and without the threat of wide-scale opposition, DORA could have been used more extensively to stop the spread of venereal disease.

Any course of action, however, required assumption of some responsibility, and the War Office did not want to assume that burden. But the War Office were more than shirkers of responsibility. They jeopardised recruitment efforts in the Dominions. They knew that a division a day was continually in hospital because of venereal disease[125] at the yearly cost of at least £400,000.[126] They were aware that the disease was as damaging to military efficiency as 'poisonous German gas'.[127] Yet, they did almost nothing to correct the situation. From the military aspect alone, the War Office were in fact irresponsible.

Notes

1. E.M. Sigsworth and T.J. Wyke, 'A Study of Victorian Prostitution and Venereal Disease', in *Suffer and Be Still*, ed. Martha Vicinus (Bloomington, Ind., Indiana University Press, 1972), pp.78-99, W. Metcalfe Chambers, 'Prostitution in Relation to Venereal Diseases', *The British Journal of Venereal Disease*, II (1926), pp.68-75. Richard Blanco, 'The Attempted Control of Venereal Disease in the Army of Mid-Victorian Britain', *Journal of the Society for Army Historical Research*, XLV (1967), pp.234-41; and Judith R. Walkowitz and Daniel J. Walkowitz, '"We are not beasts of the field"; Prostitution and the Poor in Plymouth and Southampton under the Contagious Diseases Acts', *Feminist Studies*, I (1973), pp.73-106.
2. Ibid.
3. No.142, Report from the Joint Select Committee of the House of Lords and the House of Commons on the Criminal Law Amendment Bill and the Sexual Offences Bill, *Reports*, III (1918) paragraphs 12, 86.
4. *Parl. Deb.*, HC, CCCXVI (1887), 1491-4, 1796-1830; *DNB*, 1912-21, 'Matthews', pp.370-1; *The Annual Register*, 1887, pp.145-6; *The Times*, 9 July 1887, p.14; 12 July, p.11; 23 July, p.10; 26 July, p.11; 10 August, p.5; 2 November, p.13.
5. Cd. 8189, Final Report of the Royal Commission on Venereal Diseases, *Reports*, XVI (1916), p.11 and paragraphs 9-22.
6. Cabinet (hereinafter CAB) 24/45/G. T. 3932. This source and the various

departmental records are in the Public Record Office.

7. Home Office (hereinafter HO) 45/10724/251861/26B.
8. War Office (hereinafter WO) 32/11401; WO 32/5940; P.S. O'Connor, 'Venus and the Lonely Kiwi: The War Efforts of Miss Ettie A. Rout', *The New Zealand Journal of History*, I (1967), pp.11-32, deals with aspects of the preventive question. See Cmd.322, Note on Prophylaxis Against Venereal Disease, *Accounts and Papers*, XXX (1919), for action eventually taken in prophylatic treatment.
9. HO 45/10837/331148/19.
10. No.142, Report from the Joint Select Committee, paragraoh 514; WO 32/11401. Hospitalisation varied from three to ten months.
11. HO 45/10802/307990/30.
12. HO 45/10724/251861/35.
13. HO 45/10724/251861/48.
14. HO 45/10724/251861/29A.
15. HO 45/10724/251861/102C.
16. HO 45/10837/331148/38.
17. HO 45/10724/251861/29A. See also, No.142, Report from the Joint Select Committee, paragraph 191.
18. Colonial Office (hereinafter CO) 886/7, Confidential Proceedings of the Imperial War Conference, 1917, p.197.
19. Ibid., p.198. Aside from the fact that amateurs were a medical risk, it necessarily followed that, if much of the disease was derived from them, restrictive efforts should be directed against them rather than against professional prostitutes. But the War Office and the Home Office did not want to have to deal with this possibility. See No.142, Report from the Select Committee, paragraph 472 for the comment of Ian Macpherson, the War Office parliamentary under-secretary: 'I do not think it [the above deduction] follows at all'. See ibid., paragraph 64, for a similar stand by Blackwell.
20. HO 45/10724/251861/29A. For further information on the Women's Patrols and the Women Police see HO 45/10806/309485/79-150; HO 45/10802/ 307990/156; Mary Allen, *The Pioneer Policewoman*, ed. J. Heyneman (London: Chatto and Windus, 1925), pp.20-136; Stella Newsome, *The Women's Freedom League, 1907-1957* (London: Women's Freedom League, nd), p.11; and David Mitchell, *Women on the Warpath* (London: Jonathan Cape, 1966), pp.305-8.
21. HO 45/10724/251861/99.
22. HO 45/10724/251861/89.
23. HO 45/10724/251861/96. This document reveals that 2,700 out of 30,000 in the first Canadian contingent to arrive in England had been sent back to Canada after contracting venereal disease.
24. HO 45/10724/251861/81, 83.
25. HO 45/10724/251861/96.
26. HO 45/10724/251861/88.
27. Ibid.
28. HO 45/10802/307990/89.
29. HO 45/10724/251861/88.
30. Ibid.
31. HO 45/10802/307990/2.
32. Ibid. According th HO 45/10802/307990/13, the notice was sent to all areas in April.
33. HO 45/10724/251861/96.
34. HO 45/10724/251861/89.
35. HO 45/10724/251861/102C.
36. HO 45/10724/251861/96, 100, 102, 114.

37. HO 45/10724/251861/114.
38. HO 45/10802/307990/15A.
39. HO 45/10802/307990/15B.
40. Ibid.
41. Ibid.
42. HO 45/10837/331148/all files.
43. No.7, Criminal Law Amendment Bill, *Bills,* I (1917/18); *Parl. Deb.,* HC, XCIII (1917), 61-179; and HO 45/10837/331148.
44. *Parl. Deb.,* HC, XC (1917), 1119.
45. Ibid., 1125.
46. No.58, Report from Standing Committee A on the Criminal Law Amendment Bill, *Reports,* III (1917/18); No.25, Amended Criminal Law Amendment Bill, *Bills,* I (1917/18).
47. CO 616/75/4444.
48. Ibid.
49. CO 886/7, Confidential Proceedings of the Imperial War Conference, 1917, p.190.
50. HO 45/10724/251861/89 gives this rate for the Canadians in 1915. HO 45/10802/307990/30 gives the following rates per 1,000 for Australian and New Zealand troops in Britain during the first six months of 1917; 144, Australia; 134, New Zealand.
51. CO 886/7, p.190.
52. Ibid.
53. Ibid., p.191.
54. Ibid.
55. Ibid., p.239.
56. Ibid.
57. Ibid., p.198.
58. WO 32/11404.
59. CO 886/7, p.198.
60. Ibid., p.238.
61. HO 45/10802/207990/22A.
62. HO 45/10802/307990/42.
63. Ibid. Statement by W.A.S. Hewins, the Colonial Office parliamentary under-secretary. This view was shared by Troup and by Sir John Anderson, Chief Magistrate of Bow Street. See HO 45/10802/307990/15B. See also, the contention of the Admiralty: 'if the position [were] explained public opinion would endorse drastic measures.' HO 45/10802/307990/52. Neither the *Times* nor *Lancet* had any leaders on the matter.
64. *Parl. Deb.,* HC, LXXVII (1916), 1003; ibid., 101 (1918), 799, 1934, 2080; *The Times,* 18 November 1916, p.5, are a few of the many examples.
65. *Parl. Deb.,* HC, XCIII (1917), 61-179, *passim.*
66. Cd. 8509, Prevention and Treatment of Venereal Disease, *Accounts and Papers,* XXXVIII (1917/18); *Parl. Deb.,* HL, XXIV (1917), 363, 456-66; ibid., XXV (1917), 248-54, 296-300; No.77, Report from the Standing Committee on the Venereal Diseases Bill, *Reports,* III (1917/18).
67. HO 45/10802/307990/21.
68. HO 45/10802/307990/22A.
69. *DNB,* 1941-50, 'Derby', p.826.
70. HO 45/10802/307990/22A. Doubtless Childs also had a hand in the following action by Derby: on 18 March 1918 Derby requested the War Cabinet to place French brothels out of bounds lest the failure to do so cause 'an unsavory and malodious discussion of the subject'. CAB 23/5/WC 366(13), 18 March 1918.
71. HO 45/10802/307990/30.

72. Ibid.
73. CO 616/75/35286.
74. HO 45/10802/307990/28.
75. WO 32/11401.
76. HO 45/10802/307990/37.
77. HO 45/11802/307990/36.
78. Ibid.
79. HO 45/10802/307990/39. The War Office were annoyed by this pressure from the Americans. See No.142, Report from the Select Committee, paragraph 440 for Macpherson's contention: 'London is very much better with respect to control of prostitutes than most American towns.'
80. HO 45/10802/307990/42.
81. Ibid.
82. Ibid.
83. Ibid.
84. Ibid.
85. CO 616/78/2839.
86. WO 32/11401.
87. Ibid.
88. CO 616/79/5044; WO 32/11401; HO 45/10802/307990/57.
89. CO 616/80/9485; HO 45/10802/307990/57.
90. CAB 23/5/WC 352 (10), 22 February 1918; CAB 24/41/G. T. 3598.
91. WO 32/11401; CAB 24/44/G. T. 3812.
92. WO 32/11401.
93. Ibid.
94. Ibid.
95. Ibid.
96. CAB 23/5/WC 365 (14), 13 March 1918.
97. WO 32/11401.
98. Ibid.
99. CO 616/78/28915.
100. CO 616/78/28523.
101. CO 616/78/29827; ibid., 31262.
102. CO 616/78/28915.
103. CO 886/8, Confidential Proceedings of the Imperial War Conference, 1918, p.122.
104. HO 45/10849/359931/103 gives the following figures up to 8 October 1918: 203 prosecutions (91 acquitted, 101 convicted, 1 bound over, 6 remanded, 3 put on probation, and 1 discharged under the Probation Act of Offenders).
105. *Parl.Deb.*, HC 108 (1918), 1951-67.
106. CAB 24/63/G. T. 5663. (Long's memorandum).
107. CO 886/8, p.125, statement by Newton Rowell, a Canadian representative. See ibid., p.126 for the view of the New Zealanders that 'although we do not expect our fellows to be plaster saints. . .we do expect that reasonable care should be taken of them while they are here'.
108. WO 32/11404.
109. Ibid.
110. CAB 23/6/WC 429 (16), 10 July 1918.
111. CAB 26/1/H. A. C. 7/1.
112. CAB 26/2/H. A. C. 7/2.
113. CAB 23/7/WC 455 (17), 7 August 1918; CAB 23/7/WC 460 (10), 16 August 1918; CAB 24/59/G. T. 5216 (Barnes' memorandum).
114. CAB 23/7/WC 461 (13), 20 August 1918.
115. Ibid.
116. CAB 23/7/WC 465 (14), 28 August 1918. See CAB 24/62/G. T. 5507, for

Cave's memorandum.

117. CAB 23/7/WC (14), 28 August 1918.
118. CAB 24/63/G. T. 5663.
119. CAB 23/7/WC 468 (9), 3 September 1918. The War Cabinet decided that Barnes, Cave and Cecil should frame the terms of reference and should suggest the members.
120. CAB 23/8/WC 482 (11), 3 October 1918.
121. HO 45/10893/359931.
122. WO 32/4745.
123. CO 616/78/79017.
124. See HO 45/10837/331148, various files especially 385, 389, for evidence that the chief grievance of the suffragettes was the discriminatory nature of 40D. Also, for example, most of the suffragettes supported the proposals of Lord Sydenham, the President of the National Council for Combating Venereal Disease, and of Lord Beauchamp. Both of these individuals wanted to make the transmission of venereal disease by any person a penal offence. Although the Home Office justifiably felt that omission of 'solicits and invites' from this type of measure would eliminate much of its value, it might have served as a deterrent thereby doing at least as much good as 40D. See HO 45/10837/ 331148/1; CAB 24/70/G. T. 6335 for the views of Lord Sydenham, and *Parl. Deb.*, HL, 29 (1918), 630-37 for debate on Lord Beauchamp's Sexual Offences Bill.
125. No.142, Report from the Joint Select Committee, paragraph 411.
126. HO 45/10724/251861/89. This contains the report by Dr Arthur Newsholme of the Local Government Board. Basing his calculations on an estimate of 1.5 million troops in England, Newsholme figured that there had been 54,000 cases of the disease between January and August 1915. This, he deducted, could 'scarcely imply less than 200,000 weeks of sickness at a cost of £400,000; much more than this if the loss of training is to be included.'
126. No.142, Report from the Joint Select Committee, paragraph 411.

STAFF TRAINING AND THE ROYAL NAVY, 1918-1939

Anthony R. Wells

The Royal Naval College, founded at Greenwich in 1919, was born as much from despair for what had happened in Naval Staff work during the Great War as from a fundamental desire to establish a soundly worked out course of higher professional staff training and education. The precursor to the beginnings of a Staff Course had been the indignation which Churchill had shown on assuming the office of First Lord of the Admiralty in 1911. He was shocked to find that

> . . .there was no moment in the career and training of a naval officer when he was obliged to read a single book about naval war, or even pass a rudimentary examination in naval history. The Royal Navy had made no important contributions to naval literature. The standard work on sea power was written by an American Admiral. The best accounts of British sea fighting and naval strategy were compiled by an English civilian. The silent Service was not mute because it was absorbed in thought or study, but because it was weighted down by daily routine and by its ever diversifying technique. We had competent administrators, brilliant experts of every description, unequalled navigators, good disciplinarians, fine sea officers, brave and devoted hearts but at the outset of the conflict, we had more Captains of ships than Captains of War. In this will be found the explanation of many untoward events.[1]

In 1912 he succeeded in having a staff training element injected into the courses of the Royal Naval War College which had been founded at Portsmouth in 1900, but this was in no way a broadly based staff course. It tended to concentrate on Fleet strategy and tactics. The Royal Naval War College was re-established at Greenwich after the First World War, but was soon to have its activities and student numbers pruned in the ensuing Geddes economies.

Churchill's fears in 1912 were well borne out in the war itself. The origins and development of the Naval Staff, and particularly the antipathy of Fisher to it and the growth of a corps of staff officers, is now well known. Suffice to sketch briefly here those aspects of immediate relevance to inter-war developments. In 1912 Churchill had created a Naval War Staff consisting of three divisions – Operations,

Mobilisation and Intelligence. At first this was purely advisory – to whom one may ask? The answer is simply to the First Sea Lord, as Chief of Naval Operations. In essence he and a handful of assistants ran the operational Navy. They also made all the plans. At this stage the First Sea Lord was not Chief of the Naval Staff because there was, quite simply, no staff. What war plans Fisher had were kept completely secret, not just from the Germans, but equally important from his point of view, from the Army too! When war came this body of advisors became a full war staff. In this new scheme of things the First Lord raised the Naval Intelligence Department to the senior position within the Naval Staff and the Director regained the direct access to the First Sea Lord which he had lost in the Naval Staff changes of 1909. Instead of closely integrating and expanding this staff, adding the necessary Plans Division and developing quite separate administrative and personnel staffs, other divisions were quite arbitrarily added between 1914-17 – the Anti-Submarine Division, the Signal Division, the Minesweeping Division and so on. The whole thing grew like Topsey.

Other than the Committee of Imperial Defence Britain had no formal organisation for integrating the strategic plans of the two Services. There was a fully organised but quite separate General Staff at the War Office. On 25 November 1914 a War Council was formed, and the CID went into abeyance. Much later in the war a Supreme War Council was formed. In 1917 several further changes were made. The general 'collective authority' of the Admiralty Board was maintained but it was split into two main subcommittees – operations and maintenance. Three new divisions of the Naval Staff were created (Plans, Training and Staff Duties, and Mercantile Movements). The Naval Intelligence Division now came under a new Board member, the Deputy Chief of Naval Staff (DCNS). It was laid down in the Instructions for the Naval Staff and the Technical Departments that the Divisions on the operational side and those on the maintenance side were to keep in close touch with one another. The First Sea Lord continued to have direct responsibility for the day-to-day operations of the Fleet.

In the 1917 Naval Staff structural reforms another crucial change was made in the intelligence world. In May 1917 Room 40 (the top secret code breaking organisation within the Admiralty), came directly under the Director of Naval Intelligence's control and in July 1917 became a full section of the NID, and began to send full intelligence reports to the Operations Division. In December 1917 Room 40 and E1 (dealing with German U-boats) became subsections (ID25A and ID25B) of the German Section (14) of the NID, under a single head. Above all else this was to lead to a greater protection of British merchant shipping. Of equal importance at this time was the creation of the Convoy Section of the Naval Staff (25 June 1917). Prior to this the German and enemy Submarine Sections of the NID had been kept separate from Room 40 and its cryptanalysis, and all of these from the work of the Anti-Submarine Division of the Admiralty. All of these organisations, united in the common goals of convoy protection and U-boat destruction were fully integrated. The significance of the separation of Room 40 from Sections E1 and 14 of the NID came out officially as late as the Naval Staff Appreciation of Jutland in 1922. This showed how, because of organisational failures and the secrecy attached to Room 40's work a combined picture of the U-boat threat in particular had never emerged within the pre-1917 Naval Staff.

At the end of the war the War Staff of the Admiralty was run down along with the whole infrastructure of British defence. The CID was revived, but the Naval Staff lost several of its crucial divisions. Above all the NID by the end of the twenties had become but a shadow of its former self. Its crucial code breaking activities had been taken over by the Foreign Office. Several other major developments must be mentioned here that are relevant to what ensues. The 1922 Churchill Committee rejected for the time being the idea of a 'Ministry of Defence', but proposed that the CID act as the instrument of co-ordination between the three Services. It made two other important recommendations, one that the idea of a Joint Staff and a Joint Staff College to train and educate officers for this Staff should be investigated, and secondly that certain common services of all three arms should be amalgamated in the interests of both efficiency and economy. A year later the Salisbury Committee reported. As a result of it the Chiefs of Staff Committee was created (COS). Another committee, which had been chaired by the head of the Board of Education, E.F.L. Wood, later Lord Halifax, recommended in the same year that a joint staff college be set up in London under the control of the CID. The net result of these various committees was the establishment in 1926 of the Joint Planning Committee as a subcommittee of the COS, and of the Imperial Defence College, which began its first course in January 1927 with Admiral Sir Herbert Richmond as its first Commandant.

It was indeed unfortunate that it was not until 1936 that the Joint Intelligence Committee was formed and that a Joint Services College for middle rank officers was not founded until after World War II when, as a result of pressure from the Navy, the Joint Services Staff College was founded at Latimer in 1946. The Admiralty's reasons for this will be discussed later. These developments during and in the early years immediately after the Great War were to condition the whole development of Naval Staff training and in consequence the work for which officers were ostensibly being trained at Greenwich and also, indirectly, the structure and workings of the Naval Staff and equally importantly the relationship of the Navy with the other two Services. The end result itself – the standard of performance of the Navy in its many and varied tasks, is of course the ultimate criterion by which any assessment of the value of staff training in this period will be made. It is all too easy in any large organisation to forget the main objectives, particularly one such as the Navy in peacetime, when it is easy to accept that its *raison d'être* may be to provide officers with careers rather than to fulfil other fundamental politico-military objectives.

It was ironical that in the year after the RN Staff College had been founded the Admiralty Board abolished the wearing of distinguishing shoulder straps by Naval Staff Officers. They had been introduced originally in September 1915 on the suggestion of the C-in-C Grand Fleet, and consisted of a blue cloth shoulder strap, as opposed to the aiguillettes worn by personal staff. The arguments in favour of abolishing them were that a Naval Staff officer did not have to be recognised as such, unlike the Army Staff officer 'in the field', who had to be distinguished from regimental officers, and secondly that if worn they would make staff officers a race apart from general service officers and this would lead to division. These were no doubt perfectly valid arguments, and there indeed seemed little real point to an extra piece of paraphernalia to go with the naval uniform. However, what does come out of this discussion is that the attitude of the Admiralty Board in general to the role of the staff officer *per se*, as opposed to an officer in a staff appointment (i.e. any general service officer doing any job which involved a measure of staff work), was somewhat nugatory, and this was transferred to the approach to staff training. If the initial attitude to the notion of a staff officer was at best muddled and at worst downright prejudiced and bigoted then there was little real chance that the problem of deciding the content of staff training at Greenwich would be satisfactorily solved.[2] There was an attitude still prevailing in the upper echelons of the Navy which was left over from the Fisher era that hated the idea of staff officers and staff training. This had been exacerbated in some minds during the war by the various staff shake-ups, several of which had implied direct criticism of the way in which the Navy was run. This hit home with the conservative-minded naval officer. It was the more radical and intellectual group of younger officers, led by Richmond, Dewar, Plunkett, Thursfield and Bellairs who supported Churchill in his desire to create a staff.

In a draft Confidential Order dated 11 September 1918 the role of the 'Staff' was made clear:

> The main object is to limit the Staff to those few officers who, by virtue of special training in, or actual experience, work in connection with the principles, preparation, and conduct of operations of war, are appointed to the Admiralty or to the establishments of Commands afloat and ashore to assist in the preparation for, and actual conduct of Naval war in relation to strategy, tactics, and the principles of training.

It went on to add: 'A distinction will be drawn between officers appointed to the staff for operations and those attached to the staff for technical and administrative duties.' The order made a distinction between a Chief-of-Staff (i.e. to an operational C-in-C) and a Chief Staff Officer (i.e. to an administrative and technical staff officer). The Staff was to be divided into four main sections: Operations, Mercantile Movements, Intelligence, Communications. David Beatty, C-in-C Grand Fleet, replied to the Draft order in a letter dated 7 October 1918. He had few quibbles with it. As the Director of Training and Staff Duties minuted on 22 October 1918; 'It is satisfactory that C-in-C Grand Fleet is in general agreement with the provisions of the draft CIO. With few exceptions the alterations suggested are matters of detail and wording only.' The Fleet Order was later issued.[3] It is important to note that at this stage no mention or concern was expressed about the nature of the training to be given to staff officers or the significance of either the training or staff appointments in officers' careers. Reforming staff structures was one thing, but ensuring that the right men were in the right job at the right stage in their career with all the training that was 'necessary' to do the job in a way that agreed with criteria previously established was another matter. Neither the Admiralty nor the Fleet gave any thought to this whatsoever.

In 1924 in King's Regulations and Admiralty Instructions number 224a staff officers were placed in two categories: (a) those who assist the command in the preparation for and conduct of the operations of war, entitled 'Staff Officers for Operations or Intelligence'; (b) those who assist the Command in its technical and administrative functions entitled 'Technical and Administrative Staff Officers'. The Regulations went on to state: 'Staff Officers will be selected for appointment from those who have passed through the Royal Naval Staff College (p.s.c.) or are selected by virtue of special capacity for the type of work required.' These are fundamental distinctions, yet at the same time no special regulations were laid down for the training of officers in staff work.

90

The Navy tended to leave the whole thing somewhat open-ended. It implied that special training was desirable but in certain cases not absolutely essential. Within a very short time the approach to staff training and the staff course in particular had crystallised in the minds of most Naval officers and particularly those within the promotion zone. The situation was summed up in a letter to the Director of Training and Staff Duties by the Director of the Staff College in 1923. He said that officers were afraid that they would not be promoted if they do the Staff Course when they could be at sea in a post which might be more 'promotion-worthy'. He argued that staff officers did need a formal training and that in order to produce enough staff officers Lieutenant Commanders as well as Commanders would have to be trained. He continued to say that officers' fears would have to be allayed by the Admiralty Board stating that the roster system would allow officers selected for staff training to have at least three shots at promotion before beginning the course at Greenwich. What was quite incredible was the Director's comment that officers should be allowed to withdraw from the Staff Course if they felt that it jeopardised their prospects of promotion. This final comment was eventually incorporated in a Fleet Order.[4] The basic contradictions here stayed with the Service right through the inter-war period — that if a job required training before it could be done and if that job was important in itself and also part of the regular career structure then it became a nonsense to downgrade the significance of the training and to imply that promotion would result from work in other quarters. Not only did this begin to jaundice the Service's attitude to the Staff Course, it also helped perpetuate Fisher's antiquated ideas about staff work itself which Churchill had fought so hard to dispel.

The controversy over whether or not the Royal Naval College at Greenwich was a full Naval training establishment and the emoluments of the Admiral President indicate that the Service was not yet prepared to commit itself to creating the ethos and status within the Navy for Greenwich which the Army had so successfully achieved at Camberley. In 1926 the question of Greenwich's status finally polarised around the issue of its right to fly the White Ensign or otherwise. Greenwich was classified as a civilian establishment, and the Admiral President was paid as a civilian head, not the appropriate rate for his Naval rank. It was argued by the Admiral President that Greenwich was a full Naval establishment insofar as Naval officers were under instruction there (although borne on the books of HMS *President* for pay), they still continued to come under the Naval Discipline Act, and the Admiral President was also 'in command' of the War College. Permission was eventually granted.[5] The reluctance shown prior to this (when the quite simple arguments in favour had been the need to distinguish Greenwich in the locality, to exchange courtesies with passing ships and also to bring it into line with Dartmouth), had been based on the fact that Greenwich was not seriously regarded as a training establishment which had a significant part to play in the role of the Navy or the training of officers other than the traditional technical courses which had been the Royal Naval College's bread and butter since its inception in 1873. In 1921 the Treasury had declined to increase the Admiral President's emoluments to equate with those of an Admiral Superintendent of a Dockyard because they did not consider that the responsibilities of the post warranted it. The Admiral President, Admiral Tudor-Tudor, had only the Admiralty to blame insofar as it had not raised the status of the College by giving importance to its work. The next President, Rear Admiral H.W. Richmond, CB, was more fortunate because he succeeded in merging the posts of Admiral President and Director of the War College and the Treasury then conceded despite the Geddes Act in 1922.[6] As will be seen later Richmond had quite firm views on the need to raise the status of the Staff College.

The Director of the Staff College had to fight a similar battle for Command and Entertainment Allowances. It took seven years before he received what appear to have been his just deserts. The reason for this was quite simple – the status of the Staff College did not warrant it. In 1923-4 the Treasury squashed an application for more money (although the Captain of the College, the administrator and disciplinary head beneath the Admiral President in the College hierarchy, received the higher rate). In a letter of 16 April 1924 the Treasury stated: '. . .we do not regard the post occupied by this officer as analogous to that of the Commandant of the Military Staff College, Camberley. . .'. In a letter of 25 June the Admiralty Board formally requested the Treasury to reconsider their decision. After a letter from Sir Vincent Baddeley of 20 August 1924 the Treasury made a minute concession to the Staff College's Director. On the 24 March 1930 the Treasury did finally agree to a payment of £187 per annum Servants' allowance to the Captain of the Staff College.[7] It was pointless the Navy wishing parity of pay with their Army counterparts at Camberley when they quite unequivocally stated that Greenwich's role in the Staff training sphere was low key when compared with Camberley.

When Admiral Richmond was appointed Director of Training and Staff Duties in 1918 there came to the Admiralty someone who for years had been the advocate of staff training. He had supported Churchill's Dardanelles campaign as a good idea in itself but saw it as an operational disaster because of bad staff work. His supporters, people like Captain Roger Bellairs, Beatty's Flag Captain in the *Queen Elizabeth,* were echoing his views. In a letter to Richmond dated 16 December 1917 Bellairs criticised bad convoy policy and the fact that parliament was demanding explanations from the Admiralty. He wrote: 'A careful analysis of the facts simply confirms the opinion that the whole trouble lies in the lack of a naval policy and the absence of a naval staff at the Admiralty.'[8] Richmond himself always argued that the Naval Staff were against any kind of reform or even suggestion of it because it implied criticism of their way of managing affairs. He believed in a continuing process of higher education for all Naval officers, and he carefully analysed history to discover the educational backgrounds and attainments of great seamen to guide him in his programme of Naval Education reform. He was greatly influenced in all this by Sir Julian Corbett, the Naval historian. But Richmond soon found that his own reformist zeal was not welcomed by the Admiralty – after a year none of his major plans had been accepted by the Board. A letter to Richmond dated 20 December 1918 from his own Deputy Director of Training and Staff Duties, Captain Rhys Williams, sums up the situation: 'The results of our nine months work in this Division have been depressing.' He paid great tribute to Richmond's endeavours but said that the reason for his disenchantment was the recalcitrance of the Board. He went on to say:

I hope that the fruits of our sowing will be reaped by a Board of Admiralty of the future, and that we shall live to see a Naval Staff College at Camberley, a scheme of education in which fitness for war is the ultimate object. . .I hope the Staff system as we have tried to develop it, on the lines proved in the Army to be correct, may develop in the Navy, and that the close association we have established with the Staff Duties Division will not be allowed to lapse. I also hope that the practice of nominating exceptional candidates, which gives such good results in the Army, may be adopted in the Navy.[9]

Richmond himself was so depressed by the whole situation that he considered resignation and accepting the Chair of History at Cambridge which he had been offered. Roger Bellairs advised against it and wrote him: '. . .personnel and ideas both change in the course of time, even at the Admiralty. . .'.[10]

Richmond's views on Staff training and education were simple but at the heart of the problem. He wanted the Staff Course (and the precursor to this in an officer's career training – a Junior Officers' War Course), to become a 'think tank' to provide his 'New Model Staff' with the right sort of brain power. In fact Geddes' Staff reforms were very much in line with his own ideas. Richmond had always wanted an Historical section whose function was to advise the Naval Staff by putting contemporary tactical and strategic problems in their historical context. He saw this section as belonging to the NID (Naval Intelligence Department). On 'Education' he wrote: 'Education should be lifted out of its narrow meaning. Education is confounded with instruction. As a result it is dominated by examinations and a pernicious system of cramming unintelligently acquired facts. . .'. He said that there was not enough study of war. 'In the old days they were thinking of these things when they were between twenty and thirty because they had to. Now they do not, or they ought to.' He wanted to cut the number of lectures at Greenwich and allow more time for thinking so that C-in-Cs could be made at a much earlier age. He also argued that papers produced by students at Greenwich if of sufficient merit should be used by the Admiralty War Staff, thus motivating students, involving them in a realistic way with practical problems and also sharpening the wits of the Naval Staff.[11] He made it abundantly clear when DTSD that the training of staff officers cannot be separated from the wartime experiences of the Admiralty with regard to the organisation of the Naval Staff. The main components of his Staff Course were to be: Naval strategy, tactics, history, international relations, intelligence duties, the organisation and conduct of war by sea, land and air, and the principles, theory and practice of staff work. It was essentially to be about the 'art of war'. His original ideas for the location of the RNSC had been that it should be completely separate from any other Naval Educational Establishment, it should be residential and self-contained and that it should be within easy reach of Camberley. In a minute of 15 November 1918 he had written: 'Port location for the RNSC is unnecessary. The best location is near to the Army Staff College at Camberley. A house known as Penneyhill Park, Bagshot, with 100 acres of land attached is now on the market and could be secured if it is decided to institute a Staff College for the Navy. The house is within two miles of the Military Staff College at Camberley.'[12] Richmond believed firmly in the need for constant co-operation between the two staff colleges. In 1918 there was just coming to light the lack of co-ordination between the Naval staff, and particularly the Plans Division, and the Army Staff especially concerning operations in Palestine, Salonika and the Balkans. As we know, Richmond's Grand Design came to nought.

When one looks at the professional advice that was available to the

Admiralty it becomes quite apparent that it had no one from the educational world who could offer the sort of guidance that was necessary for designing a Staff Course, establishing standards and maintaining the right sort of connections with the Naval Staff, the Fleet and civilian educational and commercial interests as well as other government departments such as the Foreign Office. In December 1921 an Adviser on Education was appointed to the Admiralty Board. During the Great War Sir Alfred Ewing, a brilliant former professor of Engineering from Cambridge and founder of the code breaking organisation, Room 40, had occupied the post of Director of Naval Education. He was a man with his feet firmly on the ground and with a vast knowledge of the Navy, Naval operations, and equally important, with a wide range of Service contacts and friends. Since 11 March 1919 Mr A.P. McMullen, a former Assistant Master from the Royal Naval College Dartmouth had occupied a temporary post of Education Adviser. This post was now confirmed by the Treasury. The incumbent was directly responsible to the Second Sea Lord for the whole of Naval Education. In retrospect it is not surprising that he was unable to assist the DTSD in the formulation of policy for the Staff Course and also influence the Second Sea Lord's policy on Staff training. He simply did not have the right sort of background and experience.

In January 1919 the office of Dean of the College was revived. His terms of reference were as follows:

> . . .to assist the Admiral President in arranging with the Professors and Instructors the time-tables of lectures, classes and examinations, and the allocation of classrooms other than those already specially allotted, and to arrange for the superintendence of examinations and co-operate as required with the office of the Adviser on Education in examination work at the College. He will not be responsible for syllabuses nor for the disposal of the services of any of the teaching staff of the College except those who are appointed to his own department.[13]

The first Dean was Instructor Captain S.F. Card. The one appointment then of a Naval Officer who could have been directly responsible for looking at Staff training as a whole, in conjunction with the Admiral President and the Director of the Staff Course, and acting as the professional link between College and the Admiralty, yet not encumbered with the day-to-day problems of running the Staff College as the Director, was merely to manage classrooms and directly instructed not to meddle in syllabuses. An opportunity was surely lost here.

However, a positive move was made when the Admiralty Board created a Chair of History and a Lectureship in History at Greenwich from 12 April 1922. The Board decided that History and English should be included in the Lieutenants' and Sub-Lieutenants' courses, and the Science content was proportionately reduced. Mr Geoffrey Callender, who had worked at both Osborne and Dartmouth, was appointed to the Chair, and from 152 applications for the Lectureship Mr Jack Bullocke was appointed. This ensured that from early on the Staff Course and later the Junior Officers' War Course (and to a lesser extent the Senior Officers' War Course) did have on the spot professional advisers on matters of educational policy and content for these courses. It was in keeping with Richmond's philosophy that the study of history was essential for the correct analysis of contemporary strategic and tactical problems. The relatively new study of international relations had not yet begun though as we shall see later considerable emphasis was placed on the study of international affairs and international law to enable students to place their military studies in the right context.

In 1924 the Director of Naval Intelligence, Admiral Fitzmaurice, proposed that the Intelligence School be incorporated with the Staff College, the idea being that if the graduates of the RNSC were intelligence trained too then at some stage in their careers they could work in the NID. The Admiralty Board decided that although this was a good idea in theory the Intelligence School would have to remain separate from the Staff College because the latter did not have sufficient turn-over to produce the number of intelligence officers required. However the study of intelligence was incorporated in the Staff Course syllabus.

The period from its foundation until 1935 was a relatively quiet one for the Staff College. It busied itself consolidating its courses and building up good relations with the other two Service Staff Colleges. There were a few minor rumblings in 1933. The Admiral President, Admiral Boyle, tried to move the tactical course to Greenwich and integrate it with the Staff Course. The Admiralty Board turned this down on the grounds that the tactical course should be near to the Portsmouth training schools, the RAF and the Fleet Air Arm. In February 1933 the Board expressed concern at the apparent lack of co-ordination and direction between the War College, the Staff College and the Imperial Defence College. The Admiral President's solution was that he should become the Director of both the War College and the Staff College. The Assistant Chief of Naval Staff (to whom the Director of the Staff College was directly responsible) ruled: 'If the

Admiral President can be placed between the Director of the Staff College and the ACNS without fettering the independent status, personality, and leadership of the Director *vis-à-vis* the students and the Commandants of Camberley and Andover (the RAF Staff College), I see no objection to this change.' However, he went on to add: 'If the President were placed in charge of all these courses then control by the Naval Staff would be inevitably weakened. Further, to exercise effective control an enlargement of the President's staff would be essential.' Admiral Boyle's argument for assuming direct control was to ensure that there was co-ordination and a common related policy for all the various courses. In addition the Admiral President wanted all training at Greenwich to be placed under the direct control of the Dean of the College, an Instructor Captain, who was to be responsible to the Admiral. In paragraph 13 in his letter to the Board he wrote:

With a view to ensuring the continued effectiveness of the instruction given by the professorial staff at the Royal Naval College to officers undergoing courses, by subjecting it to criticism by a Naval officer who possesses the necessary academic qualifications, a knowledge of sea conditions, and a close acquaintance with the attainments and requirements of the officers under instruction, I submit that the position of Dean of the College should be improved and his title altered to 'Director' or 'Superintendent' of Studies in order to make clear his position, and that it should be made quite plain that he has authority, under the President, to supervise the College instruction, and advise him on all matters connected with the administration and conduct of the instructional staff.

The Board turned down all these recommendations of the Admiral. On the latter point the Secretary to the Admiralty replied: 'Considerable difficulties might arise if all the other professors were placed under the control of the Instructor Captain, who might be a comparatively young man without great experience.' A Board of Studies continued to run the Greenwich courses.[14]

In 1935 there came the first sign that the Service was going to re-think its Staff training policy. The Director of Training and Staff Duties considered that far too many officers thought that the Staff Course was not good for their promotion prospects and the majority preferred sea appointments. As a result Naval Staff training was being regarded with complete scepticism by both the Navy and the other two Services. He wrote: 'It is proposed that an outside committee should be set up to consider the whole question of the future training of Naval officers for war.' On 28 January 1935 Admiral Pound agreed to the formation of a committee, although he made no bones about saying that he did not hold out much hope for the findings of such a committee. The members of the Committee on the Training of Officers for War were: Vice-Admiral W.M. James, Captain P. Macnamara, Commander H.G. Norman, and the Secretary was Mr J.F. Mountain of the Commission and Warrant Branch. The First Lord of the Admiralty to the Committee summarised the issues at stake as follows:

> I think that our difficulty in this matter has been partly caused by our Staff College having been started with only Army practice to guide us whereas our requirements are almost entirely different from theirs. A Commander-in-Chief in a big Fleet has a large number of Staff officers fulfilling various special staff qualifications. The majority of these officers receive their staff training in technical establishments. The only officer on the staff who is not in this position is the Staff Officer (operations) for whom a special course is necessary. It is this special course which is the basis of our Staff College; the other part of the training of the Staff College is one of general education which, while it is essential for the Staff Officer (operations) is almost equally important for the other Staff Officers. Further, there are the remainder who are unlikely to fill any staff post but require the preliminary higher education as early in life as possible to fit them for higher command and for employment at the Admiralty. I feel, therefore, that in principle the part of the course which trains officers for operational Staff Duties should be separate from the part that gives officers higher general education.[15]

A very important point was therefore raised early in the discussion — that a continuous process of higher education was essential in itself for Naval officers irrespective of their appointing pattern, and also that it was, in any case, very much complementary to the narrower field of staff training. It was therefore not surprising that the First Lord was also in favour of a three-month Lieutenants Course, which should be designed to give junior officers both the beginning of a higher education but also to spot at an early stage those who might be suited for staff appointments later and who should therefore be selected to do the Staff Course. Inherent in his comments were the notions that officers had to be trained to do staff work, that not all might be suited to this work, and that therefore the Service should take trouble to discover those with special talents for it.

The First Sea Lord's views on the James Report (as it became known) were quite clear. Instead of all Commanders taking the Staff Course, which was one of the main recommendations of the James Committee, he wanted to continue the voluntary system and confine the course to selected Commanders — thirty in number. The Second Sea Lord and the ACNS (Assistant Chief of Naval Staff) agreed with the First Sea Lord that all officers of the rank of Lieutenant over six years seniority or Lieutenant Commanders should do a three-month Junior Command and Staff Training Course. Unlike the Committee's proposal they wanted this to be held at the Tactical School in Portsmouth, and not at Greenwich. The Staff Course itself was to remain one year in duration, and not as the Committee recommended to consist of two overlapping courses each of eight to nine months duration. The method of selection for the Staff Course was to be based upon the reports of the Director of the Junior Command and Staff Training Course to the Admiralty. Commanders who earlier in their careers had not been selected to do the Staff Course were to do a four-month War Course, two of which were to be run each year at Greenwich. In none of their comments was there a hint of the place of staff training *vis-à-vis* career prospects which was the continuous issue which concerned all career minded Naval Officers and had in fact sparked off the formation of the Committee. However the James Report itself made no bones about stating the facts as they were: it said that at present those least likely to be promoted were being trained for higher command on the Staff Course, because all the better candidates were at sea. This, together with the fact that post-Staff Course appointments were not in keeping with the higher aims of the course, seemed to the Committee to be totally unsatisfactory. At the same time the Committee did not allow itself to run away with unrealistic or inappropriate educational objectives. Admiral James wrote:

Whilst much of their learning at the Staff College can be put to practical account at sea, much more covers a wider field and is, though undoubtedly useful, not essential at that particular time in their careers. In many commands the Flag Officer requires from his Staff Officers the efficient performance of certain limited duties. He expects him to be quick, accurate, level headed, able to draft signals and orders, and to be conversant with the various publications dealing with tactics. A junior staff officer's knowledge of international law, economics, and strategy will seldom be allowed to break surface in peace time. . .The Navy is a Service of action, of the ordered activities of a large personnel, and it is an officer's power of command, character and seamanship that must be the main consideration when selecting officers for promotion to Commander and to Captain or for re-employment as a Flag Officer; their knowledge of subjects taught at courses though important, is a secondary consideration.[16]

This was slightly at variance with other parts of the report. One moment it advocates a continuous process of higher education and the next it casts doubt on its validity, although it demonstrated quite clearly that an officer did need general education throughout his career, and that if he either did not receive this from an early age or what he did receive was allowed to atrophy, then his ability to perform satisfactorily in the higher appointments within the Service later in his career was being jeopardised. Churchill's words quoted earlier about the absence of 'Captains of War' in the Navy seemed to echo through the report. Reading these contradictions in the report it becomes apparent that if staff training was ever justified then this report did just that, insofar as the report was not well planned, logical, well reasoned throughout, and did not conclude in a way which left no doubts in the reader's mind, or that the conclusions were fully justified. Above all else the report seemed to have lost sight of its aim, and James himself, able as he was, seems to have lost the battle with his masters because his arguments were not cogent enough and were not followed through consistently.

On the question of the rank of the Director of the Staff College the report recommended that he be a Rear-Admiral, so that he equated with the Camberley and Andover Commandants. Admiral Colvin, the Admiral President at Greenwich, concurred with this. The Director of the Staff Course, Captain Bertram Watson was against this and indeed against most of the report. He made his position clear in a letter to the Admiralty dated 23 August 1935. 'Destruction is not too strong a word. The existing system has a definite aim, is voluntary, and is for the selected few; the proposed system has no definite aim beyond general education and is compulsory for all.'[17] He never once said why staff training was necessary or tried to analyse the relationship between what the Service actually needed in terms of trained staff officers and what the course at Greenwich purported to do. He did though make the relevant comment that if the course became a Commander's course (and not one for Lieutenant Commanders) then a greater number of higher ranking directing staff would be required. He said the end result would be a course populated with senior Commanders who would not be receptive to learning and the atmosphere would be spoilt. He failed to make the equally relevant point that if Lieutenant Commanders filled staff appointments which required training then presumably they should do the Staff Course. In other words it would be too late in the day to train people by the time they reached Commander's rank. Equally valid was Watson's point that to leave further training from the time of the new Junior Officers' Course until an officer became a Commander and did the Staff Course would result in a large gulf in an officer's education.

The Director of Training and Staff Duties agreed with Watson's main contentions, and he wanted the Admiralty to issue a statement drawing the attention of all officers of all ranks to the importance which the Admiralty attach to the Staff Course as part of the training of officers for higher rank. He wanted the Staff Course to be done only by those Commanders who had not done it as a Lieutenant Commander. He also agreed that the Staff Course should not come under the direction of the Admiral President. In the event the Admiralty Board made its position plain in a letter from the Secretary to the Board to the Commander-in-Chief Portsmouth and to the Admiral President at Greenwich. In it three items specified the Board's proposals: the Junior Command and Staff Course was to be started, lasting three months, and there were to be three a year and they were to be held in the Tactical School; the Staff Course was to continue to last one year and was to be for thirty selected Commanders. Commanders not selected for the Staff Course would do a four-month War Course, two of which would be held each year; finally Captains and Flag Officers would attend a 'refresher' course.[18] The situation remained thus until after the Second World War when the Service decided that it had little time or justification for the one year Staff Course as it stood, and Lord Cunningham's idea, supported by most of the Admiralty Staff, was to opt for more tri-Service training with a little individual RN training at the junior staff level. As a result of pressure from the Navy, the Chief-of-Staff opened the Joint Services Staff College, and although this was most certainly an advance in its own right it did ensure that the Staff Course never got off to a flying start immediately after the war because of the emphasis the Navy now placed on the JSSC.

The only way that it is now possible to ascertain how and in what subjects the Service thought staff officers should be trained is to examine the syllabuses and course programmes of each staff course during the inter-war period. From these, deductions can be made as to what were considered those areas of Naval staff work which required both specific and general training before an officer took up a staff appointment. The course did not alter fundamentally during the twenty years from 1919 to 1939 except that the emphasis on Jutland and the big fleet action that dominated naval thinking in the early twenties shifted to the big gun versus the aircraft controversy of the mid-thirties and a re-thinking of the Dardanelles campaign and combined operations in general.[19] Each course did various staff work schemes based on the conventions of Service writing. Each course had to produce several staff appreciations, the most important ones being concerned with convoy organisations and convoy operations with special emphasis on anti-submarine operations. Straightforward tactics were left out as these were dealt with by the Tactical School in Portsmouth. Each course received a long series of lectures on the English language and Naval history, but of great benefit and of a very high standard were the lecture courses on international law and the associated staff schemes in which students were required to respond to credible situations at sea using their knowledge of international law. General lectures were given on strategy, followed by specific ones on British, French and German Naval strategy. A special study was made of the Russo-Japanese War, convoy problems, the attack and defence of trade, blockading operations, the use of bases and a long time was spent looking at the staff organisation of the Army and land operations during the Great War. What may now seem unusual is that despite the general lack of preparedness in terms of material and organisation for combined operations in 1939 the RN Staff Course spent more time dealing with this subject from 1935 onwards than any other single item. Not only was the Dardanelles campaign analysed in detail but also excellent lectures were delivered by RAF and Royal Marines officers on amphibious operations. Lieutenant Colonel H.T. Newman was the star lecturer for this part of the course. A good analysis was made of the German submarine campaign of World War I and, in true Richmond vein, an exhaustive series of lectures was given on the French Revolutionary Wars and Naval operations.[20]

What is apparent from an examination of the actual Staff Course syllabus and also the way in which it was designed is that the Admiralty, although on paper it wished to have direct control of the Course through the VCNS to the Director of the Staff College, never really exerted any direct influence over the Course. If the course aimed at training men for appointments in the Admiralty and on the staffs of C-in-Cs, and also wished to update those under training with the latest picture yet at the same time encourage young officers to think and produce new ideas whilst on course which could be fed directly into the appropriate Admiralty department, then this just never happened in the way in which people like Richmond had originally envisaged. There was a procession of visiting lecturers from the various Admiralty departments but nothing resembling a dialogue between the two ever developed. These ideas soon became a pipe dream in the minds of the 'Young Turks' who survived into the twenties and thirties.[21] At no time during the inter-war period did the RN Staff College conduct a scheme or war game which was directly sponsored by a Naval Staff department or maintain a system of direct feedback other than for the content of lectures given by Admiralty Staff. The War College played a war game involving Atlantic trade protection in 1939 which was sponsored by the Director of Naval Plans. It was highly successful insofar as it threw up a number of problems which were useful to the planners in making their war plans, and at the same time involving the students in an exercise which was completely meaningful and productive. This was a rare occurrence even in the War College and in retrospect it seems such a regrettable waste of an opportunity for the Staff College that this and other similar training techniques were not used more frequently.

When one looks at twenty years of Naval staff training certain points emerge. Staff training was a controversial subject and at no stage did anyone, or any of the Admiralty departments, attempt to base the discussion and the decisions which were made upon objective criteria, although the James report made a valiant attempt at doing this.

What does hindsight tell us that the inter-war Navy should have done to solve its staff training problem? Let us start from a basic assumption that the problem should be focused on what staff officers do. A comparison of the performance of Staff and non-Staff trained officers in a range of appointments would have revealed both the usefulness of the training given at Greenwich and equally important it would have highlighted those aspects of staff work which specifically required training in addition to the teaching of general staff skills and the higher education which was the necessary support for this. In other words there was a fundamental failure to define the aim (ironically the first principle uppermost in the mind of the good staff officer) which was to ensure that staff officers performed to a defined minimum standard within staff appointments. As a result of muddled thinking the problem was not resolved along systematic lines. For example it was being argued by some that it was desirable to have all Commanders staff trained, and that a 'psc' should be a prerequisite for promotion. If this was so it was logical to argue that a non-'psc' Commander could not efficiently fill most staff appointments designated for Commander and that currently such jobs were being performed less effectively than they should. In fact there was no concrete evidence either way, although commonsense indicated that the latter point was palpably not true though it could be said that training could improve performance. All this shows that there was not a data base about jobs and standards of performance within them from which to begin an analysis. Staff jobs in the Navy were not graded either, as they still are by the Army, on the basis that a specific type of training and experience is necessary to perform each individual job. The contentious issue of the value of staff training and the fact that it took people away from sea when they were in line for promotion could have been resolved if the Service had shown that staff training was necessary for the effective performance of staff jobs, and that those jobs were important, and therefore as promotion-worthy as sea appointments. A natural corollary to this line of reasoning is that extensive research should have been done to derive content for the initial courses. Furthermore if it had been shown that the necessity to have a 'psc' for a high percentage of staff appointments was derived from objective investigation then it would have been highly likely that the attitude of most officers to staff training would have been more positive.

In modern management terms what was lacking were detailed job descriptions of a range of staff appointments and a feedback system for what were the deficiencies in training to enable the course designers at Greenwich to modify their course content. The James report mentioned selecting officers for staff training and appointments yet it had no way of deciding what sort of man was required. A detailed breakdown of jobs would have helped in this and also this would have served as a basis for assessing a man's performance in the job just as job terms of reference do. In any event the RN Staff College just could not produce enough staff officers to fill all staff appointments. For example the annual intake of Naval officers to the Staff College was reduced from 40 to 26 in 1922 when staffs were reduced and in 1930 the Staff College could accept only 32 at a time when the DTDS considered that all staff appointments (in maintenance departments as well as Naval Staff divisions) should be filled by 'psc' officers. Throughout the inter-war period this was an impossible ideal.

In conclusion several general observations can be made about the problems already discussed. The Navy tied itself to its past too much so that in the end two schools of thought emerged which did not reflect the real problems mentioned above. There was the old style Fisher school on the one hand and the Churchill-Richmond school on the other. As a result the Service tended to argue in terms of the dangers of the 'psc' qualification being seen as a qualification for promotion and forgot the real point — the efficient working of the Navy with an effective training system to meet its aims. Career structures and promotion prospects were paramount when they should have been of secondary consideration. Even the assumptions upon which the latter were built were taken at face value — no one questioned the validity of the Naval appointing or promotion system. For example, the report from the Staff College received little attention compared with the one from sea when it came to appointments, even though an officer might be going to a staff appointment next, and the Navy never examined its requirement for staff trained officers in all staff appointments but instead appointed officers to all types of staff positions regardless of whether they were staff trained or not. If officers were staff trained then this was simply regarded as being a bonus. No one ever stressed the point that the staff course could in fact equip an officer for command. Indeed the Army has always argued that it is absolutely essential for command. The notion of valuable sea time being lost whilst an officer is at the Staff College was never rooted in either fact or logic. It is quite obvious that an officer's contribution to the Service and also his own immediate effectiveness might be much more affected by something which occurs at the Staff College than by sea service. By 1939 Churchill's original aim, that the RN Staff College should become the 'brain' of the Naval Staff was still a pipedream. Furthermore the Navy had also lost the essential point that a higher education, in the traditional and widest sense, was required for those aspiring to the highest ranks. As a result staff training was left out of the major reviews of officer structure and training, except for the James Report. As an additional handicap the Navy let its appointing problems act as a ready buffer for not making radical changes.

There is no doubt that Greenwich itself did and still does have a special place in the affections of the Navy, more as a Naval University than as a centre for staff and command training. The Tactical School always detracted from the Staff College's role. The latter, with its emphasis on war in the future, requirements for war, and achieving broader aims through general strategies should have been at least of equal if not greater significance than training in the latest tactics, which were relatively easy to acquire and were part of the pattern of sea training in any case. At the end of the day the Royal Naval Staff College never matched up to the hopes of its original founders, and the responsibility for this lay firmly at the feet of the Service itself.

Notes

1. W.S. Churchill, *The World Crisis (1923-1931)*, vol.I, p.93.
2. Wearing of shoulder straps by staff officers, proposed abolition, 16 March 1920, PRO Adm 1: 8583/44.
3. Naval Staff organisation — Staffs afloat, PRO Adm 1: 8670/199.

4. Staff Course − recommendations concerning the conditions of application and selection, 28 November 1923, PRO Adm 1: 8670/199.
5. RNC Greenwich − Application to fly the White Ensign, 1926, PRO Adm 1: 8706/203.
6. RNC Greenwich − Question of President's Emoluments, 1922, PRO Adm 1: 8707/215.
7. Command and Entertainment Allowances, 1923-1930, RPO Adm 1: 8744/140.
8. NMM Greenwich, Richmond MSS 1, vol.15.
9. Ibid.
10. Ibid.
11. Staff Work and Training, NMM Greenwich, Richmond MSS 12/4.
12. Ibid.
13. RNC Greenwich Professorial Staff, PRO, Adm 116: 1850.
14. The organisation of War Courses and the Training of Naval officers for War, PRO Adm 1: 9041.
15. Ibid.
16. Ibid.
17. Ibid.
18. Ibid.
19. Details of the content of inter-war Staff courses at Greenwich, NMM Greenwich, Tennant MSS 41/11. Papers of Captain G.A. French, CBE, RN (Rtd.).
20. Lectures and Courses given in the RN Staff College, NMM Greenwich, Bellasis MSS.
21. The Young Turks were the radical intellectual group led by Richmond during the Great War which began the Naval Review and influenced Naval policy during the latter part of the war.

GERMAN AIR POWER AND THE MUNICH CRISIS

Williamson Murray

One of the most persistent myths in post-war historical literature has
been that Chamberlain saved Britain at Munich from the prospect of
immediate defeat at the hands of a German air offensive and thus won
the time necessary for the RAF to win the Battle of Britain.
Supposedly the year's grace allowed the RAF to re-equip fighter
squadrons with Hurricanes and Spitfires and extend the radar stations
to cover the whole British Isles.[1] The key question which must be
posed, even acknowledging the dreadful state of British air defences,
and which has not been answered hitherto, is whether Germany was
actually in a position in 1938 to launch a strategic bombing offensive
against Great Britain. To answer such a question it is necessary to
establish the actual balance of air power in 1938 by comparing the
RAF and the *Luftwaffe* and to discuss in detail Luftwaffe training
and support services, and strategic and tactical planning.

There are striking similarities in the development of these air
forces in the late 1930s. Both Air Staffs had to grapple with rapid
expansion, a new generation of aircraft, crew training, supply and
maintenance — all on a scale far exceeding anything previously
experienced. If anything these problems were of such magnitude as to
make the respective air forces barely fit for combat. In late 1937 the
British Air Staff reported that:

> The above picture of our state of readiness for war discloses many
> unsatisfactory circumstances, but it must be realized that the RAF
> is now in the midst of a most difficult stage of transition. We are in
> the process of expanding from a small force which mainly consists
> of light single-engined aircraft to a large force equipped with aircraft
> which are in many cases multi-engined and all of which have a high
> performance and completely different characteristics from those on
> which the bulk of the air force has been trained. Our squadrons are
> manned largely by personnel who — though enthusiastic and
> efficient — are yet lacking in experience and higher training.[2]

A German 'after-action' report on the Czech crisis indicates the same
situation existed in the Luftwaffe in 1938:

In the last months the following special measures had to be carried through at the same time: 1) equipment of many new units, 2) rearmament of numerous units, 3) early overhaul of about sixty per cent of the front-line aircraft, 4) replacement of spare parts, 5) rebuilding of numerous aircraft in the supply depots, 6) rearmament of many aircraft, 7) accelerated introduction of overhauled motor models. . .8) establishment of four new air groups and one new airfield. . .10) preparation and resupply of mobilization supplies, corresponding to the newly established units, rearmed units, and transferred units. . .The compression of these tasks into a very short time span has once more and in clear fashion pointed out the known lack of readiness in maintenance of flying equipment as well as in technical personnel.[3]

Neither air arm was prepared for the war which would come. The RAF saw future war as a rapier-like surgical operation carried out by opposing air forces on populations hundreds of miles distant. For the Luftwaffe, air war was far more involved with interservice co-operation, but according to it, too, war would be quick.

The reality of air war in the Second World War was, of course, quite different. It resembled the strategy of the First World War, although attrition was in terms of aircraft, bombs, numbers of crews, training programmes, fuel supplies and munitions production. Month after month, year after year, the crews climbed into their aircraft to fly over a darkened continent. Success was measured in drops of percentage points in bomber losses rather than yards gained. As one commentator has pointed out:

Despite the visions of its protagonists of pre-war days, the air war during the Second World War. . .was attrition war. It did not supplant the operations of conventional forces; it complemented them. Victory went to the air forces with the greatest depth, the greatest balance, the greatest flexibility in employment. The result was an air strategy completely unforeseen by air commanders.[4]

Neither air force was ready to fight anything resembling such a war in the late 1930s, for the skills, tactical training and depth required were not yet at hand. The British official history of the strategic bombing offensive puts the basic problem of air war succinctly:

Air superiority is not simply a question of being able to use an air force. It is a question of being able to use it effectively. From the point of view of the bombers, for example, it is not simply a question of getting through. It is a question of getting through and doing effective damage.[5]

Admittedly, the Royal Air Force was not ready for war in September 1938. Its rearmament programme had made little progress. Re-equipment of fighter squadrons was only beginning, while Bomber Command had no modern aircraft in production. As a contemporary pointed out:

In a word, expansion caught the Air Ministry napping, and the attempt to expand, side by side with the getting up-to-date technically, resulted in confusion and muddle so that no expansion program — and they succeeded each other rapidly — was ever punctually or completely carried out.[6]

When Bomber Command mobilised in September 1938, only ten out of forty-two squadrons possessed what at that time passed for heavy bombers. Reserve aircraft numbered only 10 per cent of front line aircraft, while barely 200 out of 2,500 pilots were fully 'operationally ready'. Many aircraft had no turrets, and spare parts were in such short supply that Bomber Command had to cannibalise some squadrons to provide parts. By RAF peacetime standards less than 50 per cent of the force was combat ready.[7]

Fighter command was in scarcely better shape. Instead of the fifty squadrons considered the minimum for Britain's air defence, twenty-nine were mobilised, and only five of these possessed Hurricanes and none Spitfires.[8] The Hurricanes could not operate at high altitudes because their guns did not have the warmers required for firing above 15,000 feet. The remaining squadrons possessed obsolete Gladiators, Furys, Gauntlets and Demons.[9] As of 1 October 1938, British first line strength was 1,606 machines with only 412 aircraft in reserve. British estimates for France were 1,454 first line aircraft with 730 in reserve; and Germany 3,200 first line with 2,400 in reserve.[10] In fact the Germans had 3,307 aircraft, including transports, but almost no aircraft in reserve.[11] The anti-aircraft situation was even less encouraging. The War Office provided the table (see next page) on anti-aircraft guns in its post Munich review:[12]

Surprisingly, the situation in Germany did not differ substantially from that in Britain. The Luftwaffe was no better prepared to launch a strategic bombing offensive than the RAF. Since the Second World War American and British advocates of strategic bombing have

Table 1

Type	Approved Programme	Available	Actually Deployed
3 in.	320	298	269
3.7 in.	352	44	44
2 pdr barrels	992	50	49
Naval 3 in.	—	96	95
Search Lights	4,128	1,430	1,280

criticised the Luftwaffe as being 'in effect the hand maiden of the German army' and for being unprepared to launch a strategic bombing offensive.[13] This accusation misses the significance of Luftwaffe doctrine and preparation for war. In 1936 the German Air Ministry issued a doctrinal statement, entitled *Die Luftkriegführung,* which based doctrine on a realistic appraisal of aircraft possessed by the Luftwaffe. German doctrine underlined four major air missions: air superiority, strategic operations, battlefield interdiction and close air support. It stressed that the air force would be part of a team rather than a service with a wholly independent mission. The Germans, moreover, seriously doubted whether strategic bombing by itself could achieve a decisive result by destroying industry or terrorising civilians.[14] Development of a strategic bombing capability was hindered by technical problems rather than by a conscious decision. In the other major fields of air power, such as close air support, interdiction and reconnaissance, the Luftwaffe would be much better prepared for the coming war.

The Germans approached the question of strategic bombing more sceptically than the British. A partial explanation lies in the German experience in Spain. Terror bombing had had, for the most part, a counterproductive effect. Captain Heye of the *Seekriegs-Leitung* reported the following on return from Spain in July, 1938:

> Disregarding the great military success accompanying use of the *Luftwaffe* for the immediate support of army operations, one gets the impression that our attacks on objects of little military importance, through which in most cases many women and children. . .were hit, are not a suitable means to break the resistance of the opponent. They seem far more suited to strengthening the resistance. . .Doubtless the memory of the air attack on Guernica by the [Condor] Legion still today produces

an after-effect in the population of the Basques, who earlier were thoroughly friendly to Germany and in no manner communistic.[15]

The strongest element, however, in the Luftwaffe's unwillingness to place the emphasis in its armament programme on strategic bombing lay in a realistic appraisal of Germany's geographic position on the continent. The RAF might have the luxury to speculate about strategic bombing when others were going to fight the land battles, but for Germany, whatever the circumstances, war meant land war as well as air war. Thus, strategic bombing had less relevance to a Germany threatened by land. It would do the Germans little good to carry out extensive long-range bombing on industrial and population centres if the Rhineland, the Ruhr and Silesia were to fall to enemy ground attacks. Even when Germany was no longer threatened by land operations, other factors constrained strategic options. A 1939 report warned that a bombing offensive against the British Isles would open up Western Germany to unlimited air attacks and make the launching of a land offensive in the west extremely difficult. Moreover, the use of fuel and munitions for an air offensive would severely restrict supplies available for ground operations.[16] The above helps to explain why the Germans were so unprepared to launch a strategic bombing offensive at the outbreak of the war.

For most of 1938 the Luftwaffe was involved in exchanging its first generation aircraft for those with which it would fight most of the Second World War. Fighter squadrons replaced their Arado Ar-68s, which were bi-planes, for Me-109s, but by the autumn of 1938 there were no more than 500 Me-109s in the regular fighter squadrons.[17] Moreover, the transition programme to Me-109s led to a high accident rate in newly converted squadrons.[18] The two bombers in production, the Do-17 and He-111, were twin-engined aircraft, which possessed neither the speed nor bomb-carrying capacity to act as strategic bombers. Their defensive armament was insignificant. Early models of the He-111 carried a bomb load of 500 kilograms, and while London was within their range, they could barely reach the industrial regions of the midlands from bases in Western Germany. The Do-17 had an even shorter range. Its first production models could reach no further than the London metropolitan area with a 500 kilogram bomb load.[19]

Bombing attacks launched from German soil would not have had fighter escort, as, even when based on Pas-de-Calais in 1940, the Me-109s hardly had sufficient range to stay with the bombers over London. The Ju-88, supposedly a significant advance in bomber construction, was not scheduled to begin production until April 1939, and would not reach full production until 1940.[20] In August 1938, most ground attack squadrons still possessed He-123s, which could carry four 50 kg bombs, and He-45s, which could carry eighteen to twenty-four 10 kg bombs.[21] In view of the scarcity of raw materials, the German aircraft industry would have been hard put to maintain its rate of production if war had broken out over Czechoslovakia.

In numbers, the Luftwaffe mustered just over 3,000 aircraft at the end of September 1938. These consisted of 1,128 bombers (none of which were Ju-88s), 773 fighters, 513 reconnaissance aircraft, 226 dive bombers, 195 ground attack aircraft, 164 naval support aircraft and 308 transports. In May 1940, shortly before the invasion of France, Luftwaffe strength was in excess of 5,000: 666 reconnaissance aircraft, 1,736 fighters, 1,758 bombers, 417 dive bombers, 49 ground attack aircraft, 241 coastal aircraft and 531 transport aircraft.[22] The differences in the strength and quality are striking.

Introduction of a new generation of aircraft brought with it considerable problems in air crew training, maintenance and supply. Throughout the summer of 1938 most of the Luftwaffe experienced a high accident rate. This resulted, particularly in the Me-109 squadrons, from troubles in aircrew training in models which were far more sophisticated than anything the pilots had hitherto handled. The Me-109 with its narrow undercarriage presented fighter pilots with an especially difficult transition problem. The following table of crew training status indicates how unready the Luftwaffe was in 1938 to fight any sort of air war, much less a major air campaign:[23]

Table 2: Air Crew State of Readiness: August, 1938:

| Type of Aircraft | Authorised Number of Crews | Crew Training Status | |
		Fully Operational	Partially Operational
Strat Recon	228	84	57
Tac Recon	397	183	128
Fighter	938	537	364
Bomber	1409	378	411
Dive Bomber	300	80	123
Ground Attack	195	89	11
Transport	117	10	17
Coastal and Navy	230	71	34
Total	3714	1432	1145

Third Air Force *(Luftwaffengruppe* 3) reported that two factors contributed to the relatively high number of partially operational crews *(bedingt einsatzfähig):* bomber crews which were not fully operational were not rated for instrument flying, while Stuka crews generally lacked fully trained radio operators and machine gunners.[24]

The Luftwaffe's 'in commission' rate for the period 1 August to 8 December 1938, indicates the extent of supply and maintenance problems. There was a significant improvement in September percentages, but this resulted from a deliberate reduction of flying and training time as the time for the invasion of Czechoslovakia approached. Third Air Force's 'after action' report on the Czech crisis admitted that the 'in commission' rate had been brought to a high level by carefully planned measures, but that losses, as well as the heavy demands of combat operations, would have quickly lowered these rates. Moreover, its units did not possess adequate reserves of spare parts to support even normal flying.[25] By December 1938, 'in commission' rates had fallen considerably. While it is hard to estimate how much strain the Luftwaffe could have sustained before overall combat effectiveness would have suffered, August 'in commission' rates could not have given the Luftwaffe staff much encouragement:[26]

Table 3: Luftwaffe 'in commission' rates:

	1 Sug	15 Aug	5 Sep	12 Sep	19 Sep	26 Sep	8 Oct	8 Dec
Bombers	49%	58%	76%	84%	89%	90%	90%	78%
Fighters	70%	78%	89%	88%	93%	95%	90%	78%
Overall	57%	64%	79%	83%	90%	94%	92%	79%

As already mentioned, the high September percentages do not indicate that the Luftwaffe had solved its maintenance problems. The chief of supply services reported on the maintenance and supply situation during the Czech crisis and concluded that:

The consequence of these circumstances was: a) a constant and, for the first line aircraft, complete lack of reserves both as accident replacements and for mobilization; b) a weakening of the aircraft inventory in the training schools in favor of regular units; c) a lack of necessary reserve engines, supplies for the timely equipment of airfields, supply services and depots both for peacetime needs as

113

well as for mobilization.[27]

One of the major weaknesses of the Luftwaffe throughout the Second World War lay in the supply system. Obviously, without an efficient supply service and competent maintenance the best aircraft and pilots cannot fly. The Luftwaffe Staff had based its concept of airpower on the belief that a flying unit was not combat ready unless it possessed modern reliable aircraft, backed up by a first-class maintenance organisation and by a supply system which guaranteed adequate numbers of replacement aircraft and reserves of spare parts. The chief of the Luftwaffe's supply branch reported in an 'after action' report on the Czech crisis that 'these three requirements were not met'.[28] There were no reserve aircraft to replace combat losses because the Luftwaffe had devoted its entire production to supplying front line units with new aircraft or to equipping newly-established squadrons.

The situation was exactly similar in all categories of spare parts. The number of aircraft engines in maintenance and supply depots represented only four to five per cent of total engines in service, an incredibly low figure. The number of built up engines was correspondingly lower. Considering the number of airframes and engines in the supply pipe lines, the supply staff doubted whether the Luftwaffe could have fought for more than four weeks.[29] Without spare parts in either depots or pipe lines, extensive combat flying could only have been maintained by mass cannibalisation of existing aircraft — a process which would have led to the slow collapse of fighting capabilities. The basic cause of this state of affairs lay in Hitler's and Göring's failure to recognise the importance of devoting a substantial portion of industrial production to supply reserves. Thus, Göring refused to follow his staff's recommendation that 20 to 30 per cent of production be devoted to providing adequate inventories of spare parts.[30] Instead, production was devoted exclusively to building up front line strength.

In September 1938, the Luftwaffe faced a complicated strategic situation for which it was not prepared. Contrary to what many pro-appeasement historians and contemporary RAF officers have supposed, the Luftwaffe's first task was to aid in the destruction of Czechoslovakia. Other tasks such as disrupting French mobilisation, protecting Germany's North Sea trade and bombing Britain were strictly peripheral to the central Luftwaffe mission: to aid the army in destroying Czechoslovakia. German planning for both *Fall Rot* and *Fall Grün* deployed the bulk of German aircraft against Czechoslovakia. Only after Czechoslovakia had been destroyed by a decisive air and land attack would the Luftwaffe shift to tasks in the West.[31] This factor must be considered in any evaluation of the Luftwaffe's capability to launch an attack against Great Britain later in the year.

The weather during the projected period for the invasion of Czechoslovakia was appalling. For the twelve days from 30 September to 11 October, there were six days of rain and six of fog in the regions surrounding the Republic.[32] During the critical first five days of the projected invasion period, the weather was even worse.[33] This was not the sort of weather with which a young and inexperienced air force could have coped without serious losses — especially in view of the fact that so many of its pilots were not yet instrument rated.

Third Air Force, assigned to support the German advance into Czechoslovakia from the southern flank, reported that it would have faced considerable difficulty. The phased mobilisation of German forces had fully alerted the Czechs to German intentions. They had, as a result, deployed their air units from peacetime bases to satellite fields, thus robbing the Luftwaffe of an opportunity to make a surprise attack. Nevertheless, Third Air Force thought that attacks aimed at the Czech ground organization and supply system would eventually have restricted Czech operations, but warned that committing large numbers of aircraft in bad weather would have resulted in unbearable losses through accidents, crashes and mid-air collisions.[34]

First Air Force, deployed in Saxony and Silesia, reported that, while the Czechs were inferior in air power, they could have caused serious difficulties. It had expected to meet a strong, well-organised Czech anti-aircraft defence system over Czech fortifications and important industrial centres.[35] Thus although the Luftwaffe would undoubtedly have played a major role in any conquest of Czechoslovakia, both because of bad weather and its own inadequacies it would have suffered losses, which would have severely crippled its capacity to meet the test of a major European war.

When the Czech crisis began to take on wider implications the Germans discovered that they were completely unprepared to launch any sort of a strategic bombing offensive. Ironically the Luftwaffe Staff had not even begun to plan for such an eventuality.[36] In August 1938, one member of Second Air Force's staff — which would have had responsibility for operations over the North Sea and against the British Isles — characterised his command's capability as no more than an ability to inflict pin pricks.[37] Another memorandum in September 1938 confessed that there was no possibility of launching successful air operations against the British Isles, which had any prospect of success.[38] As late as May 1939, General Felmy,

Commander of Second Air Force, complained that the maintenance and supply base in his zone of operations was entirely inadequate to support a major air offensive against Britain. He stressed that, should war break out before 1942, Germany would have insufficient forces for such a task, and that in 1939 preparations for such an offensive were 'completely inadequate' *(völlig ungenügend)*.[39]

In view of aircraft capabilities and aircrew technical skills, Second Air Force declared in August 1938, that Belgium and Holland would have to be seized before there would be any prospect of successful attacks on strategic objects in Great Britain.[40] This was an accurate forecast, as, even in 1940, the only way that the Luftwaffe was able to launch an offensive against Britain was through control of Belgium, Holland and Northern France. General Felmy warned the Luftwaffe High Command in late September that the measures which his command could initiate would only disturb the English. 'Given the means at his disposal a war of destruction against England seemed to be excluded.'[41] Even in May 1939, Second Air Force Staff was to come to the same conclusion.[42]

In September 1938, the Luftwaffe found itself facing a series of problems which would have severely restricted its effectiveness in any operations against the British Isles. In order to frame its weather predictions, the German weather service depended on: 1) reports from England, Iceland, Norway and Greenland; 2) ship reports from the Atlantic; and 3) reports from France, Spain and Portugal. At the end of September the Luftwaffe discovered, much to its consternation, that no alternative precautions had been undertaken to replace reports from England, France, ships in the Atlantic and North America. Thus, it was discovered that once these key reporting stations were lost on the outbreak of war, the weather service would have been operating in the dark — not only forced to base its predictions of British weather on sketchy information, but also hampered even in its ability to predict accurately the weather over Europe.[43]

Even with well trained aircrews, the Luftwaffe did not have the capability to bomb accurately in bad weather. Kesselring admitted in 1939 that the 'excellent' all-weather aircraft at the disposal of his aircrews would still not enable them to bomb effectively in bad weather.[44] Moreover, in 1938 the Luftwaffe did not possess the radio technology necessary to carry out night or bad weather attacks,[45] while most of the navigational equipment emplaced along the North Sea was designed to help aircraft operating over the sea rather than to aid bombing attacks on Great Britain.[46]

Considering that air war has proven to be the most technical, precise form of war man has waged, the technical, as well as the operational, inadequacies of the Luftwaffe in 1938 define its weaknesses. One cannot help but conclude that the Luftwaffe could not have launched a significant bombing offensive against the British Isles in 1938. In nearly every respect it was unprepared for such a task and so could not have significantly damaged the British war effort in spite of the often cited weakness of the RAFs Fighter Command. Moreover, the Luftwaffe would even have had difficulty in fulfilling its operational commitments to support German ground forces against Czechoslovakia and in the west.

Notes

1. See among others: Keith Eubank, *Munich* (Norman, 1963); Basil Collier, *History of the Second World War* (London, 1965); Keith Robbins, *Munich* (London, 1968); Lawrence Thompson, *The Greatest Treason* (New York, 1968); Sir John Slessor, *The Central Blue* (New York, 1957); Air Marshal Sholto Douglas, *Combat and Command* (New York, 1966).
2. PRO CAB 24/273, C.P. 283 (37), 29.11.37., p.141.
3. Milch Collection, Imperial War Museum, Reel 55, vol.57, Chef des Nachschubsamts, Nr.3365/g.Kdos., 3.11.38.
4. William R. Emerson, 'Operation Pointblank', Harmon Memorial Lectures, No.4 (Colorado Springs, 1962), p.41.
5. Charles Webster and Noble Frankland, *The Strategic Air Offensive against Germany,* I, *Preparation* (London, 1961), p.21.
6. L.E.O. Charlton, C.T. Garrett, and Lt Cmdr. R. Fletcher, *The Air Defence of Great Britain* (London, 1937), pp.170-71.
7. C. Webster and N. Frankland, *The Strategic Air Offensive against Germany,* I, *Preparation,* p.79.
8. Sir John Slessor, *The Central Blue,* p.223.
9. Basil Collier, *The Defence of the United Kingdom* (London, 1957), p.65.
10. PRO CAB 24/279, C.P. 218 (38), 25.10.38., p.131.
11. Air Ministry, Air Historical Branch, Translations, vol.VII, G. 302694/AR/9/51/50.
12. PRO CAB 3/8, p.2, 301-A, 14.11.38., CID.
13. See particularly: Dennis Richards, *The Royal Air Force, 19390 1945* (London, 1953), p.29; Asher Lee, *The German Air Force* (New York, 1946), pp.16-17; and surprisingly, Sir C. Webster and N. Frankland, *The Strategic Air Offensive Against Germany,* I, *Preparation,* p.125.
14. Paul D. Deichmann, *German Air Force Operations in Support of the Army* (New York, 1968), pp.9-13.
15. OKM, B.Nr., 1. Abt. Skl. la 961/38 g.Kdos., Berlin, 14.7.38., (USNA, T-1022/2957/PG 48902).
16. BA/MA, RL 2 II 24, Chef 1. Abt., 22.11.39.
17. Karlheinz Kens and Heinz J. Nowarra, *Die deutschen Flugzeuge, 1933-1945* (Munich, 1964), pp.15, 416.
18. Richard Suchenwirth, *The Development of the German Air Force, 1919-1939* (New York, 1969), p.97.
19. BA/MA RL 2 II/115, Luftwaffenführungsstab, Az. 89a Nr.3400/38 g.Kdos., 1 Abt. III, 4, 1.12.38.

20. Milch Collection, Imperial War Museum, Reel 55, vol.57, 3.6.38., "Vorläufiges Flugzeug – Beschaffungs Programm."
21. Letter from the Reichsminster der Luftfahrt und Oberbefehlshaber der Luftwaffe, 10.8.38., (USNA, T-79/24/000606).
22. Air Historical Branch, Air Ministry, vol.VII, Translation: Luftwaffe Strength and Serviceability Statistics, G 302694/AR/9/51/50.
23. Air Ministry, *The Rise and Fall of the German Air Force, 1933-1945,* Air Ministry Pamphlet #248 (London, 1948), pp.19-20.
24. BA/MA RL 7/164, Der kommandierende General und Befehlshaber der Luftwaffengruppe 3., 1.12.38.
25. Ibid.
26. Air Historical Branch, Air Ministry, VII, Translations: Luftwaffe Strength and Serviceability Statistics.
27. Milch Collection, Imperial War Museum, Reel 55, vol.57, Der Chef des Nachschubsamts, Nr.3365/38, g.Kdos., 3.11.38.
28. Ibid.
29. Ibid.
30. Richard Suchenwirth, *The Development of the German Air Force,* p.148.
31. BA/MA RL 7/64 Planstudie 1938, Hauptteil III Aufmarschund Kampfanweisung 'Fall Rot' zu Lw. Gruppenkommando 3., As Plst. 38/Ia op. Nr.450/38 g.Kdos., 2.6.38.
32. KTB Arbeitsstab Leeb (USNA, T-79/16/396).
33. BA/MA RL 7/164, Der kommandierende General und Befehlsthaber der Luftwaffengruppe 3., Ia. Nr.7829/38 g.Kdos., 1.12.38.
34. Ibid.
35. BA/MA RL 7/1, Der commandierende General und Befehlshaber der Luftwaffengruppe 1. Ia. Nr.197/38, g.Kdos., 11.7.38.
36. L.W. Gr. Kdo.2., Führungsabteilung, Nr.210/38, g.Kdos., 22.9.38.
37. Vortragsnotiz über Besprechung mit Ia des Befehlshabers der Luftwaffengruppe Braunschweig 25.8.38. (USNA T-1022/2307/34562).
38. L.W. Gr. Kdo.2., Führungsabteilung, Nr.210/38, g.Kdos., 22.9.38.
39. BA/MA, RL 7/42, Luftflottenkommando 2., Führungsabteilung, Nr.7093/39, g.Kdos., Braunschweig, 13.5.39., pp.4, 22.
40. Karl Gundelach, 'Gedanken über die Führung eines Luftkrieges gegen England bei der Luftflotte 2. in den Jahren 1938/3939', *Wehrwissenschaftliche Rundschau* (Jan.1960).
41. L.W. Gr. Kdo.2., Führungsabteilung, Nr.210/38, g.Kdos., 22.9.38.
42. Ob.d.1, Generalstab, L. Abt., Nr.5095/39, g.Kdos., 22.5.39.
43. See particularly BA/MA RL 7/50, IW/38, g.Kdos.; IW 23/29 G. Vortrags Planspiels 10-14.5.39; BA/MA RL II/101 Luftwaffengruppenkommando 2., 6.12.38., Führung Abt/IW B.Nr.129/38, g.Kdos.
44. BA/MA RL 2 II/101, Vortrag: General der Flieger Kesselring, 1.3.39.
45. Air Historical Branch, Air Ministry, AHB 6 No.VII/153, 'German Air Force Policy during the Second World War', A Review by Oberst Bernd von Brauchitsch, p.3.
46. Karl Gundelach, 'Gedanken über die Führung eines Luftkrieges gegen England bei der Luftflotte 2. in den Jahren 1938/1939', p.35.

THE INTRODUCTION OF WAR OFFICE
SELECTION BOARDS IN THE BRITISH ARMY:
A PERSONAL RECOLLECTION

Brigadier F.H. Vinden

When I consider my role in the introduction and establishment of the more scientific methods of selection exemplified in the War Office Selection Boards into the British Army, the Indian Army, Navy and Air Force, and into the British and Indian Civil Services, I am bound to conclude that sheer chance played a part.

The first chance was that instead of going to Oxford in 1914 with the intention of becoming a barrister, I enlisted in the University and Public Schools Battalion, which in a very short time became four battalions forming the 18th, 19th, 20th and 21st battalions of the Royal Fusiliers. We went to France in September 1915, and in the following June I was granted a temporary commission in the 2nd Battalion the Suffolk Regiment, then in the 3rd Division. This was part of the reserve army which was intended to follow the break through the German lines on 1 July 1916 and finish the war. Before the advent of the Navy, Army and Air Force Institutes, officers messes were dependent to some extent on local purchase of supplements to rations and drink. The long journey from St Omer, where the regiment had been training for the offensive, to the Somme had depleted our stores, and the Colonel ordered me to take the mess cart, a mule-drawn two-wheeled vehicle, to Doullens, twenty-odd miles to the rear, and fill it up. There and back was a three day trip for the mule, and I returned to find that the Battalion had been in action, suffering heavy losses. Amongst the dead was the officer who had taken my place in command of the platoon.

I had been chosen to make the trip because, before I went to Oxford, my father had decided that he wanted me to be fluent in a foreign language and had placed me in the Law School at the Sorbonne for a year. I never discovered how this idea came to my father, but it saved my life. Subsequently, through casualties rather than, perhaps, merit, I became acting adjutant and an acting brigade major at the age of twenty-one. It took me a further seventeen years to reach this appointment as a regular officer. Under persuasion from my Colonel I had been granted a commission in the regular army, not expecting to be alive; but on 11 November 1918 I thought this was, to quote Bruce Bairnsfather, 'a better 'ole' than going back to books to study for the Bar.

I served in the Suffolk Regiment in England, Ireland, Gibraltar and China, passed into the Staff College (Camberley) and held appointments on the General Staff in Britain and Malaya. Tenure of staff appointments was then three years and my time in Malaya was up in February 1940 when I was posted as general staff officer to the 1st Division in France, under the command of Major General Alexander. This was a plum for me and for my future. I arrived on 3rd April. Two days later, I felt extremely ill, was sent down to a base hospital in Dieppe where my complaint was diagnosed as meningitis. I was shipped to England the day the German attack started, spent four months in hospital and two convalescing. To my bitter disappointment, this prevented me from ever becoming a fighting soldier again. In November 1940 a medical board passed me fit for light duty and I was posted as an Assistant Adjutant General to the War Office in the Department of the Adjutant General, then Lt. General Sir H.C.B. Wemyss shortly to be succeeded by General Sir Ronald Adam, Bt. I was to be in close contact with General Adam for the succeeding twenty years both at home and in India. I formed the highest opinion of him as a soldier, a leader of men and as an administrator of a high order.

In this appointment I was head of the infantry branch responsible for the administration of the 63 regiments of the line, posting officers newly commissioned from the Officer Cadet Training Units and men called up for military service, to the regiments stationed across the world from the West Indies to China. On one of the General Adam's regular visits to his branches, I informed him that I was most concerned at the shortfall of 25 per cent in the output of the OCTUs from the 600 which was their monthly target. I was thus unable to provide the Middle East and India with their requirements let alone those of home units. Shortly after, I was transferred to AG1 (e) the branch concerned with the provision of officers.

It had been decided in 1938 that commissions would only be granted after service in the ranks. Commanding officers of all units were under strict orders to recommend every NCO or soldier whom they considered fit to hold His Majesty's Commission. Those recommended were seen by an Interview Board of which there were thirteen located round Britain and, if accepted, were posted to an OCTU. The Presidents of the interview boards were retired Colonels called back from the Reserve and were assisted by two officers from the local garrison as they happened to be available so Presidents seldom if ever had the same assistants.

I decided that I must see for myself and visited units, OCTUs and

120

the boards. The OCTUs contended that they were reluctant to reject cadets and were too lenient, but too many were well below competence and had to be returned to units. This was known as RTU. The possibility of RTU created an atmosphere of strain which was not helpful to the receipt of instruction and morale was generally low. Units found that those who returned to units, particularly NCOs, lost face and the possibility of RTU prevented some from being willing to be recommended for commissions.

At the boards, I found that no criteria for the qualities of personality or the level of ability required for effective leadership had been laid down. Interviews lasted for about 25 minutes and candidates, knowing that their fate was in the balance, were naturally nervous; in such a condition and in such short time, few could display their inherent qualities. At the end of each interview, I found that I had little information on which to make a decision and on occasions my views were contrary to those of the board though I was not prepared to back my judgement. At the end of this tour I was certainly despondent but felt that the major problem was in the interview boards although I had no clue as to how this could be put right. My last visit was to the board in Edinburgh where I spoke to a stranger in uniform in the University Club. He turned out to be a psychiatrist, Captain Eric Wittkower, who was working under Lt. Colonel Fergusson Roger, then Command Psychiatrist at the Headquarters, Scottish Command. Eric Wittkower was a refugee from Germany and before being absorbed in the Army had spent some time with the Tavistock Clinic. I talked about my problem and asked him if he knew anything about the methods of selection in the German army. Fortunately, he did. The United States Army Medical Service had obtained a document from Germany giving full details of the German methods and had passed it to our Royal Army Medical Corps where it had been received by Brigadier J.R. Rees, Consultant Psychiatrist to the War Office, who sent it to Eric Wittkower for translation. I asked him if he could set up this system and cadged £5 out of Scottish Command for the purchase of apparatus.

The German system consisted of intelligence tests; a test of hand-eye co-ordination in finer movements, speed and agility. This test was on a dotting machine in which a tape punched with irregularly spaced holes passed by clockwork under an open slot. The person under test was required to make a pencil mark in each hole as the tape passed under the slot. Another test consisted of a muscle exerciser usually fixed on a bathroom door from which keep-fitters exercised their muscles by stretching the two spring coils fitted with handles. In the German system, this was fixed to a wall behind a bench at which the 'victim' sat. He was required to pull the handles as far as he could and his pull was registered on a dial. He was then told to repeat and an electric current would pass through the handles and would increase in strength according to the strength of the pull. In performing, wrists started to shake, teeth to be gritted and signs of agony appeared on the face of the performer. There was a small slit behind the apparatus concealing a cine camera taking pictures of the facial contortions of the candidate. From the facial contortions, the interviewer gauged the courage and tenacity of the candidate. There was a further test which took place in the waiting room into which the candidate was shown on arrival. The room was furnished with seats varying from the most comfortable, through hard back chairs to a wooden stool. On a table, there were periodicals varying from heavy political to pin-up. A spy hole noted the candidate's choice. Eric Wittkower tried these tests out on some guinea pigs including myself — except of course for the spy holes — and they were then scrapped.

On my return to the War Office, I had a series of meetings with Brigadier Rees, later President of the World Federation for Mental Health, and two of his staff, Lt. Col. Ronald Hargreaves, later Professor of Psychiatry in Birmingham University and Lt. Col. Thomas Wilson, later Director of the Tavistock Clinic. The two latter had been studying the U.S. army World War I material as well as the German documents and were anxious to see the introduction of scientific methods of selection. They were pleased at my interest and anxious to help in solving my problem which they agreed was a serious one. At our meetings we appreciated the difficulties in introducing novelties and the need for finesse in achieving change. It was arranged that Lt. Colonel Fergusson Roger should test and interview an intake of officers attending the Company Commanders School in Scotland. This he did and forecasted their likely performance. His assessment was 90 per cent in agreement with the reports of the commandant and staff at the end of the course and later it was found that in the case of the 10 per cent in which there was disagreement, Fergusson Roger's prognostications were correct.

On my side, I decided that I would produce proof positive that action was necessary and urgent. I assembled the thirteen Presidents of the Interview boards at Oxford and arranged for ten candidates to be brought for interview on three successive days. Each candidate was to be interviewed by each president separately who would give his decision to accept or reject. It was an ordeal for the candidates to be interviewed thirteen times in a day, but I did my best to put them at ease by telling them that this was an experiment which might lead to fairer selection and thus help the war effort. I gave them a good lunch and they co-operated cordially. At the end of the three days, we added up the scores for acceptance and rejection. In none of the thirty cases had there been a unanimous opinion. Variations in voting ranged from 12 to 1 and 7 to 6.

I reported all this to General Adam. He arranged a meeting in Edinburgh for the following Sunday and took the chair. Present were General Sir Andrew Thorne, GOC Scottish Command, Brigadier Rees, Lt. Col. Fergusson Roger, Dr J. Sutherland and the Commandant of the Company Commanders School. Discussion went on till evening when General Adam ordered me to set up an experimental selection board.

For the next three weeks I commuted by night train between London and Edinburgh to fix accommodation, adminstrative arrangements and establishments. In all this we received warm support from General Thorne and the staff of Scottish command and we had the good fortune in obtaining permission to use the new buildings and grounds of the University of Edinburgh.

The experimental board consisted of:

President: Colonel Delahaye retired early from the Royal Artillery. He was of high intelligence with vision and warmth of personality.

Psychiatrists: Major W. Bion who had won the DSO in the First World War and later became a specialist in Harley Street and now practises in the United States.

Major Jock Sutherland holding a doctorate in psychological medicine and also in psychology.

Psychologist: Captain Eric Trist holding doctorates in psychology from universities in Britain and the United States.

Testing Officers: Three carefully chosen officers from the infantry.

Administrative: An adjutant with clerical staff and a few orderlies.

It was decided that the board procedure should occupy three days and deal with thirty candidates in a session. Candidates were to be lodged in barracks in Edinburgh and were to be brought by lorry daily, arriving on the first day at 4 p.m.

In the evening of the first day candidates were welcomed by the President who outlined the programme and they were then required to fill in a very comprehensive *curriculum vitae.* They were then given three tests, consisting of:

Raven's Matrix (1936). A test of logical reasoning without the use of language. It consists of 60 sequences of designs arranged in order of increasing difficulty. The task is to select the correct design to complete the sequence from some examples at the foot of each page. This is a test of versatility which can go all the way from simplicity to extreme complexity and is made more difficult by an ungenerous time allowance.

Verbal Intelligence test. A test of speed, comprehension, accuracy and agility with words and other visual symbols. It consists of a mixed bag of catch questions, word definitions and brain teasers. It is a searching test of verbal reasoning capacity. The major value of these tests was that their standards were graded according to the results of many thousands of serving soldiers and enabled the selector to pick out and take a closer look at the top 10 per cent or thereabouts.

Projection personality test. A specially designed modification for group use of Murray's Thematic Apperception Test. Candidates were shown four pictures of equivocal situations on a screen capable of legitimate interpretation in several ways and then a blank screen. Candidates were given four minutes to write a scenario from which the picture might have been taken, indicate an opening, a development and an ending and for the blank screen imagine their own pitcure. Stories were assessed according to the cirteria established by other candidates in terms of originality, banality, optimism, pessimism, ingenuity, dependency and fantasy. One of the chief values of this test was as a guide-line to the psychiatric interview. Its statistical reliability was quite respectable, though obviously not absolutely reliable. As a sidelight on the test, anonymous volunteers from Scottish Command took the test to help validate it. One volunteer wrote five perfect comic short stories with a wealth of imagination. Test Report: 'No idea about his complexes, chap's made a monkey of the test. Officer Quality A plus. Officer's name Eric Linklater.'

On the second day, candidates were divided into groups of ten each under a testing officer. Work began with a group discussion on a subject decided by the group. The remainder of the day and the morning of the third day were devoted to a series of outdoor tactical exercises of a simple nature. Imaginary situations were described by the testing officer. Candidates were nominated in turn as leader and were required to give orders to the rest of the group for the action considered appropriate. Time was provided for each candidate to be interviewed by the psychiatrist and president. They dispersed at mid-day. The board then assembled and each member gave his assessment. There was a free discussion in which all spoke as equals including the president who was responsible for the final decision.

Naturally there were teething troubles both administrative and technical. The major administrative one was the transport of candidates to and from the barracks located on the opposite side of Edinburgh including the return journey for the mid-day meal. Lorries broke down or were late which upset the carefully timed programme. Officers were billeted all over the town and had to find somewhere for their lunch. Colonel Delahaye suggested that we should obtain our own premises for both staff and candidates with common mess and ante rooms. Scottish Command were most helpful and provided six houses in a terrace adjacent to the site of the board and also a staff of cooks, waitresses and orderlies from the womens' Auxiliary Territorial Service (ATS). This formed the pattern for all the boards in Britain, Egypt, India and Malaya. This very practical arrangement gave rise to the widely held belief that it had been designed to discover whether candidates had appropriate table manners.

On the technical side, it was found that the tactical exercises were of no value in differentiating aspects of ability of personality amongst the candidates. They came from all arms of the service and artillerymen could not be expected to know how the leading section of an advanced guard should deploy or an infantryman how to bring guns into action. The unpremeditated action of Colonel Delahaye produced the solution to this problem too. He was accompanying a group proceeding to a tactical exercise. The group was passing a stack of heavy granite blocks intended for a statue in the University grounds. He halted the group and without naming a leader said: 'Take the top block off that stack.' Some of the group attempted to shift the block with their hands, unsuccessfully. There was general chatter about how to do it. One man who had taken no part in the discussion saw some stout poles nearby, picked one up and started to lever the block up. Others then picked up poles and the block was eventually shifted. Colonel Delahaye repeated this with other groups and was surprised at the insight he obtained into the personalities of some or all of them. To another group, Delahaye said that there had been a serious accident nearby and told them to prepare the mess room to receive casualties. He again witnessed the differences in the personalities in the group. He recounted this to the psychiatrists and the psychologist who were aware of work that had been done on leaderless group tests and these became an important part of the selection techniques. Tests were devised which required a group to achieve an objective after making a plan, the acceptance of the plan by the group and their co-operation in carrying it out. Some limited measure of physical strength was needed. The group's performance was watched by the Group Testing Officer and observation of a variety of such tests gave insight into the personality of each candidate.

A standardised form of assessment was devised and it was the effect of the candidates on each other that was of the greatest interest. No military knowledge was involved or required. Later, as additional boards were established, a variety of such tests were devised by the ingenuity of the board staffs who competed with each other in devising new ones. The tests satisfied the principle of reliability by comparing assessments on the performance of candidates at the boards with the reports of their OCTU training as assessed by the OCTU staffs. As a result GTOs gained greater confidence in their judgements and at the board discussions there was a large measure of agreement by all concerned on the suitability or otherwise of the candidates.

After the experimental board had dealt with ten batches of candidates General Adam reconvened the original meeting and watched the procedure for the three days. All participated with the board staff and were surprised at what they themselves discovered independently about the personality of the candidates which coincided with the board's decisions. Thereupon, General Adam ordered me to establish the system throughout Great Britain as fast as possible. As selection depended on the quality of the selectors, I was given *carte blanche* to select staffs and made the proviso that all must have undergone the selection procedure and approved with credit. Brigadier Rees nominated the psychiatrists all of whom I found to be men of high ability. Within four months, 18 War Office Selection Boards were in operation and two boards were later formed to deal with candidates for commissions in the Women's Auxiliary Territorial Service.

To test the attitudes of candidates towards the methods, all were given a questionnaire to be completed anonymously at the end of their three days and before they were informed of their results which were despatched to candidates' units. These questonnaires were examined independently at the War Office with the result that 95 per cent were more than satisfied with emphasis on the fairness of the procedure. An additional test of satisfaction came to my branch in the War Office where I had been receiving about 30 letters a month from parents of candidates, headmasters of schools, and commanding officers of units alleging unfairness of rejections. Most came through members of parliament and answers had to be prepared for the signature of the

Minister of War. These complaints dwindled to zero when all candidates passed through the WOSBs.

General Adam knew that there was a measure of hostility towards psychiatrists by some more senior officers and told me that part of my job was to 'sell' selection. I complied by inviting anyone I had heard of through the grape vine as critical to attend a board and see for himself. All went away satisfied. There was, however, one disturbing hurdle which gave me sleepless nights. The Prime Minister was reported to have remarked 'What is all this that I hear about psychiatrists choosing officers. Pray enquire.' It was suspected that this had been prompted by his medical adviser Lord Moran who did not fancy psychiatry in general. Anyway, Sir Stafford Cripps was ordered to investigate. I suggested that he should visit a board. He did so and attended one at Watford. He fed in the mess with candidates and staff and, since he was a vegetarian, special quantities of carrots were provided for his meals. He participated fully in a group and at the end assured me that he was completely satisfied and was surprised at what he had learned in his three days. Had his opinion been unfavourable, I have no doubt that my work would have been scrapped.

When all the cadets in the OCTUs had passed through the Boards, the numbers RTU'd went down to 6 per cent from the 25 per cent under the former system. Amongst the rejects there were some who were sick and some were sent down for bad behaviour.

In February 1943, General Adam sent for me and ordered me to go to India and establish the system for Indian candidates for commissions for the army of two million men which the Prime Minister had demanded that India should produce. The same methods were adopted for the selection of candidates for the Indian Civil Service and the home Civil service through the insistance of Ernie Bevin when he was Foreign Minister. It was also adopted by some western European armed forces and in varying degrees by industrial firms and employment agencies in Britain specialising in finding applicants for senior appointments.

A selection board is initially expensive in the salaries of staff, and not easy to organise on a temporary basis. Where, however, there is a steady flow of applicants, it is possibly cheap in the long run because of the saving in the cost of training applicants who have been accepted and then fail to make the grade.

On turning back the pages of my life, it seems strange to me that such a 'baby' should have grown to such stature in a matter of four months and continued to grow. Much of this was due to chance, but the real credit I give to the psychiatrists and psychologists who had the knowledge and produced the right nourishment. It could only have happened in wartime when money was available for new ideas which might save money in the end; and when a man of high ability and foresight, General Sir Ronald Adam, was ready to seize the opportunity presented.

LIDDELL HART AND HIS PAPERS

Stephen Brooks

Under an agreement made in 1960 Liddell Hart bequeathed his military library and military papers to King's College, London. When in 1964 Michael Howard established the Centre for Military Archives at King's it was the intention that Liddell Hart's military papers should form its nucleus. After Liddell Hart's death in 1970, Lady Liddell Hart decided that the archive would be of much greater value to historians if treated as a whole, and that it was in any case unsatisfactory to attempt to divide it into 'military' and 'non-military' material. For instance, the papers relating to T.E. Lawrence had previously been designated 'personal' and therefore 'non-military'. Therefore, under a new agreement signed in 1973, King's College purchased the military library and the complete archive,[1] and to mark this the Centre for Military Archives was renamed the Liddell Hart Centre for Military Archives.

Liddell Hart's papers and military library, which consists of some six thousand volumes, are due to be brought into King's College by about 1980; until then they remain at Liddell Hart's home, States House, Medmenham, where (as during his lifetime) the Collection is available for research.[2] This essay is intended to give an outline of the nature of the material in Liddell Hart's papers, how the task of cataloguing them was approached, and some of the problems associated with using them.

The vast extent of Liddell Hart's archive, which at present fills eleven filing cabinets and five hundred archive boxes, reflects both the immensity of his own output, and the consistency with which he preserved documents over a long period. There is an amusing early instance of this second point in a letter he wrote to his parents from France in 1915 when he urged them to 'keep my letters carefully and study them intelligently'. Not only did Liddell Hart throw virtually nothing away, but particularly from 1945 onwards he had anything he considered to be important duplicated. Some of the duplicates were kept together in readiness for sending to interested parties, but most were distributed throughout the archive in an effort to maintain a wide variety of overlapping subject, chronological, personal, business and correspondence files by the selective use of available carbon copies.

The state of the papers in 1972 owed more to the problems of sorting and housing such a vast amount of material when time and space were limited than to any over-all scheme of arrangement. The archive had been built up over many years, and during that time a number of different ways of ordering the files and their contents had been used, and in places subsequently modified on more than one occasion. Due to the efforts of Lady Liddell Hart, who coped with all the filing for over thirty years, Liddell Hart was usually able to find papers as he needed them; but to try to maintain so many different kinds of files was too great a task for one person. Various people from time to time attempted to sort parts of the archive, but it was impossible to put the whole house in order while Liddell Hart was alive, as he would never have tolerated the upheaval in his work that this would have entailed. In any case, anyone who came to help usually found himself becoming more of a research assistant, so that instead of sorting the existing papers, he was swept into the process of creating more.

It was clear that the real value of the evidence contained in the papers would only be accessible to historians when a considerable simplification had been carried out, and a comprehensive scheme for cataloguing the whole archive devised. First, a thorough search of States House was necessary to locate all the papers, stored in every part of the house; other documents were recovered from the Royal United Services Institute for Defence Studies and the strong room of Lloyd's Bank, where they had been deposited for safety. Second, over the three years in which the cataloguing was carried out, virtually all the duplicates were removed (when finally disposed of they filled thirty-five cardboard cartons). While doing this it was found that successive drafts, and manuscript, typescript and printed versions of Liddell Hart's writings had been distributed in subject and other files as if they were simply duplicate copies. These have been put together in the correct sequence, so that it is now possible to trace the development of a particular piece, sometimes over a number of years. Third, similar material in the archive was brought together under general headings, and within each category the papers were organised in the same way. Most of the headings appeared somewhere in the archive already, but usually only applied to small parts of what is now included. When a particular grouping of files or documents had a significance with regard to the way in which Liddell Hart worked their order has been respected, but files were moved so often, including immediately after his death, that this only applied to a limited number of areas in the archive. Various old lists of parts of the archive give some idea of the way in which the files were kept, but they are misleading in that a simple heading in a list may well have represented a mass of confusion within the actual file.

There were clearly three basic divisions in the archive: Liddell Hart's correspondence files; his own military writings; and the vast amount of material which he collected on military and related subjects, including over a hundred boxes of newspaper cuttings. Within the correspondence files there are a number of different types of correspondence, and these are now grouped in six Sections: Individual, General, Literary, Official Bodies, Clubs and Organisations, and Letters to the Press.

Writing letters was a way of life to Liddell Hart and took up a large part of his day. Correspondence was a way of eliciting information, of exchanging views, maintaining old contacts and friendships and establishing new ones. He revelled in controversy, and such was his skill — and staying power — that he usually had the last word. He himself answered letters promptly, and if a reply was not forthcoming after about a fortnight a reminder would be sent. Michael Howard wrote that after his first contact with Liddell Hart he was 'involved in a correspondence which barely flagged for ten years, one letter of mine evoking three from him. Even if there was no letter for him to answer he was undeterred. "On going through my files," he would write, "I notice that you have not dealt with the point raised in the second paragraph of my letter of July 17th of last year. . ." '[3]

Some of the earliest letters in the archive are those which Liddell Hart wrote to his parents between 1913 and 1916. These are full of fascinating comments on the war and insights into Liddell Hart's character, and should make an excellent starting point for any volumes of his collected letters which may be published. After he went to France in 1915 he poured scorn on the 'slackers at home' and 'doddering politicians', whilst in contrast to his later critical views of the high command he extolled the virtues of the generals — as he did in his short unpublished book, 'Impressions of the Great British Offensive on the Somme', which he wrote in the autumn of 1916. It is clear from his letters that his reaction to first-hand experience of the war was anything but one of disillusionment. In his first letter from France, dated 29 September 1915, he wrote, 'So far I have thoroughly enjoyed the experience, and though one has to rough it far more than in England it reminds me most of a great picnic.' Ten months later on 15 July 1916, three days before he was gassed at Mametz Wood, he wrote, 'Somehow I would not have missed it. It is a wonderful experience.' Liddell Hart wrote these, and most of his letters in the 1920s, by hand. From about 1933, however, he had regular secretaries to type his letters and carbon copies were retained, so the correspondence files contain both sides of discussions, not just a series of incoming letters. This fact, the time Liddell Hart was prepared to give to writing letters, and the wide variety of his correspondence make these files a particularly valuable source.

The first Section of correspondence contains files of correspondence with 780 individuals. In the ranks of these, besides service people, there are politicians and playwrights, journalists, military historians, businessmen and clergymen, with a variety of different countries represented. Many of the correspondences extend over a large number of years – the three longest are with Fuller from 1920 to 1966, Montgomery from 1924 to 1970 and Lt.-Gen. Sir John Evetts from 1922 to 1968.

In Section 2, under the heading General Correspondence, are several groups of files, including some miscellaneous letters arranged by years and correspondence with Officers and Embassies of overseas countries – included here are all Liddell Hart's files of correspondence with Israelis. Section 3, Literary Correspondence, includes correspondence with publishers, newspapers and journals, at home and aborad, and with literary agents. In Section 4, the heading Official Bodies covers government departments, military establishments, universities and such bodies as the RAND Corporation and the Institute for Strategic Studies; there is also a set of files relating to the Official Histories of the two World Wars. Section 5, Clubs and Organisations, includes various pressure groups such as the Army League and CND.

Liddell Hart belonged to groups and wrote for publications which have long ceased to exist, so in part these files form an interesting 'period piece'. The correspondence with publishers and literary agents illuminates the business side of Liddell Hart the writer – the care he took over contracts, his determination to ensure that he always got a fair return for his labours, and simply the vast amount of time that he had to give to the business side of his work. For though after 1945 Liddell Hart was independent of any government, newspaper or organisation, he was never independent of the need to earn a living. Lastly, Liddell Hart's letters to the correspondence columns of newspapers and journals, Section 6, cover a wide range of subjects, as he was never slow to take up his pen if he saw a current problem mishandled or some historical myth revived.

The second broad category of material in the archive is Liddell Hart's military writings. Liddell Hart was above all a brilliant writer, able to compose fluent narratives or detailed analyses, and a master at producing striking phrases. When he came to prepare a fresh book or article on a new topic he read widely on the subject, taking very few notes. He then wrote surrounded by a selection of sources from which he could check factual points, and these were afterwards replaced on the library shelves or in the archive. He actually wrote very slowly, polishing each phrase as he went along, sometimes crossing out alternatives several times over. Though his strongly held beliefs coloured some of his broader interpretations of history, in matters factual he had a passion for accuracy, and he would spend days weighing up conflicting evidence on a particular point to achieve a balanced judgement. He believed deeply in learning lessons from history, but valid lessons could only come from accurate history. This concern for accuracy and the pleasure he took in helping others came together in his later years in the amount of time he spent checking the manuscripts of books by younger historians, producing lengthy 'Notes and Queries' for them. In this way he influenced almost a generation of military historical writing. In a letter of 23 January 1942, Wavell wrote to Liddell Hart, 'With your knowledge and brains and command of the pen, you could have written just as convincing a book called "The Strategy of the Direct Approach" '.[4] But this would only have been true if Liddell Hart himself had been completely convinced of the wisdom of the Direct Approach. His success as a publicist lay precisely in his own massive commitment to the truth and importance of what he was writing.

It seemed that Liddell Hart's military writings could best be listed under five headings. Firstly, one Section was made for all his military writings up to 1925, involving a relatively small amount of closely interwoven material. As a whole it reveals a great deal about Liddell Hart's reactions to army life and the early development of his military thought in the field of training and tactics. The years 1924 and 1925 mark the most important dividing line in Liddell Hart's career, and this is very much reflected in the archive. In July 1924 his army career was brought to a close when he was put on half pay (he was retired in 1927). But a successful season writing on army training for the *Morning Post* led to a fresh start, and in July 1925 Liddell Hart's appointment as the Military Correspondent of the *Daily Telegraph* was announced. In the same month his first major book, *Paris, or The Future of War,* was published. The volume of his military writings expands rapidly after this. They are now divided into four Sections, though there are very close connections between all of them; the arrangement in each case is broadly chronological.

Firstly, the manuscripts, proofs and reviews of his books. Between 1925 and 1970 Liddell Hart wrote twenty-eight books and edited three. Several were republished over the years with fresh material added and under different titles, particularly *Strategy: The Indirect Approach,* which began life in 1929 as *The Decisive Wars of History.*

This book, and many others, have been translated into numerous foreign languages. Liddell Hart never parted with the copyright of anything he wrote, and several of his books are composed almost entirely of previously published articles; *The Ghost of Napoleon* was based on his Lees-Knowles lectures at Cambridge. In other cases the manuscripts of books are written out in longhand — that of *Sherman* covers 787 sides. Some of the proofs of his books are noteworthy in that they have the comments of people whom he asked to vet the book; the galley proofs of three books from the Second World War are annotated by Robert Graves. In the case of three books — *T.E. Lawrence — In Arabia and After, The Other Side of the Hill* and *The Tanks* — there are large collections of material related to the subjects of these books catalogued with them.

Secondly, other published material, including articles in newspapers and journals, book reviews and forewords to other people's books; these number over two thousand. From 1925 to 1939 Liddell Hart wrote regular articles as the Military Correspondent first of the *Daily Telegraph,* then of *The Times.* During the Second World War he wrote war commentaries for the *Daily Mail;* after 1945 he wrote numerous articles on military history and current affairs, but only on a freelance basis. In fact he had been considering giving up regular journalistic work in 1934, having already grown tired of the pressures of news gathering and producing 'scoops' for the *Daily Telegraph.* Then the offer came to move to *The Times* as Military Correspondent and adviser on defence as a whole, with wider scope for more general comment on defence problems. However, his relationship with *The Times* became strained over the issues of the Spanish Civil War and appeasement as his views diverged from those of the Editor, Geoffrey Dawson, and the Assistant Editor, Robin Barrington-Ward. This is fully documented in Section 3 of the archive in *The Times'* files.

In his biography of Barrington-Ward,[5] Donald McLachlan criticises Liddell Hart for showing 'a certain failure to understand the requirements of a newspaper office, which aims at forming and publishing a collective rather than a personal attributable view.' And he quotes Geoffrey Dawson's statement in 1913, 'I hold most strongly that *The Times* should stick to its old practice of anonymous journalism, and that the members of its staff should be as far as possible unknown by name to the world at large.' If this was the case it is strange that on the day that Liddell Hart's first article appeared in *The Times*, there was the following announcement on the opposite page: 'Captain B.H. Liddell Hart, the well-known writer on problems of defence, has joined the staff of *The Times* as its Military Correspondent and adviser on defence in general. His contributions, according to the tradition of the paper, will appear anonymously.' Even stranger that this was then made into a circular and widely distributed by the paper – there are several copies of this in the archive at States House.

In a diary note quoted by McLachlan, Barrington-Ward says 'whether we like it or not questions of defence are coming to the fore. . .Liddell Hart is almost alone, by his own exertions, in that field'. Clearly he wanted the weight of Liddell Hart's reputation behind defence comment in *The Times,* as much as Liddell Hart wanted a platform for, as he put it, 'expressing in the most carefully weighed form the fruit of prolonged reflection on current problems'.[6] So when Liddell Hart threatened to resign, to quote his Memoirs, 'as usual B-W was so reasonable and persuasive and reassuring about future freedom to comment, that I agreed to defer my resignation and see how things worked out'. If, as McLachlan says, there was any failure on Liddell Hart's part to 'understand the requirements of a newspaper office', it was because Barrington-Ward preferred to fudge the issue rather than risk losing him.

The third category of Liddell Hart's military writings consists of his notes, records of conversations, reflections and memoranda. Some of the memoranda were subsequently made into articles or chapters of books, and excerpts from the notes of conversations were incorporated into the Memoirs, but the bulk of the material remains unpublished.

The first time Liddell Hart made a record of a conversation was in December 1916 after talks with Geoffrey Butler, one of the Chiefs of the Intelligence and Propaganda departments at the Foreign Office, who had been his tutor at Cambridge, and John Buchan, who was then on the GHQ Staff. In this note Liddell Hart recorded with approval such comments as 'GHQ is a collection of many of the cleverest brains in the world today' and 'Haig is not only a great general but also a great statesman'. Apart from a few jottings, there is then a gap until 1926 and 1927, in which years Liddell Hart kept a very full diary. In a later note he explained, 'these notes were kept as an aide memoire – not really as a diary. While a few of the longer entries were made as an historical record of sidelights on general affairs, most of the entries were intended simply as a reminder to myself of engagements, incidents, impressions and the personal attitude of various people. For after succeeding Colonel Repington as Military Correspondent of the *Daily Telegraph* in 1925, I decided to make it the platform for launching a campaign for the mechanisation of the army. It was thus important to keep a record of the effect of the case I put forward, stage by stage, as the campaign developed.'

After this Liddell Hart mainly kept simply appointments diaries, though there are some fuller details added in places. However, these are supplemented by large numbers of separate notes of talks, reflections and comments on current events. These are very full during the 1930s, and in the twelve months, August 1937 to July 1938, during the period when Liddell Hart was unofficial adviser to Hore-Belisha, there are notes of over ninety talks with Hore-Belisha alone. There are also a large number during the Second World War when he was gathering information in readiness for writing his history of the war. During this time from 1940 he began to call them 'Notes for History'. After the war there are detailed notes of his talks with the German generals whom he went to see when they were prisoners of war, and he used these to write *The Other Side of the Hill*. After this the 'Notes for History' dwindle, reflecting Liddell Hart's decreasing involvement in current affairs.

In some of the notes Liddell Hart records information on historical points or current events given to him in the course of conversation. In others he tries to reconstruct both sides of a discussion, giving a summary of what he himself said. Only in the case of Hore-Belisha did anyone check through Liddell Hart's records of his talks with him. Though some of the records bear the heading 'Note for History', they share with all diaries and reports of conversations certain limitations as an historical source. One must consider the prejudices of the person with whom Liddell Hart is talking, and how likely he is to have accurate information or to be passing it on 'undoctored'. Equally important, one must be aware of Liddell Hart's own strongly held opinions and consider how these might have influenced the kind of information he recorded and the way in which he recorded it.

Although he had a healthy scepticism about official records, Liddell Hart perhaps placed too much faith in what people told him,[7] particularly if he was in sympathy with them. A quotation from his *Memoirs* confirms this point when he wrote of his friend T.E. Lawrence, 'He withstood my cross-examination so well that I was perhaps inclined to give him a shade too much the benefit of the doubt on points I could not check. That effect was reinforced because the more I probed into the reasons which guided his actions in the war, the more I found them to coincide with my own military philosophy.' When Robert Graves wrote to Lawrence that a London newspaper had recently asked him to write a short memoir to file away against T.E.'s death, he replied, 'They were right in applying to you rather than Liddell Hart, who seems to have no critical sense in my regard.'[8]

Bearing in mind these reservations, if viewed with a critical eye, and checked where possible with other sources, then the Notes, based as they are on Liddell Hart's wide contacts over a long period, can provide the historian with invaluable insights into the workings of government and the armed forces, Liddell Hart's own views, and particularly people's private opinions of events and personalities.

The fourth, and last, Section of Liddell Hart's military writings contains what might be called 'spoken' material – lectures, speeches, broadcasts and interviews. There is much of interest in these, though they are far fewer in number than his articles, and are often derived from them. Liddell Hart's way of speaking was not sufficiently clear for lecturing to be one of his strong points. Guy Chapman, in his book *A Kind of Survivor,* recalls how he invited Liddell Hart to give a lecture in 1943 at the Army School of Education in North Wales, but 'except in the common room after dinner he was inaudible to all but the front row of his listeners'. Nevertheless, when, in his seventieth year, Liddell Hart was appointed Visiting Professor of History at the University of California, the student audience for his lectures on the Second World War actually increased as the term progressed, which was considered a notable achievement.

The third broad category in the archive consists of all the material collected by Liddell Hart on military affairs, politics and society; this has been given the heading 'General Evidence'. The files are organised by subjects, and the majority of them are composed of newspaper cuttings. However, in the inter-war period some of the files, such as those on disarmament, deal with matters with which Liddell Hart was closely involved in his own career. Many private memoranda and confidential documents were passed to him, and he also preserved all the schemes for army exercises from 1924 to 1939, some of which have his handwritten notes on them. Also included under the heading 'General Evidence' are over two hundred military manuals, marked typescripts and proofs of books sent by their authors to Liddell Hart for vetting, a cabinet of maps, and collections of papers given to Liddell Hart by their owners, notably those of Chester Wilmot, Maj.-Gen. Sir Percy Hobart and Maj.-Gen. George Lindsay.

There are also two Sections in the archive containing material concerning Liddell Hart's career, Section 8 for the early years up to 1925, and Section 13 covering the period 1925 to 1970. Finally there is a Section for Liddell Hart's 'non-military' interests – religion, sport and fashion, including his writings on each of these subjects.

Reviewing the archive as a whole, it is obvious that for Liddell Hart his work was his overwhelming preoccupation, and the library and papers are very much a monument to this. The archive is Liddell Hart orientated, and self-consciously created, reflecting aspects of his character. This orientation has been accentuated to some extent by separating his writings from the other material in the archive. The advantage of this, with the chronological organisation, is that it makes it possible to get a much clearer idea of the development of his military thought; and when an index for the archive has been completed it will be possible to study all the papers on a given subject, or on the various aspects of a particular period, in their correct context.

As Liddell Hart laid great stress on his foresight over many different issues this is particularly important. One of the problems of using his papers is that he was both an historian and a significant figure in important historical events, and he took frequent opportunities to be the historian of his own words and actions. He would work over his own writings, picking out what he considered to be the important points, and producing lengthy memoranda on controversial episodes and ideas. In many ways by doing this he made it more difficult for other historians to consider his career objectively, and it is quite essential to distinguish between what he wrote at the time and what he wrote after the event.

For instance, in 1948 Liddell Hart wrote a note about two meetings he had had with Patton in 1944. Briefly the note says that on his first visit Patton was despondently talking about having to return to slow 1918-style warfare in France. Liddell Hart reminded him about Sherman's campaigns, and 'I think the indirect argument made some impression. At any rate, when I spent another evening with him in June, just before he went over to Normandy, he was no longer talking about 1918 methods, but on much bolder lines.' The implication here is clearly that Liddell Hart's little talk did the trick; but this is really pure conjecture. Looking back now to the original notes which Liddell Hart made at the time of these two meetings, there are only jottings from the first one on 14 March 1944, but for the second on 19 June there is a three-page typed note. There is certainly a reference to Sherman in the first note, but as Liddell Hart recorded it it is in the second one that Patton talks of returning to 1918 methods — 'he argued that it was necessary for us now to go back to 1918 tactics, with the infantry moving ahead of tanks'. Evidently the note written in 1948 does not tally with the notes made at the time.

It is clear from the archive that Liddell Hart was obsessed by his own place in history. His consciousness of this developed very early — he wrote the draft of an autobiography in 1920 — and thereafter he was always seeking to establish his claim to that place. His principal way of doing this was by collecting, and often in effect soliciting,

138

tributes to his work and influence — such as Guderian's statement that he was one of Liddell Hart's 'disciples in tank affairs' — and ensuring that they reached the widest possible audience. Michael Howard has written of Liddell Hart's quest for such tributes as coming from the 1940 period when his reputation sank after he had been identified with the 'Maginot mentality': 'For the rest of his life he was to display an almost pathetic need for praise and appreciation, treasuring every scrap of evidence of his influence and every tribute to his abilities in a way that surprised his disciples who took them for granted and occasionally exasperated his dearest friends.' In fact, though 1940 does form a watershed in Liddell Hart's career, he had been amassing tributes for many years before that.[9]

When challenged on the subject of these tributes and testimonies, Liddell Hart's justification was that he was simply establishing facts for the sake of history. He sincerely believed in the reality of his own achievements, and he did not believe in false modesty. He felt that if he did not publicise the tributes which were paid to him people would not appreciate the value of his life's work. At certain times he also hoped that they might have some practical effect. In a letter to Chester Wilmot in 1953 over publishing a particular tribute reported to have been made by Rommel, he wrote, 'Having devoted my life to the service of military thought, and to preaching the need for it, it does not seem right to me to suppress striking evidence of its effect for fear of causing offence. . .If reason prevailed, it would be natural that anyone whose ideas have once achieved a striking effect, especially in a field vital to national survival, would be provided with the opportunity and means of doing some more useful thinking. But that "isn't done" here in any sense.' Chester Wilmot replied, 'I am afraid that I disagree with your general approach to this whole question. You are not going to persuade people to listen to you now by ramming down their throats that they didn't listen to you last time. All you succeed in doing is creating resentment and that harms your cause.' But this was a point of view Liddell Hart could not accept.

The influence of thought and writings on people and events is a very difficult thing to establish, and to some extent it must rest on the testimony of those claiming to have been influenced. But historians who come to write about Liddell Hart will have to examine the evidence in the archive with great care, and consider how far friendship, gratitude or less worthy motives might have caused people to exaggerate his influence on them when they saw how much these tributes pleased him. They will not be short of criticism to weigh against the praise, as that too was filed away in the archive. Liddell Hart never tried to censor any of the material which went into his archive, and he is revealed there with all his strengths and weaknesses. In every way the Collection reflects the complexity of Liddell Hart's character and the wide variety of his interests and activities in a very full life. It is as unique as its creator.

Notes

1. With the exception of a small amount of family and business correspondence. Also excluded is Liddell Hart's collection on fashion, women and manners, though spare copies of his own writings on these subjects are included in the archive in the Section devoted to his 'non-military' interests.
2. Intending readers must make applications in writing to the Librarian of King's College, stating the purpose of their research; the application must be supported by a recommendation from a person of appropriate standing.
3. In his article 'Liddell Hart' in *Encounter,* June 1970, p.37.
4. Quoted by Jay Luvaas in his chapter on 'The Captain who Teaches Generals: Captain B.H. Liddell Hart' in *The Education of an Army* (Cassell, 1965), p.421. Liddell Hart Papers 1/733.
5. *In the Chair. Barrington-Ward of The Times, 1927-1948* (Weidenfeld and Nicolson, 1971).
6. In a letter to C.S. Kent, the Manager of *The Times,* 6 Oct.1939. Liddell Hart Papers 3/109.
7. For instance, the controversial reference in Liddell Hart's *History of the Second World War* to a meeting between Molotov and Ribbentrop in 1943 to discuss peace terms was based solely on the claim of a German major, whom Liddell Hart met briefly at a prisoner of war camp in 1945, that he had attended such a meeting.
8. See Liddell Hart Papers 9/13/14.
9. The quotation is again from Michael Howard's *Encounter* article, p.41. What, therefore, were the origins of Liddell Hart's need for praise is as much a matter for a psychologist as for an historian.

REVIEW ARTICLES

THE ARMY AND ITS CRITICS IN
SEVENTEENTH CENTURY ENGLAND

Ian Roy

L.G. Schwoerer, *'No Standing Armies!.' The Anti Army Ideology in
Seventeenth-Century England.* Johns Hopkins. (Baltimore and London
1974). x + 210 pp. £5.50.

J. Childs, *The Army of Charles II.* Routledge and Kegan Paul (London
and Toronto, 1976). xii + 304 pp. £9.

J.T. Johnson, *Ideology, Reason and the Limitation of War: Religious
and Secular Concepts, 1200-1700.* Princeton UP (Princeton, N.J.,
1975). x + 291 pp. £7.30.

C.R. Boxer, *The Anglo-Dutch Wars of the 17th Century, 1652-1674.*
National Maritime Museum, HMSO (London, 1974). iv + 68 pp. £2.

W. Seymour, *Battles in Britain and their Political Background.* Sidgwick
and Jackson (London, 1975-76). 2 Vols. I, *1066-1547.* II, *1642-1746.*
Each 232 pp. Hardback £6.50, paperback £3.75.

In 1589 England was fully engaged by land and sea in a major conflict
with the leading military power in Europe, over whom, in the previous
year, she had gained a remarkable success. An English army, 5,000
strong, was fighting in the Low Countries alongside the Dutch. The war
was to continue for a further decade and a half. Although there was,
for home defence, a serviceable militia of over 100,000, the English
sovereign was advised to continue this continental commitment, and to
encourage 'men of account' to serve in the land forces sent overseas. It
was 'a more profitable course' for the enemy to be met and defeated
abroad, than awaited at home.

In 1689, having survived a great political and military crisis the year
before, involving the leading power in Europe, the nation was once
again waging war on the continent. An English army, soon to grow to
20,000 strong, was fighting in the Low Countries alongside the Dutch.
This struggle was to continue for the better part of two decades. During
this time English sovereigns were advised that neither the fleet nor the
militia (60,000 men) could ensure the safety of the realm, but that a

land force, sent to engage the enemy abroad, could. England had enjoyed two wonderful '88s, wrote a leading minister, but she might not be allowed a third, unless her regular army was kept in being.

But in the century between these two definite military commitments and positive expressions of support for such a policy, the nation, favoured by its geographical position, and to a lesser extent by its constitutional traditions, for long periods felt able to do without a land force at all, and sent one abroad only on rare occasions. The navy and the militia were considered sufficient for national security. The case for the maintenance of a permanent force in peacetime was never made by the early Stuarts, and when, by accident, the nation acquired one in mid-century, the unpleasant fact was concealed so far as possible by subsequent governments. Soldiers and soldiering were condemned by many, and service in the ranks remained unpopular. Nor were the precepts of the military advisers of Elizabeth carried out: at the height of Queen Anne's War it was argued that 'men of estate neither served in the fleets nor armies'. But this was a partisan statement, as we shall see. The burdens of long and costly warfare, particularly on the continent, were wherever possible avoided, and if inescapable, most unwillingly borne. Even military success did not still criticism, and opposition to the army rose following the victories first of William III, then of Marlborough.

England's military preparedness, its defects and its critics, and more generally warfare and the limitation of war in this period, are the subject of the books under review. Mrs Schwoerer's is the most ambitious. The author, known for her work on the pamphlet literature of the standing army debate of 1697-9, has extended her study to the rest of the century. By tracing the historical precedents of the later controversy she attempts to show the existence in England of a long-standing 'anti-army ideology'. While we may be grateful that she has brought together the findings of recent research, otherwise scattered in learned journals, and material long buried in older works, such as those of Fortescue, Clode and Walton, it cannot be said that she fully establishes her thesis.

The main difficulty is that, in considering supposed opposition to a standing army in Stuart England, for half the period there is no standing army. The debate can hardly take the form it does later in the century until a permanent force emerges from the confusion of the Civil War and Revolution in the 1640s. Significantly, the terms 'the army' and 'plunder' both enter the language at that time. For the first half of the seventeenth century the author must rest content with an examination of the origins of a hypothetical anti-army ideology in the writings of English Machiavellians, whom she admits had a rather restricted influence. Not till the appearance of Harrington's *Oceana* in the 1650s, and the emergence of the 'classical republicans', with their belief in the virtues of a citizen militia and the dangers of a professional army allied to tyranny, did these views reach a wider audience.

Nor are matters improved when she comes to examine that audience, in Parliament and the country. She assumes too readily, from the criticisms of Charles I's military policy, and his attempts to reform the militia, that an anti-military bias was general. In fact the Elizabethan military tradition died hard. If James I was distinctly un-military (he had been horrified as a child by the brawling of the Scottish nobility), his elder son was, until his early death, a keen young militarist, whose circle led the fashion for martial activities. Military books, manuals and histories continued popular, although less so than in the previous reign. The old chivalric code and a more modern code of honour reveals itself in Stuart literature and the behaviour of quite unquixotic Englishmen. Artillery 'gardens' in the capital were well used before the Civil War, and a typical City merchant dressed up as an HAC officer to have his portrait painted. If the old aristocracy were being weaned away from their delight in the killing affray at this time, there was no shortage of sprigs of the nobility and other young gentlemen willing to volunteer for military service overseas.

The commitment, begun by Elizabeth, to the defence of the Netherlands not only introduced a large number of Englishmen to the best school of modern warfare in Europe — a link which was interrupted but never severed during the whole of the century — but provided the means whereby in moments of crisis the English monarch could call for military aid (1587, 1626, 1638-42, 1665, 1678, 1685 and 1688 — the last, like that at the start of the Civil War, being a largely unsuccessful appeal). The Anglo-Dutch brigade and other mercenary armies on the continent permitted the continuance in military service of certain important families, refreshed and rewarded their consuming martial interests, and helped transmit the latest ideas on war and its conduct to the nation at large. The *Swedish Intelligencer* and Monro *His Expedition* brought home to Englishmen, and Scotsmen, the perils of the Thirty Years War and the part played by their fellow countrymen in it. The families of Conway, Cecil, Vere, Sidney and Goring are simply the best known of the many who participated in this European tradition and naturalised it. They, or their kin, were to be available to both sides at the beginning of the Civil War. They not only provided some of the leading soldiers of the wars but some of the most formidable (and influential) ladies, such as Lady Brilliana Harley, defender of Brampton Bryan for Parliament, the daughter of a Conway who named her after the Dutch stronghold of Brill where he commanded and she was born; or Lady Fairfax, Vere's daughter, also raised in the Netherlands, who married the Lord General of the New Model, another Dutch-trained soldier, and had the temerity to interrupt the trial of Charles I.

Given the existence of a military tradition, and a continuing interest in martial affairs during the year of peace before the Civil War, where do the Parliamentary debates of the 1620s fit in? On this question Mrs Schwoerer adds nothing to what Dr Boynton said, some years ago, on the grievances expressed in the Petition of Right, and Dr Stearns more recently on the poor quality of the troops raised. The attack on the government over the militia, billeting and martial law are less a sign of an incipient anti-army ideology, let alone adherence to Machiavellian principle, than the muddled reaction, by no means unanimous, of the country gentry in Parliament to ministers and policies which aroused hostility because of their inefficiency, extravagance and misguided aims. The critics of Buckingham's expeditions (who had warmly supported his conversion to a warlike posture a year or so before), were reflecting their constituents' grievances about the burdens placed on the Southern shires by the movement of ill-disciplined troops; they were *not* providing an overture for the Whig pamphleteers of the 1690s. MPs, all of whom carried swords, none of whom was a republican, objected equally and on the same practical grounds to the use made of the militia by the King against the rebel Scots. There was little reluctance on their part to place their own nominees in charge of the militia in 1642, or take an active part in the Civil War if events forced them to. They then endured the greatest military and financial burdens, so long as they approved the ends to which the forces were put, and they had consented to those measures. What emerges clearly from the controversies of the period is less the importance of a sustained criticism of armed forces in England, than the essentially neutral attitude of the political nation to such forces. What mattered was the way in which the government handled the military, and what end it had in view for them, once raised.

It is particularly difficult to see the events of the 1640s in terms of pro- and anti-army attitudes, and this chapter of the book is the weakest. With the creation of the New Model Army one might suppose that anti-military critics would have had a field day: but the author finds it difficult to uncover more than one or two pamphlets which suit her purpose. The fact is, again, that politicians hostile to the New Model objected to its policies, its revolutionary fervour, not to the existence of all armies. The critics in the Parliaments of 1656 and 1658 relfect the unease (similar to that of their Caroline predecessors) about the use to which the new forces being raised by the Protectorate were put. They attacked the war against Spain, until it produced results acceptable to them. The Major-Generals were unpopular with the gentry because they usurped the functions and style of the former magistrates. There is little consistency in anti-military argument during the Interregnum. Those influenced by classical republican ideals must have approved of the Army leaders purging, then dismissing, the Long Parliament, executing the King and founding the first English Commonwealth; later they disapproved of Cromwell as Protector, fearing a return to one-person government. They joined with the Generals to overthrow Cromwell's son Richard, whose régime could no longer be thought of, as his father's had been, as owing something to the New Model. Their triumph was short-lived. Another military *coup,* which brought about the Restoration, was engineered by the commander of the army in Scotland, George Monck. It could be argued that this last military revolution shows that regular forces need not be unpopular with taxpayers and MPs, if they are used for desirable political ends. Monck's soldiers were fêted in the City.

Monck, as Duke of Albemarle following the Restoration, occupies an important place in the transition from the politics of the first half of the century to the new issues raised in the second half, and it is appropriate that his swarthy features decorate the cover of a new book on the army of Charles II, by John Childs. Dr Childs' study (in which I must declare an interest, as supervisor of the doctoral thesis on which it is based) may be conveniently discussed at this point, for it complements the argument put forward by Mrs Schwoerer. The Restoration army, largely the creation of Monck, was a poor thing in comparison with the large forces at the disposal of Cromwell. Dr Childs shows how King and Parliament agreed to disband the old army,(though the piffling riot of 1661, known as Venner's rising, was used by the government to retain a larger force than was originally intended, euphemistically described thereafter as 'Guards and garrisons'), and so reduce military taxation and the chances of further military intervention in politics. At the same time Parliament readily agreed to confirm the Crown's rights over the militia, something Charles I had never been able to achieve. But Charles II had few military ambitions. Although he had seen a good deal of warfare by the time he was 21, he was too indolent to take a close and continuing interest in the army. His relative poverty (Parliament was unwilling to supply large sums for the armed forces), and his complaisant foreign policy (he was content to remain a client of Louis XIV), kept his army small. In a crisp and workmanlike manner this study outlines the main features of the army, which was stationed not only in England, Scotland and Ireland, but provided garrisons for Tangier, Bombay and Portugal. These colonial and foreign postings helped to conceal from MPs' prying eyes the true strength of their armed forces.

Dr Childs devotes a separate section of his book to Parliament and the army, but here it is disappointingly slim in size and content. No very clear picture emerges of civilian attitudes to England's first peacetime standing army. While service in hellholes such as Tangier was highly unpopular and probably fatal, there were more than enough applications for places in the Guards, and commissions generally were over-subscribed, by a generation hungry for office. Dutch (and French) service continued to be an excellent school for English soldiers. It came to be realised that the army, if it remained small and manageable, had its uses. Remote garrisons could receive unwanted radicals such as Old Cromwellians; new levies for service abroad provided an opportunity to be rid of jailbirds, vagabonds and others displeasing to the civilian magistracy (a continuation of the policies of an earlier period); units stationed in Britain and her first colonies demonstrated to the propertied classes their value as police forces, or in aid to the civil power — Covenanters in Scotland were hunted down, and the politically recalcitrant anywhere had troops billeted on them, in moves reminiscent of Louis XIV's *dragonnades.* But an ill-disciplined soldiery could be as great a threat to law and order, as this book shows, and on two occasions (1673, 1678-9) 'Country' Whigs in Parliament attacked the army when it had been enlarged for a war no longer popular.

Another view of England's armed forces at this time is afforded by Professor Boxer's study of the three Anglo-Dutch Wars. As might be expected from the hand of this eminent historian, the text of this little booklet is exemplary; it is concise, learned and readable, and firmly based on Dutch sources as well as English. The illustrations, drawn from the National Maritime Museum's superb collection of portraits, medallions and battle scenes, are equally admirable. The only regret must be the price (£2): when the Museum last produced a pamphlet on the Second Dutch War, similar in size and format, it cost 6s.6d.!

On the whole the navy emerges with some credit from Boxer's pages. English warships impressed observers by their size and strength; the naval commanders (often old army officers, like Rupert and Monck) showed skill and courage; and the men endured terrible conditions with great patience, particularly as so many of them were victims of the press gang. Pressed or not, at least they were native English: over half the men serving in Dutch warships were foreign.

The navy, of course, offered no threat to political liberty (if we except the freedom of those pressed for service), and we must return to the army in the last quarter of the century to conclude this discussion. With the accession of James II the army embarked on a period of rapid growth, and after the Revolution of '88, of increasing involvement in continental wars. In the relations between the standing army and its political critics in the seventeenth century, this period forms a natural climax, when the debate takes its classic form, and the guidelines of future controversy are laid down. It is the centrepiece of Mrs Schwoerer's book, and it is particularly unfortunate that she was unable to use two masterly studies, bearing on these problems, which appeared in 1972: J.R. Jones, *The Revolution of 1688 in England,* and J.R. Western, *Monarchy and Revolution.*

What is clear from these recent studies of the 1680s is that James, of very different stamp from his brother (a pupil of Turenne, deeply interested in militaria, a competent Admiral during the Dutch Wars), aimed to set up absolute monarchy in England, and designed an enlarged army for this purpose. He was aided in this by the unpopularity of radical critics at his accession, and the outbreak of the Monmouth rebellion, which allowed the government to increase its forces with little protest. The natural supporters of the monarchy feared subversion more than an enlarged standing army. Arrangements in this army, as with the navy, suited them well enough. Many regiments were virtually owned by their Colonels, who benefited from the abuses which were countenanced by the government. Abuses which were, however, burdensome to society, such as billeting and martial law, were remedied as far as possible; without purpose-built barracks, of course, not a great deal could be done.

Opposition in Parliament to these moves was feeble, and Professor Jones has shown that the King was in a fair way to packing the Parliament he would have called had his régime not been overtaken by events. It was not so much civilian resistance which caused James's downfall as a countervailing military force – the army of William III. The failure of James to recruit his forces from among the Anglo-Dutch brigade veterans, and their use by William, is a crucial factor. Nor did Parliament do much better in limiting the Crown's use of a standing army and dominance in foreign policy once the Revolution had occurred. Like his uncle James, William was 'first and foremost a keen soldier' (Western, op.cit., p.239). He was autocratic, reserved, old for his years, and represented the old Orange military tradition in the United Provinces. He was dedicated to war with Louis, and English politicians were unlikely to be able to stand in his way. It is a myth,

147

faithfully repeated by Mrs Schwoerer, that the Bill of Rights transferred sovereignty over the forces from the Crown to Parliament, or that the passing of an annual Mutiny Act placed them under Parliamentary control. Professor Western and others have shown conclusively that William disposed of the army largely as he wished in the wars with France, and the standing army continued in being during the years (1697-1702) when no Mutiny Acts were passed.

What Parliament did control was the money supply, and when politicians could harness a general war-weariness and resentment of high taxation, and at the same time, following victories in the field or at sea, could promote the feeling that the nation was no longer threatened by a foreign power, they had sufficient influence to reduce the size of the military establishment. This is what happened in 1698, after the Peace of Ryswick, and in a different form in 1711. It is a pity that Mrs Schwoerer did not project her study forward, to embrace the arguments of Swift and the Tories in Queen Anne's reign, rather than backwards.

The press and pamphlet campaign over the standing army issue, in 1697-9, is certainly of great interest, and repays study. One can see developing the two sides of so many later controversies — the argument for land forces and commitment to continental allies on the one hand, and on the other the 'Blue-Water' School, arguing for colonial and maritime warfare as cheaper and less dangerous to political liberty. The classical republican tradition made its contribution to the debate on behalf of the army's critics. One of the principal writers, Moyle, drew his inspiration from ancient Rome and Sparta, modern Switzerland and Poland. Machiavelli and Harrington were much quoted; translations of the former, and the latter's *Oceana*, were reprinted at this time. While the pro-army apologists, such as Somers and Defoe, may be said to have had the better of the argument (pointing out Louis's continued strength, the defects of the militia, the complexity of modern warfare, which required trained professionals), their opponents' views chimed with the discontent of the country gentry and the backbenchers in the Commons. The government was defeated in its attempt to keep a force in peacetime as large as that which had fought in the war. Did the pamphlets of Trenchard and Moyle work this change, as Mrs Schwoerer suggests? She does not essay any evaluation of the complex political situation of the time, or the conflicting pressures on MPs.

In any case the success of the army's critics was only temporary. By 1700 Tory backbenchers were loudly condemning the government for being too accommodating with Louis. One of the most popular tracts of 1701 was 'The Dangers of Europe from the Growing Power of France'. By the time of William III's death the threatening continental situation had both alerted the government and alarmed Parliament. From 1702 Britain built up her armed forces on an unprecedented scale: there were 70,000 men in arms by 1711. This huge force (by the standards of the time) was backed up by a much enlarged military bureaucracy. The Board of Ordnance grew enormously, as did the market for supplies and munitions of all kinds. England witnessed the growth of a 'military-industrial complex'. In its train came important political changes. The government now had more political patronage — commissions in the army and navy, contracts to suppliers, lucrative offices in the expanded administration — to dispose of. After the experience of William III, Parliament began to exercise control over this cumbrous military machine, and the political nation began to see the benefits of the continued existence of a standing army. The gentry, particularly those with pressing need of office, looked on army and, to a lesser extent, naval service, as a principal avenue for advancement. Henceforth, army officers form an important element in the House of Commons.

It is against this background of growing acceptance of the army, and realisation of its uses, that the party warfare over Marlborough's forces, 1708-11, should be viewed. It was at this time that Tory spokesmen for the hard-pressed landed classes argued that only the despised monied interest had profited from the war; 'men of estate' had not generally served in the enlarged army and navy which their taxes had paid for. But while politicians, once they had come to power on a wave of war-weariness, might replace unpopular commanders and alter the direction of the war, the long-term tendencies were irreversible. The Tory government in 1711 had its own military and naval projects and its own nominees to carry them out. When peace was made the army offered an even more attractive career, as the hazards were less. The greater regulation and the more established position of the eighteenth-century army further promoted this trend. The Hanoverians, like James II and William III, were 'warrior-kings'. Their growing empire required policing: fear of slave insurrection in the West Indies made the regiments sent there welcome. At home, too, the vaunted political stability England achieved in the early eighteenth century was more firmly based on bayonets than is commonly realised. A dragoon regiment billeted on the South Coast might spend up to a third of its time suppressing smuggling or dealing with riots. Conscription into the army, especially overseas, of those unwanted by civil society continued as a form of social control, a corollary to the transportation of criminals. Suspicion of the costly and dangerous armed forces, so created, of course lingered for some time, especially on the back benches of the

Commons. The building of barracks was constantly postponed, until the Napoleonic Wars: proper housing for the army at home was considered too obvious a sign of the permanence of military occupation, indeed a 'badge of slavery'. So one criminal class, the soldiery, continued to be billeted on another, innkeepers. With this neat solution the political nation had to rest content, and in general the army's critics remained muted throughout the century.

Armies were being brought under greater control and their use regulated almost everywhere by 1700. In part this was due to the development of thinking about the relations between states, the morality of going to war and the code of behaviour governing those engaged in war. The evolution of these ideas in the late Medieval and Early Modern period, in Western Europe, is the theme of Professor Johnson's important and original study. He shows how the classic just war doctrine of the Middle Ages bifurcated, and how from one half of this tradition there sprang the modern secular concepts of international law, grounded on natural law. The author considers particularly the contribution made by English writers in the sixteenth and seventeenth century to this development. John Locke, for instance, extended the limitations of what was permissible in war on the basis of his thinking about natural justice. Professor Johnson disentangles these fine threads with great skill and admirable clarity, but he does not place them in their historical context (the biographical appendices in his book are hardly an adequate substitute), and he is a little shaky on points of detail (Paul's Cross was not a parish church).

For those who like to explore England's military history on foot Mr Seymour's smartly presented guide to the battlefields of Britain, from Hastings to Culloden, will be welcome. 'On foot' is perhaps a misnomer: it is clear from these two volumes that the light aircraft and the car are the most essential tools. The guide's most distinctive new contribution is the aerial photograph, which provides a clear and panoramic view of each battlefield: and the modern motorist's route to each is given in detail. In an otherwise convincing and accurate description of the Civil War campaigns there is one oddity. A portrait of Maurice of Nassau is included among others captioned 'Royalist commanders'. I have argued above the importance of the Anglo-Dutch brigade in fostering the English military tradition, but this is going too far: by 1642 the Prince had been dead for seventeen years!

ARMED FORCES AND THE STATE:
THE HISTORICAL ESSAYS OF OTTO HINTZE

Peter Paret

Otto Hintze was not a specialist in the history of war; but the study of
military institutions and of the violent and non-violent uses to which
they are put is a major theme of his historical work. In his writings he
firmly integrated the study of European administrative history with
the comparative history of political systems and of the development
of the modern state — an achievement whose value to scholarship has
become increasingly apparent since Hintze's death in 1940. The first
publication in English of a selection of his essays thus provides an
occasion to explore the military elements in the work of a significant
interpreter of the history of the state and of the European state
system.[1]

Hintze's scholarly production falls into three periods.[2] The first
extended from 1888 to 1910, during which time he participated in
the publication of the *Acta Borussica,* editing nine volumes on the
Prussian silk industry in the eighteenth century and on the Prussian
bureaucracy in the first years of Frederick the Great's reign. While
acquiring an exceptionally thorough knowledge of the workings of
the administrative machinery in Prussia and other states in early
modern Europe he also wrote synthesising analyses, for example the
essay 'Prussian Reform Movements before 1806' (1896), which refuted
the accepted view that Prussian reforms after her defeat by Napoleon
constituted a nearly total break with the past. Hintze showed, on the
contrary, that both civil and military innovation built on intellectual
and institutional elements that predated the disaster. In 1910 he
withdrew from editorial work on the *Acta Borussica* to devote more
time to the comparative analyses of administrative, legal and military
institutions 'within the framework of general European history', which
he had begun with such essays as 'Military Organization and the
Organization of the State' (1906). His longest work during this period,
however, concerned a single state: *Die Hohenzollern und Ihr Werk,*
which appeared in 1915 and remains one of the best histories of Prussia
in the literature. In 1920 he retired from his chair at the University of
Berlin, and during the last twenty years of his life turned to explicitly
theoretical studies, which sought to combine approaches of modern
sociology and economic history with the methods of political and

institutional history. In what came to be some of his most important articles he applied his new theoretical insights to specific historical developments, for example in 'Calvinism and Raison d'Etat' and 'The Preconditions of Representative Government in the Context of World History', both published in 1931. At the beginning of this last phase of his career he also published his most significant study of a conventional topic in the history of war: 'Delbrück, Clausewitz, und die Strategie Friedrichs des Grossen', an austerely logical, somewhat narrow rejection of Hans Delbrück's thesis that Clausewitz had established the dominance of two strategic systems in the history of warfare – the 'strategy of exhaustion' and the 'strategy of annihilation', the former exemplified by Frederick, the other by Napoleon.[3]

Even this brief outline indicates the crucial role that Prussia played in Hintze's historical thinking. Although he never regarded himself as a specifically Prussian historian, and indeed wrote his dissertation on a Dutch theme, he approached the European past from a Prussian base. Occasionally his background and outlook led him into distortions – of an atmospheric rather than of a factual kind. For example, his discussions of France and England during feudalism and in the early modern period emphasise the agencies and structure of governmental power at the expense of a full appreciation of the varied political impulses coursing through their societies. Despite these limitations in his work, however, Hintze's analyses of the methods by which an increasingly effective central administration fused disparate and largely underdeveloped territories into the Prussian monarchy gave him an exceptionally clear understanding of the mechanics of state-building even in the more complex societies of Western Europe. The growth of Prussia provided a relatively simple model for the general development of centralised government and of the nineteenth-century nation-state.

In this development, Hintze argued, the relationship of the particular state to its neighbours assumed critical importance. External pressures helped determine the political organisation of society, and shaped its military and administrative organs, which in turn were a source of its political ideals – as, in his view, the Brandenburgian army and its supporting institutions contributed special features to the Prussian *raison d'état.*

We can gain a clearer picture of his manner of interpreting the dynamic and continuous relationship between foreign affairs and internal conditions, between army and state, by tracing the main arguments in two of the essays that are included in the present volume. Both are comparative analyses. The first, the already mentioned article 'Military Organization and the Organization of the State' (1906), ranges over the whole sweep of European history.[4] The other, 'The Commissary and his Significance in General Administrative History' (1919), is an exploration of one of the tools employed in the process of military-administrative centralisation, with an emphasis on developments in Brandenburg-Prussia and France.[5]

The essay on 'Military Organization' opens with the assertion that 'all state organization was originally military organization, organization for war. This can be regarded as an assured result of comparative history.' As tribal structures grow more complex, military activity becomes a specialty, and issues of political organisation and civil-military relations arise. Hintze draws on Herbert Spencer's two basic types of state and social organisation, the 'military' and the 'industrial', to indicate the 'polar opposites between which the political life of mankind takes place'. But he cautions that movement toward the one or the other ideal is determined less by internal strife and class conflict than by conflict between nations, and draws on examples from antiquity to support his claim. The history of Rome, in particular, permits him to explore links between the size of the state's territory that must be defended (always an important consideration in Hintze's thinking), class structure, military organisation, tactics and political institutions.

The decline of the Empire, 'initially barbarized by the army', marks a point of departure for a new stage in the history of Europe, divided by Hintze into three epochs, in which types of military and political organisation appear linked: (1) the epoch of the tribal or clan system, which antedates the Roman Empire; (2) the feudal epoch; and (3) the epoch of militarism. This last is further divided into three periods: (i) from the end of the fifteenth to the middle of the seventeenth century, when 'the mercenary system was not yet firmly and permanently integrated with. . .political institutions, nor was the organization of the state itself yet solidified into the absolutist-centralist state'; (ii) to the end of the eighteenth century, when absolutist states and standing armies matured on the continent, while England moved in the direction of Parliamentary government, local home rule, and greater reliance on the militia; and (iii) the nineteenth century, which saw the emergence of the inter-related principles of universal military service and constitutional government, 'while the militia system. . .continued and naval forces assumed greater significance'.

After comparing the political and social characteristics of armies and navies, Hintze concludes his study by returning to the 'military' and 'industrial' types of society, whose further development he views in a light very different from Spencer's optimistic liberalism. In the twentieth century, he believes, a

> general adjustment of differing political and military institutions is beginning to take place. The opposition between land powers and sea powers, between peoples that govern themselves and peoples that are governed from above, will become less and less rigid and obvious. The military and industrial types of society will probably experience not a sharpening of their differences, but a gradual blending and increasing similarity of institutions. . .In the foreseeable future, matters will remain as they have been throughout history: the form and spirit of the state's organization will not be determined solely by economic and social relations and clashes of interests, but primarily by the necessities of defense and offense, that is, by the organization of the army and of warfare.

The second essay traces the development of the commissary, an official holding a special, temporary commission, whom Hintze regards as a principal agent in the innovations between the fifteenth and eighteenth centuries that created the modern state. Hintze's attention had been drawn to the commissary by his studies of eighteenth-century Prussian administration, whose characteristic features derived 'from the commissarial authorities that had chiefly developed out of the military commissaries'. In Brandenburg they first appeared in the seventeenth century as agents of the elector, supervising the military entrepreneurs who raised and led his troops. Other commissaries were in charge of military administration, justice, fortifications and also of the collection of taxes that maintained the army. As the mercenary forces gave way to a standing army in the second half of the seventeenth century, the military commisars became permanent bureaucrats in the service of the central executive. Gradually their duties became inseparably entangled with those of the civil bureaucracy as they took over the collection of additional taxes from the estates and other local and provincial authorities. Simultaneously they infused the bureaucracy with a new absolutist and professional ethos. The tradition of officials vested with extraordinary and temporary powers continued to play a role in the subsequent modernisation of the Prussian administration during the first decades of the nineteenth century.

Prussian officialdom developed in a unique manner; but, Felix Gilbert notes, Hintze recognised the Prussian phenomenon to be merely a particular form of the European-wide process leading to the establishment of modern bureaucracies. Hintze first points to officials in sixteenth- and seventeenth-century France, the *intendants de justice ou d'armée,* who accompanied troops in wartime, and like the Prussian commissaries were 'pioneers of the [royal] police state that undermined the bulwark of the old legal order'. Similar officials, holding temporary commissions and combining civil and military functions, can be found in other states of early modern Europe. To discover their origin, Hintze investigates the all-pervasive distinction in European administrative theory and law between office and commission – the one, a regular appointment for a fixed period or for life; the other, an executive, temporary charge. Applying this distinction as a touchstone, Hintze finds the first ancestors of the commissary among officials of the medieval Papacy and of other medieval bureaucracies.

The significance of the commissary, Hintze concludes, is that 'wherever public administration came up against new and extraordinary tasks, which the ordinary officials did not have the equipment to cope with, at first extraordinary officeholders were outfitted by commission with power adequate to these new tasks'. If the need persisted these officials tended to become permanent.

> In this way the primitive district administration of bailiffs and officeholders throughout Europe was displaced by a new organization. . .The institution of the commissary was especially a means of exerting monarchical discipline and the authority of the absolutist state in administration. . .The commissaries represent a new type of public servant, corresponding to the spirit of absolutist reason of state, who did not completely supplant the old officialdom but, in amalgamation with it, after a long struggle, effected profound changes in its nature which have their impact to the present day.

In these two articles, and indeed from his earliest writings on, Hintze appears determined to pursue the interactions between the many forces that together created the unities of political power. He saw the past as a whole. But he expressed his universalistic view not in allusions or by analysing one institution or policy in detail and then briefly suggesting possible implications in other areas. On the contrary, each new component of his structural, genetic and comparative analyses of power in European history was treated with the same specificity. That would scarcely have been feasible had not his historical thinking clustered around an organising principle: the state, with its primary function – as Hintze saw it – of gaining and maintaining power. Armed force was an essential element in carrying out this functon, internally as well as in the state's foreign relations. As Hintze demonstrated repeatedly

155

from a great variety of episodes, to gain control over the resources needed to support the army meant an increase in the power of the state at the expense of regional and local authorities. A stronger, more complex military establishment led to an expanded state apparatus, more effective internal control and perhaps territorial acquisitions. The reciprocal relationship between army and executive, whose workings were revealed with special clarity in the development of the centralised state, persisted, although in somewhat different form, in the matured nation-state.

This major motif in Hintze's work may suggest that he was essentially a historian of civil-military relations, but that is not the case. Much as the relations between different institutions interested him, he was equally fascinated by the genesis and nature of the institutions themselves — institutions, which in the final analysis, he believed, were moved by a concern for power, and which were brought into contact or conflict with other institutions by this same concern.

It was self-evident to Hintze that these relationships could be understood only on the basis of the specific characteristics of the institutions involved. Unless their routine were mastered, interpretation of their policies and actions remained insubstantial and formalistic. Consequently when Hintze analysed armies he interpreted them not only as instrumenents of power and as open or implicit claimants of social and political authority; he also studied their organisation, their economic and technological conditions, their social composition, and — by no means least — their tactics and their strategic doctrine. The dreary compartmentalisation that inhibits too many historians today is entirely lacking from his work, which at first glance seems frozen in the narrow channels of administrative analysis. He would have derided any separation of 'military history' from other kinds of history, and he would have shown little patience with scholars who insist that one area of their discipline is innately superior or inferior to the rest. Like his friend Friedrich Meinecke, whose work on the history of ideas is joined by extensive explorations into military organisation, strategy and the conduct of war, Hintze did not hesitate to immerse himself in the details of company tactics and administration. Only an understanding of everyday business made possible the construction of over-arching interpretations. The intellectual environment in which he worked will never return, and his writings cannot serve as specific models for others, but they continue to exemplify the potential and strengths that are inherent in the historian's universalistic concept of his task.

Notes

1. *The Historical Essays of Otto Hintze,* translated by Hugh West and Robert B. and Rita Kimber, edited with an introduction by Felix Gilbert, Oxford, 1975, pp.vii + 493. Some years ago sections of one of Hintze's essays, 'The Character of Feudalism', which is not included in this volume, appeared in English translation in *Lordship and Community in Medieval Europe,* edited by Fredric Cheyette, New York, 1968.
2. The following is based on Felix Gilbert's excellent introduction to *The Historical Essays,* which further refines Fritz Hartung's evaluation in the first volume of the German edition of Hintze's collected papers, *Gesammelte Abhandlungen,* Göttingen, 1962.
3. The article, which is not included in *The Historical Essays,* appeared in the *Forschungen zur Brandenburgischen und Preussischen Geschichte,* XXXIII (1921).
4. *The Historical Essays,* pp.178-215.
5. Ibid., pp.267-301.

ASPECTS OF WAR IN THE NINETEENTH AND TWENTIETH CENTURIES

Brian Bond

An outstanding new book at the beginning of the period is Peter Paret's *Clausewitz and the State* (Oxford University Press) which was available in proof shortly before the *Yearbook* went to press. As it is hoped to include a review essay on this study together with the new translation of Clausewitz's *On War* by Paret, Michael Howard and Bernard Brodie in the next issue, only a brief advance notice is called for here. Paret is concerned with Clausewitz's private and professional life, the development of his mind and his writings but not his posthumous influence or his relevance today. With impressive scholarship and subtlety Paret places Clausewitz's contribution to the theory of war firmly in its cultural and historical context. Appropriately the culminating point of the study is Paret's masterly account of how *On War* was written and what Clausewitz was trying to achieve. Reviewers should employ the accolade of 'definitive' rarely, if at all, but Paret's brilliant study will certainly remain essential reading for students of military theory for a very long time.

Roger Parkinson, though not in the same league of scholarship as Peter Paret, anticipated him with his popular biography of Clausewitz. He has recently produced an equally lively life of Marshal Blücher entitled *The Hussar General* (Peter Davies, £5.75, 264 pp.) which, though not impeccable in its handling of sources and historical detail, provides graphic descriptions of Blücher's principal battles and makes the most of his eccentricities.

The chief novelty in D.W. Davies' carefully researched and well-written book *Sir John Moore' Peninsular Campaign, 1808-1809* (The Hague: Martinus Nijhoff, G52.50, 290 pp.) is his emphasis on Moore's error of judgement in marching into Spain, though he also describes the better-known retreat, exploding several myths along the way. This is clearly a labour of love by a scholar who knows the terrain as intimately as the archives and it can be strongly recommended to students of the Peninsular War.

Unlike many books about weapons, B.P. Hughes' *Firepower: Weapons Effectiveness on the Battlefield 1630-1850* (Arms and Armour Press, £4.50, 176 pp.) is primarily concerned with their tactical employment. The development, capabilities, methods of deployment and potential of various weapons are first described and then illustrated in detailed accounts of several battles. The book is fully illustrated with tables, diagrams, charts and contemporary drawings.

My only real regret about the second volume of the Marquess of Anglesey's *History of British Cavalry* (Leo Cooper, £15, 542 pp.) is that the price will unduly restrict the readership of a very interesting study. This volume covers the period 1851-71 and therefore devotes a good deal of attention to the cavalry's role in the Crimean War, the Indian Mutiny and the colonial campaigns of the 1860s. But its scope is wider than the title may suggest and in fact it conveys a good general impression of the British Army at that time. Admirably based on contemporary documents this study makes a significant contribution to mid-Victorian social history. The same tribute cannot be paid to William McElwee's *The Art of War: Waterloo to Mons* (Weidenfeld and Nicolson, £4.50, 352 pp.), which has the air of a book written to order by someone not very familiar with the sources for the period and even less *au fait* with modern scholarship on topics such as Clausewitz and his posthumous influence. Though not entirely without value as an introduction, the beginner would do better to consult the relevant chapters in the *New Cambridge Modern History* (vols.X and XI).

Except for endless accounts of the Mutiny, the Indian Army has been surprisingly neglected by modern historians, but two recent books go some way to fill this gap. Philip Mason's very well written and stimulating study, *A Matter of Honour: an Account of the Indian Army, its Officers and Men* (Cape £5.75, 580 pp.) is strongly influenced by the author's long and distinguished career in the Indian Civil Service. While he does not ignore the more conventional aspects of military history, his main concern throughout is with beliefs, emotions and ideas. Why, he asks, were so many Indians proud to serve under foreign officers and give their lives for a foreign flag? He shows how the early trust built up under the rule of the East India Company was undermined by a combination of factors which eventually resulted in the explosion of the Mutiny. Thereafter the Indian Army was reconstituted and mutual esteem largely restored, except that in the late Victorian period the British fostered the dogma of martial and non-martial races. Mr Mason stresses the Indian Army's contribution to the two World Wars and shows to what a remarkable extent it remained impervious to the inroads of nationalism. T.A. Heathcote's *The Indian Army: the Garrison of British Imperial India 1822-1922* (David and Charles, £5.25, 215 pp.) is one of a series on Historic Armies and Navies intended in part, so the dust jackets states, for the benefit of war gamers. This may account for the arrangement of chapters (Fighting Arms, Supporting Troops,

159

Reserves, etc.), and for the concluding chapter describing operations in Afghanistan in 1880. The rationale of the precise dates in the subtitle is not clear. Compared with *A Matter of Honour* this is a rather prosaic book, but it does contain much well-researched information.

A good example of the kind of work which the *Yearbook* wishes to encourage and publish is Hugh Cunningham's *The Volunteer Force* (Croom Helm, £6.50, 168 pp.). It explores the social and political significance of an organisation which in purely military terms was hardly impressive. In fact Dr Cunningham shows that relationships both within the Force and between the Volunteers and the civilian public illuminate many aspects of British life between 1859 and 1908. The Force sprang into existence in 1859 in response to the invasion scare and at first its rank and file was predominantly middle class. Within a few years its role was in doubt and it suffered from both neglect and abuse. Yet the remarkable thing is that, except for the years 1869-73, its numbers generally increased year by year. Increasingly, however, the ranks were filled with working men as the middle-class membership declined. This transformation causes Dr Cunningham to ponder what caused working men to give up their leisure and even risk losing their jobs for the sake of exceedingly amateur soldiering. He concludes that patriotism was not the answer; the main purpose of the Force was to provide recreation. After the Boer War the military value of the Force came increasingly under queston: it would take too long to mobilise to counter an invasion and was too weak to be regarded as a reserve for the regular expeditionary force. Yet so strong was its Parliamentary lobby that no reformer before 1914, including even Haldane, could bring it into line with national military policy.

Early twentieth-century British military writers provide the starting points for two stimulating lectures now available in booklet form. In his 1974 Neale Lecture, *The British Way in Warfare: a Reappraisal* (Cape, 75p, 24 pp.), Michael Howard's chief target is Sir Julian Corbett who was an eloquent exponent of the theory that from the sixteenth century onwards superior sea power and the favours of geography had enabled Britain to pursue a conscious strategy of limited liability. Michael Howard argues that continental and maritime strategies have in fact been complementary rather than alternatives. Economic pressure was at best a slow and clumsy instrument of policy and an increasingly blunt one against great continental land-based powers. Furthermore amphibious diversions, though often brilliant in conception, resulted in 'an almost unbroken record of expensive and humiliating failures' *vide* my review of Piers Mackesy's account of the Helder expedition of 1799 in this volume.

Though only half as long and more polemical than Howard's well-documented essay, Correlli Barnett's Spenser Wilkinson Memorial Lecture, *Strategy and Society* (Manchester University Press, 75p, 12 pp.) can also be strongly recommended. Barnett sees Wilkinson as one of the few British students of war (Major-General J.F.C. Fuller was another, and he might have added the late Alastair Buchan), to have understood the need for a 'total strategy' taking account of national economic and industrial resources as well as the more traditional components of 'strategy'. After a crisp historical survey the author contends that armed forces are today ever less capable of solving international problems, such as the oil crisis, and that the West in general and Britain in particular should reappraise their defence forces in the light of the Communists' skilful employment of 'total strategy'. In the few pages available Barnett can do little more than pose important questions, but he does so with characteristic verve.

Of several new books on the First World War, Norman Stone's *The Eastern Front: 1914-1917* (Hodder and Stoughton, £5.50, 348 pp.) is remarkable for its scholarship, originality and coruscating style. He contraverts the long-accepted view that Russia's collapse was due to industrial backwardness manifesting itself specifically in a chronic shell shortage. On the contrary he shows that Russia was actually experiencing a phase of rapid industrial growth which in many respects lasted until the beginning of 1917. Her munitions production was impressive but the results were frittered away by incompetent staff work and administration. The main cause of the collapse in 1917 was soaring inflation; this caused the peasants to withhold their produce from the cities and chaos resulted. Dr Stone is less impressive when dealing with military techniques and operations. His contemptuous attitude to virtually all the Russian generals and staff officers produces some blistering phrases but does not further our understanding of their problems. It is also a pity that after devoting excessive space to summarising the military operations on the Eastern Front in 1914-16, he stops abruptly on the brink of the revolution and does not describe the final military disintegration.

Guy Chapman's posthumously published autobiography *A Kind of Survivor* (Gollancz, £5, 288 pp.) should be mentioned in connection with the First World War because his experience on the Western Front remained an important influence for the rest of his life. 'To the years between 1914 and 1918', he writes, 'I owe everything of lasting value in my make-up. For any cost I paid in mental and physical vigour they gave me back a supreme fulfilment I should never otherwise have had.' He admits engagingly that he tended to judge men's characters by whether or not they had served at the front. By this criterion (Sergeant) R.H. Tawney is a hero in his eyes and W.H. Auden a dud. His own account of his experience, *A Passionate Prodigality,* remains among the best written and most penetrating of all the war memoirs. *A Kind of Survivor* is a splendid, zestful book about a delightful man.

In *Goughie* (Hart-Davis, Macgibbon, £8, 403 pp.) General Farrar-Hockley has written a very good biography of one of the last of the gentlemen warriors of the Victorian era. Only twice did General Sir Hubert Gough's career impinge on great national events: in March 1914 when he played a leading role in the Curragh incident; and precisely four years later when, as Commander of the Fifth Army, he was made the scapegoat for the German breakthrough. The author is illuminating on both these episodes, and for an extremely busy soldier the depth of his research is impressive. He excels in recreating the regimental atmosphere in the Edwardian era, and puts his own experience to good use in conveying the changing nature of the problems Gough had to deal with as he rose in the Army hierarchy.

The chief strength of Captain Eric Bush's *Gallipoli* (Allen and Unwin, £7.25, 334 pp.) is that he took part in the campaign as a very young midshipman. Thus, though he adds little to — and does not compete with — Rhodes James's more scholarly account, he does convey very vividly what it was like to be there. Nearly half his book is devoted to the initial naval operations with a very full account of the landings on 25 April 1915. As an eyewitness he has surely written the definitive verdict on why the Anzac landings on that day went fatally off course.

The seven collections of letters from the Great War, skilfully edited by Michael Moynihan in *A Place Called Armageddon* (David and Charles, £3.50, 200 pp.) were all written to convey day-to-day impressions to the writers' families and were certainly not intended for publication. This selection represents experience in France, Gallipoli and Mesopotamia and from members of all three services — or four, counting the Royal Marines. The letters are remarkably frank about such matters as living conditions and casualties, and they reveal widely differing attitudes to the war. This is a fascinating and sometimes moving volume.

Turning to the inter-war period, D.C. Watt's *Too Serious a Business* (Temple Smith, £3.50, 200 pp.) is based on the author's Lees-Knowles Lectures and suffers from excessive compression. He shows that, in contrast to pre-1914, the European military leaders in the 1930s would readily have accepted Clemenceau's maxim that 'war is too serious a business to be left to the generals'. Almost to a man they tended to be pessimistic about their country's chances in the coming war and to exaggerate their opponents' strength and preparedness. Maurice Cowling's *The Impact of Hitler: British Politics and Policy 1933-1940* (Cambridge University Press, £15, 561 pp.) takes the interesting line that in the 1930s foreign policy was for once the dominant issue in British politics; consequently Chamberlain's foreign policy must be viewed in the context of party politics. So far so good, but the author pursues this thesis so relentlessly and in such detail (with no less than 116 pages of references at the end), that events and personalities outside Britain hardly get a look in. This reviewer's reaction was that the book would have benefited from ruthless editorial pruning. Ritchie Ovendale has filled an important gap in historiography with his *'Appeasement' and the English Speaking World* (University of Wales Press, £9, 353 pp.). Though some of his conclusions are unnecessarily tentative while others do not seem to follow from his evidence, he has performed a useful task by thoroughly documenting the reactions of the Dominions and the United States to British foreign policy between 1937 and the outbreak of war. The late Sir John Wheeler-Bennett's *Knaves, Fools and Heroes* (Macmillan, £3.95, 218 pp.) suavely chronicles the author's acquaintance with some of the topmost people in Europe between the wars. There are illuminating and occasionally hilarious accounts of his meetings with such worthies as Trotsky, Seeckt, von Papen and the exiled Kaiser Wilhelm II at Doorn. There seems to have been a glut of knaves and fools but a paucity of heroes.

'The Politics and Strategy of the Second World War' is the title of a series currently being published by Davis-Poynter in which scholars reappraise controversial or neglected episodes for a serious but non-specialist readership. Robert Cecil, for example, has been remarkably successful in providing a concise analysis of the reasons for *Hitler's Decision to Invade Russia* (192 pp.). Charles Cruickshank, who has also recently published a well-researched history of *The German Occupation of the Channel Isles* (OUP, £6.50, 392 pp.), contributes to the series a very critical account of British errors in policy and execution in the Balkans and Crete in *Greece 1940-1941* (206 pp.). Brian Bond's *France and Belgium 1939-1940* (Davis-Poynter, £3.75, 206 pp.) focuses attention not so much on the German breakthrough as on the friction and misunderstandings which characterised Anglo-French-Belgian relations from before the outbreak of war to the debacle in May 1940. More specifically this study seeks to show that most historians of the campaign have misrepresented Belgium's political situation and under-rated her military achievement. P.M.H. Bell's *A Certain Eventuality* (Saxon House, £4.50, 344 pp.) takes up the story of Anglo-French relations roughly where the previous book stops — at

Dunkirk — and thoroughly analyses the break-up of the alliance in the summer of 1940. Arthur Marder highlights one of the more tragi-comic episodes in this break-up, namely the abortive Anglo-Free-French attempt to seize Dakar. This is the main subject of his *Operation Menace* (OUP, £7.50, 289 pp.), but for good measure he adds a long essay on the dismissal of Admiral Sir Dudley North from his command at Gibraltar (which was marginally linked to the failure at Dakar) and the interminable controversy that ensued. *In Vichy France: Old Guard and New Order 1940-44* (Barrie and Jenkins, £4.95, 399 pp.) Robert O. Paxton argues that Petain's Government, contrary to comforting myth, obtained for Frenchmen no better treatment than that accorded to fully occupied countries. The text of Marcel Ophuls' controversial film *The Sorrow and the Pity,* which subtly suggested the considerable extent of collaboration in Clermont-Ferrand and the present inhabitants' unwillingness to admit it, is now available as a Paladin paperback (£1, 194 pp.).

More than 500 letters of the secret wartime correspondence between *Roosevelt and Churchill* have been published with an extensive introduction and commentary by F.L. Lowenheim, H.D. Langley and M. Jones (Barrie and Jenkins, £10, 805 pp.). Informed glimpses of Churchill relaxing away from the blitz at Ditchley Park are given by its owner, Ronald Tree, in his interesting recollections *When the Moon was High* (Macmillan, £4.95, 216 pp.). Charles Ritchie, a colourful Canadian diplomat, provides a detached and highly individualistic description of London during the Second World War in *The Siren Years: Undiplomatic Diaries 1937-1945* (Cape, £6.50, 344 pp.).

In *The Road to 1945* (Cape, £6.50, 344 pp.), Paul Addison has made a major contribution to our understanding of British politics and society during the Second World War. His main thesis is that the great shift in political power which produced the landslide Labour victory in 1945 happened much earlier than was previously believed, in fact between 1940 and 1942. He also shows how Churchill's concentration on the role of war leader and grand strategist unwittingly weakened his party's position in domestic politics — which were far from dormant during the war. Dr Addison's scintillating prose and clear, crisp judgements reflect the admirable influence of his research supervisor, A.J.P. Taylor.

To conclude with four more general books — Jock Haswell's concise history of *The British Army* (Thames and Hudson, £4.50, 192 pp.) is essentially an illustrated introductory volume, accompanied by a workmanlike text which gallops through British military history from the Saxon fyrd to the present trouble in Ulster. Two recent symposia contain valuable essays on economic aspects of war. J.M. Winter (ed.), *War and*

Economic Development (CUP, £7.50, 295 pp.) consists of eleven essays ranging in time from war taxation in the early fourteenth century to the Beveridge Report in the Second World War. Those in between include four studies relating to economic aspects of the First World War and a reconsideration by Phyllis Deane of the controversial question of the relationship between war and industrialisation. Geoffrey Best and Andrew Wheatcroft have edited a slimmer volume containing eight essays under the catch-all title of *War, Economy and the Military Mind* (Croom Helm, £5.95, 136 pp.). All the essays are concerned with British and European history between 1815 and 1918 and all attempt to relate military affairs to wider political, social and economic considerations. The two essays which seemed most original to the reviewer were Richard Luckett's on pre-revolutionary army life as described in Russian literature, and Geoffrey Best's on some moral aspects of the debate on how war should be conducted between about 1870 and 1918. Finally, Richard Clutterbuck's *Living with Terrorism* (Faber and Faber, £3.50, 160 pp.) presents a concise *vade mecum* of contemporary terrorist movements with practical suggestions on how to deal with them — not least important in his view is the handling of the mass media. The author makes no secret of his own standpoint: most terrorist groups he believes to be Marxist or anarchist in inspiration with a negative attachment to violence and disruption as ends in themselves. He describes terrorism as a 'disease' which is unlikely to be 'cured' by the discovery that in political terms its activities are for the most part counterproductive.

CLAUSEWITZ AND THE AMERICANS: BERNARD BRODIE AND OTHERS ON WAR AND POLICY

Reginald C. Stuart

Bernard Brodie is the elder statesman of American strategic analysts. He has consistently stressed that military policy in the United States must be oriented toward a defensive, rather than an offensive mentality, because in the atomic age it is ludicrous to think in terms of victory over any adversary. In *War & Politics* he validates Peter Paret's point that Carl von Clausewitz has more to say to our century than he did to his own time. Brodie accepts as thesis, theme and near dogma the fabled Clausewitzian dictum that 'war is a mere continuation of policy by other means' and insists that American policy-makers will experience continual frustration unless they accept the logic of this advice.[1] Brodie extends the thrust of his earlier arguments on the need to find a viable place for force in international affairs under the atomic umbrella. He rejects deterministic interpretations of the causes of war and sees it as a conscious political act which must be intelligent.

Richard Barnet and John Donovan would disagree since they fall into the revisionist camp of scholars. Both analyse America's policy-making bureaucracy which has expanded and flourished in Cold War soil. Barnet is a conventional revisionist who finds a counter-revolutionary American socio-economic imperialism behind American policy and hence contemporary wars. Donovan accepts Barnet's analysis of the policy élite, which both see as ideologically homogeneous, but rejects economic determinism in favour of a self-defined world mission to rescue men from the clutches of communism to explain America's conflicts since 1945. Both authors see wars arising from the common assumption that implacable antagonism existed between the Soviets and the United States. Barnet finds this assumption fueled by a desire for markets and power, but Donovan believes it was self-delusion arising from the apparent historical lessons of the twentieth century as viewed from the United States. Brodie would find Donovan more acceptable than Barnet, but he would reject the argument that only wholesale internal change will prevent the United States from initiating further wars to protect her interests.[2]

Brodie believes that the ghastly spectacle of modern war has flowed from the failure of statesmen to relate means and ends, to realise that military action must have political purposes. Nuclear technology has created strategic circumstances in which general war seems increasingly less likely, and thus limited aims must replace total victory as diplomatic objectives. With Clausewitz as guide, though not commander, statesmen may avoid catastrophe. His insistence that political purpose must dominate military usage may be slightly misplaced. Herbert Butterfield pointed out some time ago that a crusade along ideological lines for total victory could be termed a war of policy by those waging it.[3] Brodie distinguishes between total and limited war by arguing that the latter is based on policy where the former is not. But 'policy' is an elastic term founded on perceptions of vital interests. Brodie knows how elastic those can be, but apparently fails to carry man's subjectivity and irrationality to definitions of policy, despite their applicability to any inderstanding of vital interests.

In Part I Brodie scans wars since 1914 in the light of Clausewitz's theories. He even ushers morality into the discussion, a theme upon which revisionists such as Barnet and Donovan have insisted. Brodie does not know quite how to juxtapose morality with strategy, but it is refreshing to see the issue raised by an establishment scholar. In the hands of some, such as Herman Kahn, with whom Brodie takes issue over American survival in a nuclear encounter, strategic studies ignored humane considerations, as the terms 'megadeath' and 'overkill' suggest. Modern statesmen have failed in Brodie's view because they ignored Clausewitzian lessons. Recent war, with all its attendant excess, can be blamed upon flawed individuals, not flawed man or flawed ideologies. Brodie skims along on this premise, skirting oversimplification by compression and arguing too much to his thesis. With World War II he stumbles over the old myth that the Americans were less 'political' than the British. He accepts unconditional surrender as a rational Allied goal, even though it was a product of the old American tradition of a policy of victory which happened to suit the circumstances. Brodie also dismisses an important historiographical controversy when he sweeps aside the revisionist arguments that America dropped the atomic bomb on Japan to impress the Russians. Brodie has a duty to address the issue since it raised the moral questions about the use of such force which Brodie himself believes deserve a place in strategic analysis.

Brodie is especially effective with the limited-war concepts of the 1950s. Those familiar with the literature and Brodie's other work will find little new here. But it is analysed with such clarity, force and insight as to constitute mandatory reading for any student of strategy. American frustration began to build up with Korea because of a national conviction that war was a heretical contradiction of nature which demanded total victory. Yet the Truman administration deliberately fought a restricted conflict in Korea and this led to the development of flexible strategic theories which discredited the doctrine of massive retaliation. America did not win the Korean war, and a Senate committee thus observed: 'We believe that a policy of victory must be announced to the American people to restore unity and confidence. It is too much to expect that our people will accept a limited war.' This was the real challenge to American strategy taken up by Brodie and others, such as Robert Osgood and Henry Kissinger.[4] American leaders faced the problem of public acceptance of such doctrines, however, and Vietnam demonstrated the difficulties encountered by a democratic society waging limited war. Osgood, pointing to the eighteenth century, suggested that war could be restrained by limiting aims. Brodie accepts this, but realises that it is only part of the answer. Civil supremacy is also vital, and he believes that the military has gained too much influence over policy formation.

Barnet and Donovan agree, but to them the question of who is in command makes little difference, since all policy élites have displayed militancy, despite their dominantly civilian composition. Barnet in particular believes that American leaders have understood the link between war and policy only too well. While manipulating public opinion, they have used martial violence to protect America's economic empire. Brodie, Barnet and Donovan have all found that Vietnam was convincing proof of their particular theses. Clearly, history does not speak for itself. Withal, the American people found limited war as baffling in Vietnam as they had in Korea, an important factor in the American decision to disengage.[5]

Brodie should have probed deeper into the past. He would have found that limited war is not new to the American experience. Most of the Founding Fathers saw war as a limited instrument of policy. Brodie sees the Quasi-War with France (1797-1801) as merely undeclared, but President John Adams actually requested and received from Congress a careful definition of the conflict. The War of 1812 had limited aims, as did the Mexican War (1846-8).[6] While crusading rhetoric punctuated these early wars, this cannot obscure the limited-war mentality of the policy-makers. Brodie also dismissed previous American guerrilla and counter-guerrilla experience found in the War for Independence, the Civil War and the Indian Wars.

On the other hand, Brodie finds the twentieth century an enormous watershed for the development of American doctrines. Policy-makers absorbed the 'lessons' of history and developed the 'Munich mentality', which produced a post-1945 determination to resist aggression in order to avert political and social disaster.[7] This led to the Cold War and

Vietnam just as surely as World War I shaped the paradigm in which the Munich 'surrender' seemed a viable policy option. This underscores one of Brodie's primary points — statesmen must select lessons from history. No advice, not even from Clausewitz, can be followed slavishly. But the apparent lessons of the past, a move away from static conceptions of massive retaliation in the 1950s, the rise of military technocracy and systems analysis under Robert McNamara, traditional American self-confidence at problem solving, the personality defects of American leaders, and their failure to appreciate Clausewitz all combined to produce the quagmire of Vietnam. Given time, the American people recoiled. The giant United States was bound like Gulliver by many fine threads which collectively rendered it helpless. Brodie's analysis of the Vietnam dilemma is one of the best in print.

Part II of *War & Politics* is a series of variations on the central theme. Brodie examines changing attitudes toward war and rejects psychological-biological imperatives, yet still manages to view man's penchant for conflict as an acquired trait. The tone is less urgent here because we abandon the United States for the larger context of western civilisation. Brodie fails to clarify the relevance of this discussion. He may also be off the mark when he suggests that resort to war may not be as common in the future. He has strong support here, from Russell Weigley, Louis J. Halle, and Merlo Pusey, and is probably correct in terms of atomic warfare.[8] But the current balance cannot be mistaken for peace and all sides do not share the same assumptions and fears. Butterfield's point that a crusade can be a state policy, technological developments which may upset the present stasis, nuclear proliferation, rising military budgets in Third World countries, and the cosmetic quality of *detente* are all disturbing disclaimers.

Brodie has no theory of his own about causes of war, save to stress 'selective inattention' and reiterate man's irrationality. He rightly rejects all pat theories. Stupidity, not malice or 'economic original sin' explains modern wars. Any understanding of causation must be broad, eclectic and rooted in historical circumstances. He suggests, as he did before in *Strategy in the Missile Age,* that men may have more success by abandoning efforts to eliminate war and concentrating instead upon preventing each conflict as it threatens. This supports other scholars who have suggested that war may have a larger place in man's affairs than liberal humanists have been willing to admit.[9]

When analysing vital interests, Brodie points out that as American power has expanded, the perception of vital interests has been correspondingly elastic. With global commitments and the means to intervene, Americans have found themselves in global entanglements.

A dedication to world leadership, with its concomitant need for unblemished prestige, has robbed leaders of flexibility. Brodie argues that the United States cannot disregard its world role, and this is why Clausewitz is of such importance. Barnet would not agree, but other critics of current policy, such as Arthur Schlesinger, Jr., Pusey and Jacob Javits have been more concerned about the democratic control of the war power than with the fundamental demands of the revisionists. All except Barnet advocate the judicious use of force. But Brodie would dismiss him as a scandal monger and probably naive as well since Brodie believes that the international world is a Darwinian jungle. Only the wary and prepared can survive. America must apply force judiciously, therefore, since simple restraint is insufficient to limit war. Survival depends upon a willingness to use force, even though the primary utility of America's atomic hardware lies in its non-use.[10]

Brodie closes with the nuclear problem, but spends little time on deterrent theories. He conventionally proclaims the lunacy of atomic war and exhorts statesmen to develop fresh diplomatic methods. Above all, they must keep Clausewitz in mind and control the military, although militant, uninformed and scheming civilians have done easily as much damage as headstrong and unrestrained generals.[11] Soldiers have their uses, but Brodie finds them committed to efficiency and victory for their own sakes — both unremarkable points. After all, it is the soldier's job to fight and win efficiently. But if such revisionists as Barnet and Donovan are correct about bureaucratic homogeneity in America, and the psychologists and biologists are correct about human aggression, Clausewitz may make little difference and civilian control effect few changes. Brodie is so intent upon Clausewitz that he does not consider the problem of the power élite which has captured the attention of critics from C. Wright Mills onwards.

The major shortcoming of this book is, therefore, its restricted focus, incredible as that may seem given Brodie's vast knowledge and his intellectual peregrinations. He has not questioned his own assumptions seriously enough and he has failed to penetrate the American past as thoroughly as he might. He also fails to appreciate that 'policy' can be irrational as well as rational. Although the premises of containment were perhaps wrong, statesmen tried to relate means and ends. In retrospect, it is hard to see how adherence to Clausewitzian principles would have made much difference for Cold War diplomats, given their assumptions and the climate of opinion in post-war America.

The major strengths of this book are its clarity, its compression, its erudition and its penetrating analysis of American military policy since World War II. Although there is no formal bibliography, the footnotes constitute an excellent list of sources for each chapter. *War & Politics* is clearly the best work of its kind. Brodie has brought Clausewitz to the American context with authority. Along with other efforts to analyse America's wars in the twentieth century, he has made a major contribution to our understanding of war and policy. One can only hope that he will continue to produce work of this calibre.

Notes

1. Bernard Brodie, *War & Politics* (New York: The Macmillan Company, 1973). Brodie's writings are extensive. For his work in context see Russell F. Weigley, *The American Way of War: A History of United States Military Strategy and Policy* (New York: The Macmillan Company, 1973), Chaps. xvii-xviii. Brodie's earlier works include *Sea Power in the Machine Age* (Princeton: Princeton University Press, 1941): Brodie (ed.), *The Absolute Weapon: Atomic Power and World Order* (New York: Harcourt Brace, 1946); and *Strategy in the Missile Age* (Princeton: Princeton University Press, 1959). Peter Paret, 'Clausewitz and the Nineteenth Century', in Michael Howard (ed.), *The Theory and Practice of War* (London: Cassell & Co., 1965), p.39.
2. Richard J. Barnet, *Roots of War: The Men and Institutions behind U.S. Foreign Policy* (New York: Atheneum, 1972), pp.3-8; John C. Donovan, *The Cold Warriors: A Policy-Making Elite* (Lexington: D.C. Heath, 1974), pp.259-85. In his last sentence, Donovan stresses 'the enduring reality of human arrogance and perversity', ibid., p.285. The revisionists are diverse and a recent discussion is in Warren Kimball, 'The Cold War Warmed Over', *American Historical Review*, LXXIX (1974), 1119-1136. Other useful studies pertinent to this topic are Merlo J. Pusey, *The Way We Go To War* (Boston: Houghton Mifflin, 1971); Jacob Javits, *Who Makes War: The President versus Congress* (New York: William Morrow & Company, 1973); and Arthur Schlesinger, Jr., *The Imperial Presidency* (New York: Atlantic Monthly, 1973).
3. Herbert Butterfield, *Christianity, Diplomacy, and War* (New York: Abingdon-Cokesbury, 1953), pp.28-30, 116.
4. Senate committee cited by Brodie, *War & Politics*, p.88. Robert Endicott Osgood, *Limited War: The Challenge to American Strategy* (Chicago: University of Chicago Press, 1957). Limited war in the eighteenth century was more complex than the stress on limited aims might imply. For good analyses see Hans Speier, 'Militarism in the Eighteenth Century', in Speier, *Social Order and the Risks of War* (Cambridge, Mass.; Harvard University Press, 1969), pp.230-52; John U. Nef, *War and Human Progress: An Essay on the Rise of Industrial Civilization* (New York: W.W. Norton, 1963), pp.182-267; Butterfield, *Christianity*, pp.89-95.
5. Barnet, *Roots of War*, p.283. A representative of the American Legion was interviewed on television at the time of the final withdrawal from Vietnam by American forces. He emphasised with some bitterness that next time the United States must not fight a so-called war of policy, but must fight to win. See also Weigley, *American Way of War*, pp.464, 466-7.
6. Pusey, *Way We Go To War*, pp.49-53. On the Mexican War see Charles A. Lofgren, 'Force and Diplomacy, 1846-1848', *Military Affairs*, XXXI (Summer, 1967), pp.57-65. See also Maurice Matloff, 'The American Approach to War, 1919-1945', in Howard, *Theory and Practice*, pp.217-9. Elements of the eighteenth-century's limited-war mentality survived in unlikely places. See

Grady McWhiney, 'Jefferson Davis and the Art of War', *Civil War History*, XXI (1975), 101-112. Walter Millis, *Arms and Men: A Study of American Military History* (New York: G.P. Putnams, 1956), pp.322-5, sees World War I as the beginning of a total-war mentality.

7. Donovan, *Cold Warriors*, pp.270-74. See also Ernest R. May, *'Lessons' of the Past: The Use and Misuse of History in American Foreign Policy* (New York: Oxford University Press, 1973), Part One.

8. Brodie, *War & Politics*, p.274. See also Pusey, *Way We Go To War*, p.156; Weigley, *American Way of War*, p.477; Louis J. Halle, 'Does War Have A Future?', *Foreign Affairs*, LII (October, 1973), 20-30. Barnet, *Roots of War*, p.237, argues that the powerful international corporations will likely prevent general war in the future since they want to exploit the world's resources peacefully. Martin Edmonds, 'The Horizons of War: Problems of Projections', in Roger A. Beaumont and Martin Edmonds (eds.), *War in the Next Decade* (Lexington: University Press of Kentucky, 1974), pp.1-20, suggests that internal struggles are highly probable in the near future. Stephen Garrett, 'Prospects of Peace or War', *Virginia Quarterly Review*, LII (1976), 24-40, notes that Istnan Kende has counted 97 non-declared civil and international wars from 1945 to 1969. He is pessimistic about improvement.

9. Arthur N. Gilbert, 'Philosophical Pessimism and the Study of War', *Virginia Quarterly Review*, LI (1975), 347-359, suggests that scholars may be doing themselves a disservice by assuming that all wars are evil and that the institution must be exorcised. See also Roger Beaumont, 'Polemology: Promises and a Problem', in Beaumont and Edmonds, *War*, pp.202-10. J. Glenn Gray, *The Warriors: Reflections on Men in Battle* (New York: Harcourt Brace, 1959), is an important, but rarely cited work which discusses war's attractions for men in chapter ii.

10. Pusey, *Way We Go To War*, p.151, agrees. But Barnet, *Roots of War*, p.33, suggests the revisionist view that the existence of weaponry creates pressures for its use.

11. Brodie, *War & Politics*, p.478. Barnet argues that since all share common beliefs it does not matter who is in charge. The institutional dominance of American policy is explored in Keith L. Nelson, 'The "Warfare State": History of a Concept', *Pacific Historical Review*, XL (1971), 127-143.

172

REVIEWS

THE STRATEGY OF OVERTHROW 1798-1799. *Piers Mackesy.*
Longman, 1975, £7.50, 340 pp.

Piers Mackesy is a thorough military historian who prefers to
concentrate on a short well-defined period rather than range over a vast
panorama. He quotes with approval the maxim of the French naval
historian Admiral Castex – *peu de surface, beaucoup de profondeur* –
and illustrates it in this excellent volume.

This is a chronicle of great diplomatic conceptions and blighted
military plans. In 1799 the Second Coalition evolved an ambitious
strategic plan designed to overthrow the French government and restore
peace to Europe. Beyond that there was no agreement, and ample scope
for discord, among the potential allies – Britain, Austria, Russia and
more doubtfully Prussia. The main impetus was supplied by the British
Cabinet, and within the Cabinet by the Foreign Secretary, Lord
Grenville. Grenville's great scheme was for a combined Austrian and
Russian force to expel the French from Italy and Switzerland and to
invade France from the latter. Meanwhile an Anglo-Russian
expeditionary force would land in Holland and thrust forward into
Belgium with the ultimate aim of reaching Paris. The author permits
himself an occasional analogy with the Second World War and there is
indeed a good one between Grenville's assumption that the Dutch were
only waiting for an Allied gesture as a signal to rise up and expel the
French, and de Gaulle's belief in 1940 that the Dakar garrison would
immediately rally to his side when his appeal was seen to be backed by
overwhelming force.

The outcome in 1799 was almost an unmitigated failure. British gold
sufficed to lure a raggle-taggle Russian contingent into the North Sea,
but Austria had already defaulted on repaying her debts and her
diplomacy remained wayward and unpredictable. Prussia, almost as
much at odds with Austria as with France, refused to be drawn in. Thus
in the event the Austrians withdrew their Army from Switzerland
leaving Korsakov's Russians to be badly mauled by Massena. On the
northern flank there were long delays while troops and transports were
collected and alternative landing plans discussed. Ironically the initial
British commander, Abercromby, decided to land at the Helder which
had not been considered by the Cabinet. After a hazardous landing the

improvised British contingent fought reasonably well but the Russians turned out to be a badly-led rabble. The advance was checked after only a few miles and the Duke of York was probably fortunate to be allowed to capitulate and re-embark.

So much for the bare outline of events. Mr Mackesy is clearly the master of all accessible material and skilfully extracts the telling phrase or anecdote. Minor digressions from the main narrative, such as the delays and perils faced by Tom Grenville in trying to reach Berlin on a diplomatic mission, tell us a great deal about the practical difficulties of co-ordinating a coalition strategy at that time. The author's microscopic concern for relevant detail is also well displayed in such matters as the number and quality of troops in each regiment and the advantages and disadvantages of each of the mooted landing places in Holland. The main actors, including Pitt, Grenville, the Duke of York, Abercromby, Henry and David Dundas are all vividly characterised. Perhaps most impressive of all is the author's concern to understand and be fair to his characters, however badly they appear to have failed. On several occasions, after weighing up all the evidence, Mr Mackesy takes a more moderate view of the decisions made by the Duke of York, Abercromby and others than previous historians of the campaign such as Sir John Fortescue. As he remarks in the preface: 'who is victorious in the chronicles of wasted time? In the end the victors go under with the vanquished, for life has no victors.' Readers of this splendid volume will look forward to the promised sequel in which we shall see Britain's strategy 'recast to meet realities and achieve a modest success, the forerunner of more spectacular ones'.

Brian Bond

A MILITARY HISTORY OF GERMANY FROM THE EIGHTEENTH CENTURY TO THE PRESENT DAY. *Martin Kitchen,* Weidenfeld and Nicolson, 1975, £5.50, 384 pp.

Dr Kitchen has produced a somewhat uneven and disappointing account of the military history of Germany. One of its major themes — the deepening divisions within German society as the nineteenth century progressed, with the ruling Junker élite and its 'militaristic' traditions entrenched in the army — has already been thoroughly researched and analysed by historians and Dr Kitchen's contribution, both on this and on the German army during the Hitler régime, adds little to our knowledge of the subject. To be fair, his chapter on the Wilhelmine Empire, a subject he has already made an area of special study, is much more interesting and mature than the rest of the book. The last chapter, on the period after 1945, in which he strives, on the basis of flimsy evidence, to show that the Bundeswehr is but the old Prussian army, with its entrenched élites, in disguise, is best passed over in silence.

However, although this book, which contains no footnotes, will be of little value to the professional historian, it can be recommended to the general reader as a background survey.

M.L. Dockrill

A HISTORY OF RUSSIAN AND SOVIET SEA POWER. *Donald W. Mitchell,* André Deutsch, 1974, £6.50, 657 pp.

The author leads us through a complete history of Russian sea power, beginning with the Varangians and taking us up to the present day. However, he wisely moves on to Peter the Great's naval activities on page 16 of his narrative, concentrating suitably on Peter the Great as the father of the Russian Navy. Because of their concentration on a land army, the Russians relied heavily in their early history on British, and even more on Dutch, developments in naval techniques. Indeed, many British sailors worked for the Russians during and after the time of Peter the Great. Men like Admirals Saunders and Greig had distinguished careers in the Russian Navy. On balance though, the Dutch seem to have contributed more in the long run. I am reliably informed by a lexicographer that there are many more words from Dutch than from English in Russian nautical terminology.

Mr Mitchell takes us carefully through the centuries, devoting most emphasis to Russian naval wars with the Turks, the Swedes, the French in the Napoleonic wars and of course in the Crimean war. In doing so with considerable detail and accuracy, the author gives western readers an idea of the extent to which Russian naval history has been neglected. Ignorance has in the past led to an attitude of supercilious disdain for Russian achievements. Who in the west, for instance, could think of the Russian equivalent for the battle of Trafalgar on the Eastern front in the Napoleonic wars? The answer is the battle of Athos in 1807. The greatest Russian naval victory of all time, the battle of Chesma in 1770 against the Turks, is virtually unknown outside the annals of Russian and Turkish history.

The author makes some interesting points that are original. He points out, for instance, that the Tsarist régime built up naval stocks in the last third of the nineteenth century, but consistently neglected to ensure a highly qualified personnel in order to run the ships. The naval authorities also left the sailors idle in harbours instead of sending them out on exercises. This is perhaps one of the reasons for the frustration and subsequent revolutionary activity on the part of the Russian sailors. On the subject of the Revolution itself, Mr Mitchell has little that is novel to say, except to point out that when the infant Soviet Union withdrew from the Baltic states, one of its greatest naval triumphs, though in defeat, was the withdrawal of its considerable Baltic fleet to Leningrad. This meant that the early Soviet navy was not quite so weak as it might have been otherwise. Indeed, the lighter vessels were used to brilliant effect in river battles on the inland waterways of Russia during the Civil War. It is often forgotten that the Caspian was a British-dominated inland sea in 1918.

There are interesting sections on Russian naval exploration, particularly in the eighteenth century. Again, names of important Russian discoverers are virtually unknown outside Russia, although they made many significant discoveries, particularly in the Antarctic (Bellingshausen being the most permanent name). There are one or two errors in these sections. On page 43 Behring is referred to as a Russian, though of course he was a Dane. On page 364 mention is made of the Arctic Russian river deltas as outlets for export to other countries as from 1912. Mr Mitchell does not mention, or has not noted, the considerable achievements of Captain Wiggins at the end of the nineteenth century in this field.

This history takes us right up to the present day. Many other writers have considered post-war Soviet naval strategy, and Mr Mitchell makes no significant contribution in these chapters. However, his naval history of World War II is very useful and is given in full detail. On the subject of the Second World War he comes to the same conclusion as with regard to the last third of the nineteenth century, i.e. that ships were produced very rapidly but the trained personnel to put them to good use was not created at the same time. As a result, Russia's World War II naval record was poorer than in many of her previous conflicts.

This book is a mine of useful information on Russian naval history, and fills a considerable gap in the area, particularly with regard to earlier periods. There is a series of interesting maps, illustrations, and a long bibliography. There is also a very thorough index divided into three sections, including an index relating to ships alone.

Roger Pethybridge

176

THE GREAT WAR AND MODERN MEMORY. *Paul Fussell,* OUP,
1975, £6.50, 363 pp.

The author of this highly original and stimulating study is an American
professor of English. His detachment from British cultural assumptions
and his literary approach are conducive to insights which, on balance,
outweigh the defects that stem mainly from his inadequate knowledge
of history. Professor Fussell's simple but profoundly significant starting
point is that the traumatic experience of the Great War was transmitted
in Britain by a generation which brought to it a distinctive outlook,
culture and, above all, language. Intensive educational development had
produced by 1914 a highly literate society with the consequence that
not only officers, but also many of the soldiers, were familiar with the
language and imagery of the Bible, Shakespeare, Milton, Bunyan and,
not least influential, the *Oxford Book of English Verse.* Thus a central
chapter is entitled 'Oh What a Literary War', and at one point the
author exclaims 'Sometimes it is really hard to shake off the conviction
that this war has been written by someone.'

However from another point of view the inflated language (or 'high
diction') of the Augustan era (by which a friend is always 'a comrade',
the dead are 'the fallen', etc.) was ill-suited to describe the horrors and
sordid reality of the Western Front. Indeed as Michael Howard remarks
(Times Literary Supplement, 5 December 1975), 'The Edwardians
brought to the war a starry-eyed vision in which the horrors were seen
through a golden mist.' This gulf between language and reality created
tensions and ironies which not only permeated the literature of the day
but also, as Professor Fussell skilfully demonstrates, continue to this
day to influence our attitude to the war.

Another source of tension, common to all the belligerents, was the
unbridgeable gulf between the Front (i.e. the men who actually
experienced trench warfare) and the Rear (i.e. rear echelons, the staff
and civilians). Guy Chapman's posthumously published memoirs, *A Kind
of Survivor* (Gollancz, 1975), are a moving illustration of how the front-
rear dichotomy could provide the basic criterion in human relationships
for the whole of a man's life.

Professor Fussell excels in analysing the symbolism of the pastoral
tradition applied to the war with its emphasis on poppies and roses,
shepherds, nightingales and larks. The author's literary range is wide
and intensive but he surprisingly omits Isaac Rosenberg's poem
'Returning we hear larks' which precisely illustrates his theme of the
ironic counterpoint of security and danger, beauty and squalor.

There is a brilliant section on what the author calls the 'homo-erotic' tradition which flourished before the war in the works of Gerard Manley Hopkins, E.M. Forster, and, most importantly for the later war poets, A.E. Housman. Housman's rather morbid emphasis on the early deaths of his 'Shropshire lads' assumed a new and more tragic significance for the young officers who had read him and then helplessly witnessed their own fair-haired lads dying horribly in droves. Wilfred Owen was himself a Shropshire lad, and his own near-obsession with homo-eroticism is well brought out. Professor Fussell also excels in exploring some of the methods by which various writers came to terms with the problems of poetic diction and an uncomprehending public by employing the devices of irony, euphemism, understatement (though here he surely underestimates the influence of the Public School ethos) and theatricality. In contrast to his sympathetic handling of Wilfred Owen, Blunden, Sassoon and Graves, Professor Fussell is irritatingly obtuse in his comments on David Jones's *In Parenthesis*. Surprisingly he fails to grasp that, whatever its flaws, this poem comes closest to providing the answer to what he rightly sees to be a crucial problem; namely how to place the unique experience of the Great War in a wider historical context. David Jones by making an imaginative leap into the distant past shows that what he terms 'the discipline of the wars' has been continuous. If the experience of the Great War is still 'contemporary', a hundred or a thousand years hence it too will merge with a historical tradition.

Professor Fussell's unimpressive treatment of David Jones may be due in part to his limitations as a historian as distinct from a literary critic. Many of his historical errors are comparatively trivial: for example, in the first line of the book his calculations are a month out; his account of the causes of the war are naively inadequate; he is confused and confusing as to which was the first Allied defeat in 1915; and he is wrong as to the date of the first use of tanks. More seriously, by ignoring recent military history, particularly the American Civil War, he exaggerates the novelty and uniqueness of the siege conditions of trench warfare on the Western Front.

Finally, in tracing the influence of the Great War and its myths on present day writers the author, while making several highly perceptive and persuasive analogies (especially in discussing Heller's *Catch 22)*, also makes some comparisons which to this reviewer seem strained, far-fetched or irrelevant. In particular I share Michael Howard's opinion, in the review referred to earlier, that Professor Fussell is in error in believing that only with the present freedom to use obscenities can the horrible reality of the Great War be fully described. After all the pastoral idiom and the high diction prevalent in 1914 did not prevent some of the authors quoted extensively and others only mentioned in passing (such as Guy Chapman and Frederic Manning) from conveying not only the war's beastliness but also the pity, terror, compassion and dignity in English that was both elegant and undefiled.

Brian Bond

THE BRITISH CAMPAIGN IN IRELAND, 1919-1921: THE DEVELOPMENT OF POLITICAL AND MILITARY POLICIES. *Charles Townshend,* OUP, 1975, £8.50, xiv + 242 pp.

A TERRIBLE BEAUTY IS BORN: THE IRISH TROUBLES, 1912-1922. *Ulick O'Connor,* Hamish Hamilton, 1975, £4.95, ix + 181 pp.

In times when the wherewithal for research is increasingly hard to come by, it is interesting to find two books which, in their very different ways, provide a justification for spending public money on historical scholarhip. Dr Townshend's study of the British campaign in Ireland, 1919-21, is based on his doctoral thesis and, like the thesis, is a thoroughly researched and balanced account of the 'troubles'. As an Oxford Historical Monograph it is unlikely (as Dr C.C. O'Brien remarked once) to 'make the rafters ring in Roscommon', though it is a very readable and at times wryly humorous piece of work. But it does give an accurate and dispassionate account of a sorry episode in Anglo-Irish relations. The picture that Dr Townshend paints is one of confusion and muddle in British military and political policy, with a Cabinet, hard-pressed by a plethora of post-war problems, choosing to 'apply military force without reference to military logic' – or, in layman terms, asking its soldiers to achieve the impossible.

Mr O'Connor's approach is completely different. He is a biographer, with good books to his credit; but he simply is not able to ask, and answer, historical questions. He does not analyse, he preaches. Thus, in his version, Ireland was a country 'paralysed by centuries of oppression', getting another taste of typical British military frightfulness; whereas Dr Townshend, while not denying the brutality and irresponsibility of the British reaction to IRA terror, demonstrates beyond cavil that the Crown forces were 'placed in a false position, and were never controlled by a definite and realistic policy'. Again, Dr Townshend concludes that the terrorism practised by the Crown forces was 'significant out of all

179

proportion to its size'; but to Mr O'Connor the 'policy' was one of 'scorched earth'.

Dr Townshend lists an impressive array of source material. He has used official material in the Public Record Office, and some interesting private collections, such as the papers of Sir Hugh Jeudwine and Major A.E. Percival. Mr O'Connor has contented himself with secondary works, but he has also interviewed former members of the IRA who participated in the events of 1919-21. These interviews have yielded some interesting information on the way in which Michael Collins's agents infiltrated the enemy; and they convey (perhaps unconsciously) the ruthlessness of Collins's men. But most of the book is merely a rehash, concocted from printed works, and since Mr O'Connor does not use footnote references, it is impossible to tell when he is using a particular source, and when he is simply writing off the top of his head. It would be unfair to dismiss Mr O'Connor's book altogether. There is an interesting section on the Easter Rising of 1916, where the author brings out the romantic and theatrical nature of the episode.

Dr Townshend's book will stand the test of time. I doubt if he will need to worry about the revisions which the release of new official papers in the year 2022 may necessitate; but more unfortunate is his choice not to extend his thesis to deal with events in the north of Ireland in the years 1919-21. Here the Crown forces were faced with not only a tricky political situation, with guerrilla warfare and urban terrorism, but with riot control thrown in for good measure. A complete history of the British campaign cannot be said to have been written until these aspects of the subject have been investigated with the same energy and thoroughness that Dr Townshend devotes to affairs in the south. Mr O'Connor, for his part, also steers clear of the IRA's campaign in Ulster in these years, but perhaps that is just as well.

Dr Townshend's study of the British campaign in southern Ireland is, therefore, a kind of antidote to Mr O'Connor's hurried and inaccurate book. It proves that time spent on honest, professional, painstaking historical research is absolutely necessary if historical myth-making such as Mr O'Connor's is not to win the day. And yet I am haunted by the reflection that, after all, Mr O'Connor's preaching may indeed make the rafters ring in Roscommon. But that will not be Dr Townshend's fault.

D.G. Boyce

TOO SERIOUS A BUSINESS. *D. C. Watt,* Temple Smith, 1975, £3.50, 200 pp.

Professor Watt sets out to chart the geography of the attitudes of the military élites of the four great powers left in Europe after 1918 – with occasional references to the role played by their equivalent in Soviet Russia. As Ben Jonson said of Bacon: 'the fear of every man that heard him was lest he should make an end', and these all too brief lectures provide a synthesis of a vast mass of documents scattered across many archives, and of books in several languages, which will be of great value to all students of modern European history.

The argument that the years since 1914 witnessed the unravelling of European society in a prolonged civil strife, both in peace and war, is not new; but to pin part of the responsibility on the General Staffs for their failure to sustain the role of guardians of the true order – the *pays réelle* – is. While the transnational society of the 1900s, with its common social and political links, its common culture, and its effective military balance, acquired an irresistible nostalgia during the 1920s, the military in each country succumbed to the attacks of disarmers, populists or League of Nations men, becoming alienated minorities, sharply divided into *nursoldaten,* 'politicians', or patriots – usually of crypto-Fascist tendencies. None of the General Staffs was able fully to cope with the advanced technology of the 1930s, although the Germans, in developing *blitzkrieg,* the British the radar-fighter screen, and the Japanese the aircraft carrier, ensured the greatest measure of success when war broke out. As a beleaguered minority, serving frequently unstable governments, whose basis of popular support differed profoundly from that before 1914, increasingly pessimistic about the impact of the coming war, mistrustful still of the European left and the new populist right, the General Staffs failed to inculcate in any country a unified military strategy. In Germany, some opposed Hitler and were subordinated to his will (with exceptions like Canaris and Oster who helped stir Britain into activity in 1939); in Italy and France, morale deteriorated; in Russia the High Command, having tried to do its duty, was ruthlessly purged; and in Britain it was ground down in pursuit of financial rather than military requirements.

It is a depressing story, livened only by splendid aberrations, such as the plans of the Canadian Colonel 'Buster' Brown, for invasion of the United States in the late 1920s, and Mussolini's attempt, in 1939, to order a head count of aircraft, in order to establish the actual size of the Italian airforce. The interweaving of grand strategy, the social and political behaviour of the military élites, and the course of events leading to war is admirably done. In the end, it seems, the

General Staffs were unable to act otherwise because they had no recourse: lacking the old dual role, in domestic as well as foreign affairs, the socio-political leverage of the late nineteenth century, they could only have appealed to the *pays réelle* — as the German High Command had in 1918, as the French army tried after Indochina and Algeria, as the Armed Forces Movement was to do in Portugal in 1974. Irresolute support for and disengagement without conviction from civilian régimes looking for mass support led equally to Vichy or Nuremburg. In Britain, according to Professor Watt, the General Staff came nearest to success; yet even there, in 1937-8, they came close to abdicating their functions to the requirements of a masterful Prime Minister and a dominant Treasury.

R.K. Middlemas

'APPEASEMENT' AND THE ENGLISH SPEAKING WORLD. BRITAIN, THE UNITED STATES, THE DOMINIONS, AND THE POLICY OF 'APPEASEMENT', 1937-1939. *R. Ovendale,* University of Wales Press, 1975, £9.00, 353 pp.

BRITISH PUBLIC OPINION AND THE ABYSSINIAN WAR 1935-6. *D. Waley,* Maurice Temple Smith in association with the London School of Economics and Political Science, 1975, £6.00, 176 pp.

Noting the contradictory claims made by contemporaries as to the influence of the Dominions and the USA on the British government's support for 'appeasement', and the silence, until recently, of historians on this aspect of British diplomacy, Dr Ovendale has rightly perceived the need for a book which will settle the conflict of opinion and fill an historiographical gap. Short though his time-span is — from the Imperial Conference of 1937 to the entry of the Dominions into the war in September 1939 — he has unearthed an impressive mass of evidence to support the view that the opinions of English-speaking democracies were constantly being referred to by British policy-makers, all of whom valued their support but also appreciated the limits to their willingness to be associated with British initiatives of any kind. Certain Dominions and Foreign Office files have unfortunately been destroyed, but within the existing British archives, the press, and printed sources from America and the Dominions, there can be few such references left uncovered. The material presented is thus very useful, both as a corrective to earlier histories which ignored it, and as an amplification of D.C. Watt's work and K. Middlemas's *Diplomacy of Illusion,* (London, 1972).

In assessing the effects of such considerations on British policy decisions, Dr Ovendale stresses an 'important' distinction which he feels should be made between Dominion 'influence' and 'responsibility' This might have been a useful starting point, but the distinction is neither clearly made (p.8), nor strictly adhered to. He rejects Watt's view that the Dominions' determination in 1937 to keep out of Europe was 'decisive' in prompting Chamberlain to proceed with appeasement; although all but New Zealand favoured the policy, they 'were not responsible for it: dominion opinion only confirmed Chamberlain on a course of action on which he had already decided'. In later chapters dealing with the Czech crisis and Munich, fear of Commonwealth dissolution is alternatively 'a factor' and 'a considerable factor' in British policy. We learn that in March 1938, when the idea of a guarantee to Czechoslovakia was rejected, 'Britain was limited by the attitude of the dominions. There was no question of British policy being dictated by the dominions: their opinion was rather one factor that had to be considered. In this instance it was, perhaps, a major factor.' When it came to September 1938, 'Chamberlain saw the reluctance of the dominions to fight, and the consequent break-up of the commonwealth, as decisive'. Such judgements, while creating the firm impression that Dominion or American influence was a reality which fluctuated, go insufficiently far towards explaining either what 'responsibility' involves or why Dominion views sometimes carried more or less weight.

The assessment of 'influence' might have been more finely drawn and carried greater conviction if the chronological and documentary perspectives had been wider. It is inadequate to discount Dominion or American influence upon Chamberlain's early commitment to appeasement — or that of any other Cabinet minister — on the basis of a document such as his foreign policy memorandum of 2 April 1937. There is no sense in this book that policy-makers' memories were lengthy. British statesmen were well aware of the Dominions' long struggle to emancipate themselves from British control in the sphere of foreign and defence policy, and naturally calculated accordingly. In the Dominions, ignorance of European affairs pales in significance when compared with suspicion of British intentions, as Smuts' recollection of Chanak at the moment of the guarantee to Poland shows. More particularly, one may wonder whether Chamberlain's adoption of appeasement, and Dominion influence between 1937 and 1939, can be fully understood without scrutinising the nature of his imperial sentiments. Attitudes long in formation — the 'unspoken assumptions' — deserve more consideration than they receive here, for 'influence' is no more always immediate, any more than 'responsibility' is necessarily only direct. Even a backwards glimpse at the Abyssinian crisis would have been instructive. The United States' attitudes to the League and sanctions against Italy only foreshadowed her reluctance to participate which blighted any prospect of economic sanctions against Japan in 1937; from the Dominions, even action under the aegis of the League met resistance in places. It is against the background of the League's patent failure in 1936, the collapse of collective security, and the desire not to 'provoke' Italy, that subsequent Dominion attitudes, American suspicions, and a good many British calculations must needs be measured.

The discussion of 'influence' also betrays at times a want of scepticism. For example, the conclusion that the influence of the Dominions was 'decisive' at the time of Munich is based upon the fact that 'it was the attitude of the Dominions which had weighed most heavily in the account that Chamberlain had given of the situation to the Cabinet on 27 September 1939'. This cannot necessarily be taken as evidence of Chamberlain's priorities and beliefs, nor can it be assumed that this apsect of Chamberlain's account weighed heavily with other members of the Cabinet. A general point about Cabinet minutes is perhaps in order here, quite apart from any speculation as to the efficiency of the Cabinet's Secretary. Speakers could fill various roles, as the representative of particular departments, as raising points forgotten by colleagues, as political rivals, or as expressing their own personal convictions; what was involved at any one moment is therefore often unclear. On the question of appeasement, the position for the historian is further complicated by the fact that the well-known inclinations of America or the Dominions could be twisted to support the case for either side. Whatever one's reasons for favouring appeasement, Dominion attitudes could provide an additional and superficially respectable argument for it. 'The Dominions' could also be flung at those like Eden, Duff Cooper, or the French, if they were thought to be pressing ill-directed, prematurely aggressive, or needlessly provocative courses. It was nothing new to employ arguments in which one did not really believe to help a cause which one had for other reasons espoused. For others, the same Dominion attitudes necessitated militant action now; Duff Cooper complained that 'if we waited until there was complete unanimity with the Dominion Governments. . .we should never go to war', and feared that meanwhile, with scarcely a march on his own part, the enemy would have stolen others' marches, both weakening and threatening Britain further.

Problems of influence and motive remain to the end. In September 1939, the Dominions all went to war alongside Britain, some at least, like Canada, without obvious grounds for doing so. Dr Ovendale gives much useful comment and evidence as to their views, but is ambiguous in his conclusion. That America was warmly sympathetic, and the Commonwealth united was 'largely' due to their education in the realities of European affairs, and to their awareness that all other courses had been tried — attitudes which, it is here argued, were fostered deliberately by Britain in 1939. 'But', one discovers, 'perhaps, . . .what counted most were ties of sentiment and kin.' If this was so, then the education was surely less relevant, and some of Chamberlain's critics may not have been simply 'high-handed' in suggesting that too much attention could be paid to the rest of the English-speaking world.

This is a full and useful contribution to the published work on appeasement, but one which leaves the reader much to do for himself, whether it be to revise the frequent and incorrect usage of 'cede' and 'disinterest', to make up the lack of hyphens clearly in short supply west of the border, or draw some of his own conclusions. D.C. Watt's essay on South African attempts at mediation in *Studies in International History* edited by Watt and K. Bourne; M.P. Lissington's *New Zealand and the United States 1840-1944* and *New Zealand and Japan 1900-1941*; and C. Edwards' book on Bruce are strange omissions from the bibliography.

Dr Waley's book, the polished product of a very experienced historian (albeit one who enters this field for the first time), is by contrast written for the connoisseur of mid-1930s historiography, for those who seek what the author confesses are the 'byways of history', and whose adrenalin will flow at the slightest new undulation in a landscape they have long known intimately. Seeking first, as he puts it, 'to gauge or perhaps explain the volume of sound that proceeds from the articulate' concerning Abyssinia and the collective security system of the League, he then assesses its influence on the policy of the National Government; chapters are also included on the organisation of and impact made by both the League of Nations Union and pro-Italian propaganda. He demonstrates well the immunity of Ministers and MPs to popular pressures. These external pressures, whose volume then and since has, we are told, been much exaggerated, were helpless unless, as happened over the Hoare-Laval proposals, backed by a similar movement of opinion within the House of Commons. MPs, though for reasons all their own, also called for the rejection of Hoare's schemes.

In 1936, however, when support in the country for sanctions was still strong, MPs ignored it and sanctions were abandoned. Plenty of detail is given about such things as the size of MPs' postbags and LNU letters to those in charge of foreign policy, but this is scarcely stirring stuff. It is, moreover, a very short work and published at a price which, notwithstanding the patronage of the London School of Economics, compares most unfavourably with the product of the University of Wales Press. One cannot but wonder whether articles might not have served the purpose more cheaply and quite as effectively.

Andrew Porter

OPERATION 'MENACE': THE DAKAR EXPEDITION AND THE DUDLEY NORTH AFFAIR. *Arthur Marder,* OUP, 1976, £7.50, xxv + 289 pp.

The thoroughness of Professor Marder's research and the clarity of his narrative are likely to make this the definitive account of the Dakar expedition of September 1940. As the repercussions of the removal of Admiral Sir Dudley North from his command at Gibraltar did not subside until 1957, the opening of the official documents under the thirty year rule and full access to the Churchill papers at Cambridge may provide additional significant detail, but Marder's evaluation of the affair is unlikely to be challenged. Although, as he himself admits, there is the possibility of documentary evidence emerging of Churchill's influence on the stubborn refusals by post-war governments to grant North an official enquiry which would amend his present verdict that such influence was minimal or even non-existent. This judgement is largely based on the personal recollections of those involved in the matter, a type of evidence used extensively throughout the book to add to the great weight of public and private papers which Marder has consulted. As emerges in his narrative, such recollections, produced some thirty years after the events, are liable to be confused or contradictory, and they should not be given the same evidential value as written documents. As the two elements of the book are treated separately there is a certain amount of repetition and the self-indulgent use of very lengthy footnotes reduces the impact of the otherwise gripping main narrative.

The fundamental reason for the failure at Dakar goes beyond the usual military difficulties of combined operations which Marder so clearly analyses, and is of considerable importance in the study of war.

The political factors leading to the timing and nature of the expedition were in contradiction to the military realities. When the basic political assumption that all that was needed to assure the acceptance of de Gaulle's authority was a show of force, was shown to be completely untrue, nothing that the military commanders could have done with the resources available to them could have brought success. This was particularly true in the light of de Gaulle's insistence that there must be no major fighting between his forces and the Vichy troops. If the dictum that war is the continuation of policy is developed into the imposition of political restraints on the resources and courses of action available to military commanders, then failure is virtually inevitable. History contains as many examples of this as it does of professional military incompetence. Churchill decided that the potential political gains of the capture of Dakar, particularly in establishing de Gaulle's authority as the leader of an independent France, was worth the risk of despatching an ill-prepared expedition on the basis of unreliable political intelligence. The consequent failure was due not so much to Marder's 'fog of war' as to the frequent contradiction between military and political factors which are inherent in the nature of war itself.

The book's verdict on the North affair, that the Admiral was dismissed primarily because the first Sea Lord, Dudley Pound, had lost confidence in his professional competence, rather than as a scapegoat for the failure at Dakar, is probably right. It is however equally probable that if Dakar had been a success, his removal would not have been effected in so clumsy a way and the subsequent unedifying dispute between him and the Admiralty avoided. The emergence of new evidence may throw further light on the personalities involved but not on the substance of the matter.

Bryan Ranft

THE WAR AGAINST THE JEWS, 1933-1945. *Lucy S. Dawidowicz*, Weidenfeld and Nicolson, 1975, £10.00, 18 + 460 pp.

The title of this magnificent effort to describe the destruction of European Jewry is slightly misleading: what Professor Dawidowicz does is to analyse the background of Hitler's anti-semitism and its place in Nazi ideology, and she then proceeds to tell the story of German and East European Jews during the Holocaust. She does not deal with the Balkans, or South, North and West European Jews, who comprised about one third of pre-war Europe's Jewish population. Nor does she try to deal with the problem of the bystander — the Poles, the Germans, the Frenchmen, or the Allied Powers, the Churches and so on. The book in actual fact is compressed into 353 pages, because the rest consists of brief descriptions of the fate of the Jews in different countries; these descriptions will probably prove quite useful for the undergraduate student, but are no addition to our knowledge of the problems discussed.

The author believes that the murder of European Jews was present in Hitler's mind from 1919 on, and marshals a great deal of documentary evidence to prove her case. The point is very cogently argued, but remains unconvincing — while there is enough evidence to show that there was a predisposition in German, and indeed European, culture to accept the murder of the Jews, there is no conclusive evidence that this became a coherent plan in Hitler's mind, or anyone else's mind, before the outbreak of World War II. Professor Dawidowicz then goes on to analyse with great exactness and compactness the rise of anti-semitism in modern Germany, the anti-Jewish legislation, and the SS, as the instrument of murder. Expertly summarising the available literature, she arrives at the conclusion that Hitler's policy of expansion eastwards and his murderous Jew hatred were closely interconnected phenomena. An identical conclusion by the great German scholar Andreas Hillgruber *(Die Endlösung und das deutsche Ostimperium,* in: Vtljhrshefte für Zeitgeschichte, April 1972, pp.133-53) was probably not known to her; the justification for the conquest of the East lay in the superiority of the Germanic race. This could be proved satisfactorily only by destroying what Nazism saw as the anti-race, the embodiment of the Anti-Christ in Nazi pseudo-religious terms.

The second part of her book deals with Jewish life and death in Eastern Europe. A very concise and on the whole accurate description of ghetto life, of the Jewish Councils and the attempts at organising social and cultural activities is followed by a very interesting description of the underground movements. Much of what could be faulted with earlier historical treatment of the same topics is corrected here, but there still seems to be too much of a tendency toward generalisation of what was a very differentiated development, in which ghettoes like Vilna, Kovno, Minsk, Lublin, Lodz or Warsaw differed from each other in practically everything except the external formal organisation and the final murder.

Professor Dawidowicz's treatment of Jewish armed resistance is perhaps the weakest part of the book. Apart from many inaccuracies, such as in the description of the Warsaw uprising (where she says, for instance, that the Jews received ten 'guns' when what is meant are revolvers – p.319), she simply does not mention armed resistance in places like Minsk (where the Judenrat was part of the resistance), Tarnow, Lachwa, Zetl and a host of other places. One would hardly conclude from her account that some 10,000-15,000 Jewish partisans emerged from the Eastern forests at liberation, or that of the partisans roaming Polish forests in 1942-3, close to half were Jewish. More importantly, the problematic nature of Jewish armed resistance in the midst of a basically hostile environment is analysed in only some of its aspects. The lack of a unified political and military leadership is emphasised, but the whole problem of the relationship with the gentile surroundings, including the Polish and Russian underground movements is only cursorily treated. The reason for this seems to be that the author did not use the many publications and theses written on this subject in Hebrew. On the other hand, there are moving descriptions of some of the rebellions, such as that of Vilna, described here perhaps for the first time in English.

It is a moot point whether a history of the holocaust can be written at this stage. Despite some basic faults, this is certainly one of the best attempts yet.

Yehuda Bauer

THE SOVIET VIEW OF WAR, PEACE AND NEUTRALITY.
P.H. Vigor, Routledge and Kegan Paul, 1975, £6.50, 256 pp.

This is a disappointing book. Peter Vigor, of the Soviet Studies Centre at the Royal Military Academy Sandhurst, has a well deserved reputation as an analyst of Soviet military thought, based on his thorough understanding of the language and his wide knowledge of the historical and contemporary Russian military literature. The concept of the book, of providing an explanation of contemporary Soviet strategic and military doctrine based on the analysis of the relevant portions of Marxism-Leninism and the historical experience of the USSR is admirable. This is especially true with the continuing debate on the significance of *detente* at a time when Russia is within sight of military equality if not superiority to its capitalist rivals, for the first time in its history. The importance of understanding the interplay of ideological, national and technical factors in shaping the USSR's military policies and actions is, quite literally, vitally important to those concerned for the survival of alternative forms of society.

Mr Vigor has assembled the material for providing such an understanding in his detailed discussion of the military thought of Marx and Engels, its development by Lenin and its continuing contribution to Soviet thought and policies today. His central theme is that the use of violence in appropriate forms has always figured largely in Marxist-Leninist thought, on the premise that it should only be used in pursuit of ideologically correct political aims and when the total circumstances are such as to make success certain. This, he maintains, will be the point of view of Russia's leaders today and tomorrow, and their evaluation of the objective circumstances is likely to be such as to make the resort to major war unlikely. But if they do go to war, it will be total, in the sense both of being nuclear and having the political aim of the destruction of capitalism and the political superstructures built upon it.

This interpretation is well worthy of attention, but unfortunately Mr Vigor's presentation is unlikely to bring it home clearly to 'the ordinary Western reader' at whom his work is aimed. The organisation of the book produces tedious repetition and the style, affected perhaps by that of the publications of the Moscow Foreign Language Publishing House with which he is so much at home, is repellently hortatory and discursive. The more specialist reader should of course be ready to endure this, but unfortunately the depth of philosophical analysis and historical judgement does not provide an adequate reward for the effort needed. He will however find the detailed references and the selective but intelligently critical bibliography useful.

A shorter, leaner and more disciplined book would have conveyed Mr Vigor's important message far more effectively.

Bryan Ranft

THE ELECTRONIC WAR IN THE MIDDLE EAST 1968-1970. *E. O'Ballance,* Faber & Faber, 1974, £3.30, 148 pp.

ARAB GUERRILLA POWER 1967-1972. *E. O'Ballance,* Faber & Faber, 1974, £5.25, 264 pp.

The title of the first book is misleading. It has very little to say about electronics, but much about President Nasser's determination to avoid, at no matter what cost to his people, the negotiating table with Israel.

Having launched — most probably, by mistake — a disastrous war against the latter, Nasser nevertheless succeeded in playing a major role in the Arab Summit Conference of August 1967, where the famous resolution was passed: 'No negotiations, no recognition, no peace'. War Nasser would have, and war was what he got. In the form of the closure of the Suez Canal, the ruining of her tourist industry, the diversion of desperately needed resources to support the war effort, and a refugee problem running into the hundreds of thousands. Egypt was made to pay the price.

The so-called War of Attrition had its ups and downs, and those who are interested in a blow by blow account of events will find it in Major O'Ballance's book. Since the author's main sources are the daily papers, there is little that is new; since he apparently knows neither Arabic nor Hebrew, some very bad errors occur in the transliteration of names, etc. His conclusion that electronic warfare is with us to stay can hardly be called revolutionary, and his anxiety to secure the widest possible reading public prevents him from saying anything very interesting about the subject that forms the title of his book. More significant than these rather vapid observations, however, is the fact that, while the war cost Israel hundreds of casualties, Egypt paid for it with the lives of up to 10,000 men; still, in the end, nothing was achieved. A ceasefire, arranged with American mediation, was established and promptly violated; time to prepare for the next bloody round.

Though marked by many of the shortcomings of the previous book, Major O'Ballance's study of the Arab guerrillas is more interesting. To the bewildering array of emerging, conflicting, fusing, disappearing terrorist organisations he has succeeded in bringing some order; which is probably more than can be claimed by Mr Arafat himself, faced as he is with a seemingly endless array of groups, splinter groups, and sub-splinter groups, that are born, live and die in the teeming alleys of the Palestinian refugee camps.

When the Palestine Liberation Organisation was set up in 1965, its avowed aim — which it has to date refused to renounce — was the destruction of the State of Israel and the establishment in its place of what is known as a 'secular Palestinian State'. In view of this fact, it is interesting to find that the vast majority of the terrorists' resources — and therefore most of the pages in Major O'Ballance's book — are devoted, not to any actions of the guerrillas against Israel (though there have been plenty of those as well) but to their disputes with other Arabs. Palestinian guerrillas have tried to hijack an Egyptian airliner; murdered a Jordanian prime minister; been involved in heavy fighting against the Lebanese army; and killed numbers of their own people in order to prevent them from going to work in Israel. In response, King Hussein has killed more Palestinians than have the Israelis; indeed, such was the solidarity between Arab and Arab that scores of terrorists preferred crossing into Israel rather than face the tender mercies of the Arab Legion. The rich Arab Countries, led by Saudi Arabia, have paid the terrorists vast sums to be rid of their interference; other Arab States, including Syria, Egypt and Iraq, have kept the Palestinians on so short a leash that Israel is now probably the one place where three of their newspapers can appear with relative freedom from interference.

In addition, the Palestinian guerrillas have hijacked and blown up – some in mid-flight – American, British and Swiss planes; killed nobody knows how many innocent bystanders of all nations; and carried their murderous activities to every corner of the globe, culminating in the infamous attack on the Israeli athletes at the Munich Olympics. Attitudes towards them have varied from open and indeed vociferous encouragement to a cowardly refusal to deal with the problem; in recognition of their achievements, their leader – gun in belt – was invited to address the Assembly of the United Nations, there to demand the extinction of a member State. From its origins to the present moment, Arab guerrilla power has spelt nothing but murder and more murder; surely, it is time for the world to rid itself of this pest.

M. van Creveld

THE MILITARY IN THE THIRD WORLD. *Gavin Kennedy,* Duckworth, 1974, xiii + 368 pp, appendices, bibliography.

MILITARY REGIMES IN AFRICA. *W.F. Gutteridge,* Methuen & Co., 1975, Hardback £3.50, paperback £1.90, 195 pp, bibliography.

The literature on the military in developing countries is already vast and still expanding. Much of it is devoted to filling in the gaps, crossing the 't's' and dotting the 'i's', or slightly altering the emphases of some of the earlier seminal studies by Finer, Janowitz, and others. The books under review are no exception. A major attempt at redefining the problems of civil-military relations in the Third World has yet to be made.

In *The Military in the Third World,* Kennedy relies heavily on the work of others, particularly in the first and less satisfactory part of his substantial study, where he analyses military intervention in politics (Chapters 3-8). Using different language, he expounds Finer's basic thesis, as developed in *The Man on Horseback,* stressing the central importance of legitimacy as the basis for a stable system of government. His recipe for the ingredients of a *coup,* 'ability, conditions and motive' (p.87) may be compared with Finer's 'motive, mood and opportunity'. Some of the case studies, such as the Mexican and Turkish experiences, are excellent, others, like his treatment of military intervention in Syria and Iraq, are sketchy and difficult to follow.

Military Régimes in Africa is a development and refinement of Gutteridge's earlier book, *The Military in African Politics.* So many post-*coup coups* have taken place and so much more information has come to light in the six years' interval between the publication of the two books, that the author shifts his focus to the military's performance in government. Some of the contents have a distinctly *déjà vu* flavour for those who are familiar with his writings.

However, each book also makes its own contribution to our understanding of civil-military relations in the developing states. As an economist, Kennedy devotes the second half of his study (Chapters 9-16) to a very interesting and revealing examination of the economics of defence in those countries. With a wealth of statistical material and through careful analysis he disposes of many popular misconceptions. He shows, for example, that high defence budgets are not necessarily at the expense of social welfare budgets, and, conversely, that low defence expenditure does not necessarily mean increased expenditure on socially valued programmed. Case studies do not indicate an obvious relationship between growth rates and the percentage of the GNP allocated to defence, nor is there an unequivocal answer to the question whether defence is a burden. When analysing the impact of war on the economies of Nigeria, Southeast Asia, Israel, Egypt, and Pakistan, the author concludes that it was not uniform in its effect and that the connection between war and economic development is not simply a matter of whether a country wins or loses.

The three chapters (14-16) which deal with the production and supply of arms are perhaps the most important of the whole book. The one dealing with 'Local Arms Races' pulls together a lot of useful material without telling us anything very new. The subsequent two on arms production in developing countries offer many interesting insights into the relationship between various types of armament industries and economic development. The concluding chapter of the book, entitled 'Disarmament', makes some pertinent points which are then followed by the gloomy conclusion that violence and war are endemic in the human species. This excursion into philosophy is very debatable and does not add anything to the book.

Apart from a special contribution to the study of economic factors in the civil-military relations of developing nations, Gavin Kennedy makes many thoughtful and provocative observations. For instance, he suggests that 'Guerrilla warfare is, in effect, a product of the organisational inadequacies of the Third World in general rather than some special characteristic of revolutionary strategy' (p.247). The book might have been more effective and readable if he had tightened the organisation and had concentrated more on the economic analysis. As it is, it conveys an overall impression of haste, an impression borne out by small errors in the text and the fragmentary structure of some chapters.

William Gutteridge's much shorter work does not suffer from such defects. It is polished and very readable. Its chief contribution is as an antidote to glib generalisations about civil-military relations in Black Africa. He has an interesting discussion of the British and French legacies in an assessment of the military's role after independence. The main body of the book consists of studies of individual countries. The author is clearly more at home in the Anglophone than in the Francophone regions. The chapters on Dahomey (Benin) and Zaire are primarily descriptive, whereas those on Ghana and Nigeria contain many insights. The chapter on Uganda, brief as it is, is an excellent account of the background from which Amin rose to power. Gutteridge has written a very handy introduction to African military politics for students of this subject.

Wolf Mendl

NOTES ON CONTRIBUTORS

John B. Hattendorf is at present a graduate student at Pembroke College, Oxford. He was a serving officer in the U.S. Navy for seven years, including spells in Atlantic and Pacific Fleet destroyers, and ashore in the Office of Naval History and on the Strategy Faculty of the Naval War College. With Rear-Admiral John D. Hayes he edited *The Writings of Admiral Stephen B. Luce* (1975).

V.G. Kiernan has taught at Edinburgh University since 1948 and has been a Professor of History since 1970. The most recent of his numerous books is *Marxism and Imperialism* (1975).

Neil A. Wynn is a Lecturer in History at the Polytechnic of Wales. The article published here is based on his book *The Afro-American and the Second World War* (Paul Elek, 1976).

Suzann Buckley took her doctorate at Duke University in 1972 and is at present a member of the history department of the State University of New York at Plattsburgh. She has published several articles, including 'Attempts at Imperial Economic Co-operation' in *The Canadian Historical Review* (September, 1974).

Anthony R. Wells is a serving naval officer who took a doctorate at London University while on the teaching staff of the Royal Naval College Greenwich.

Williamson Murray received his doctorate from Yale University in 1975 and is currently a member of the history department there.

Brigadier F.H. Vinden served in the British Army from 1914 to 1946. He subsequently held various appointments in UNESCO, UN and OECD. He has lived in France since 1971.

Stephen Brooks read modern history at Oxford and took an MA in War Studies at King's College, London. As a member of the latter's library staff he spent three years reorganising and cataloguing the Liddell Hart Papers. He is currently archivist at the Royal Institute for International Affairs.

BOOKS RECEIVED

G. Parker, *The Army of Flanders and the Spanish Road, 1567-1659.* Cambridge UP (London, 1972; paperback edition, 1975). xx + 309 pp., £2.25.

K. Nebenzahl, *A Bibliography of Printed Battle Plans of the American Revolution, 1775-1795.* University of Chicago Press (Chicago and London, 1975). xiv + 159 pp, £6.60.

C. Hibbert (ed.), *A Soldier of the Seventy-First. The Journal of a Soldier in the Peninsular War.* Leo Cooper (London, 1975), xv + 121 pp, £3.95.

J. Fabb, *The Victorian and Edwardian Navy from Old Photographs.* Introduction by A.P. McGowan. Batsford (London, 1975). Unpaged. 172 photographs. £4.45.

W.P. Trotter, *The Royal Navy in Old Photographs,* Dent (London, 1975). Unpaged. 190 photographs. £4.50.

E. Belfield, *The Boer War.* Leo Cooper (London, 1975). xxvi + 181 pp, £4.75.

J. Ellis, *The Social History of the Machine Gun.* Croom Helm (London, 1975), 186 pp, £5.50.

A. Lloyd, *The War in the Trenches.* Hart-Davis, MacGibbon (London, 1976), 200 pp, £4.95.

G. Thomas and M. Morgan-Witts. *The Day Guernica Died.* Hodder and Stoughton (London, 1975), 319 pp, £4.95.

K. Macksey, *Guderian, Panzer General.* MacDonald and Jane's (London, 1975), xii + 226 pp, £4.95.

A. Seaton, *Stalin as Warlord.* Batsford (London, 1976), 312 pp, £5.95.

J. Keegan, *The Face of Battle.* Jonathan Cape (London, 1976), 352 pp, £6.50.